Hard Press

THE HISTORY OF ROME, BOOK II

From the Abolition of the Monarchy in Rome to the Union of Italy

by

THEODOR MOMMSEN

Preparer's Note

This work contains many literal citations of and references to
foreign words, sounds, and alphabetic symbols drawn from many
languages, including Gothic and Phoenician, but chiefly Latin and
Greek. This English Gutenberg edition, constrained to the characters
of 7-bit ASCII code, adopts the following orthographic conventions:

1) Except for Greek, all literally cited non-English words that do
not refer to texts cited as academic references, words that in the
source manuscript appear italicized, are rendered with a single
preceding, and a single following dash; thus, -xxxx-.

2) Greek words, first transliterated into Roman alphabetic
equivalents, are rendered with a preceding and a following double-
dash; thus, —xxxx—. Note that in some cases the root word itself
is a compound form such as xxx-xxxx, and is rendered as —xxx-xxx—

3) Simple unideographic references to vocalic sounds, single
letters, or alphabeic dipthongs; and prefixes, suffixes, and syllabic
references are represented by a single preceding dash; thus, -x,
or -xxx.

4) Ideographic references, referring to signs of representation rather
than to content, are represented as -"id:xxxx"-. "id:" stands for
"ideograph", and indicates that the reader should form a picture based
on the following "xxxx"; which may be a single symbol, a word, or an
attempt at a picture composed of ASCII characters. For example,
—"id:GAMMA gamma"— indicates an uppercase Greek gamma-form followed
by the form in lowercase. Some such exotic parsing as this is
necessary to explain alphabetic development because a single symbol
may have been used for a number of sounds in a number of languages,
or even for a number of sounds in the same language at different
times. Thus, -"id:GAMMA gamma" might very well refer to a Phoenician
construct that in appearance resembles the form that eventually
stabilized as an uppercase Greek "gamma" juxtaposed to one of

3

lowercase. Also, a construct such as —"id:E" indicates a symbol that with ASCII resembles most closely a Roman uppercase "E", but, in fact, is actually drawn more crudely.

5) Dr. Mommsen has given his dates in terms of Roman usage, A.U.C.; that is, from the founding of Rome, conventionally taken to be 753 B. C. The preparer of this document, has appended to the end of each volume a table of conversion between the two systems.

CONTENTS

BOOK II: From the Abolition of the Monarchy in Rome to the Union of Italy

Chapter

BOOK SECOND

From the Abolition of the Monarchy in Rome to the Union of Italy

—dei ouk ekpleittein ton suggraphea terateuomenon dia teis iotopias tous entugchanontas.—

Polybius.

CHAPTER I

Change of the Constitution—
Limitation of the Power of the Magistrate

Political and Social Distinctions in Rome

The strict conception of the unity and omnipotence of the state in all matters pertaining to it, which was the central principle of the Italian constitutions, placed in the hands of the single president nominated for life a formidable power, which was felt doubtless by the enemies of the land, but was not less heavily felt by its citizens. Abuse and oppression could not fail to ensue, and, as a necessary consequence, efforts were made to lessen that power. It was, however, the grand distinction of the endeavours after reform and the revolutions in Rome, that there was no attempt either to impose limitations on the community as such or even to deprive it of corresponding organs of expression—that there never was any endeavour to assert the so-called natural rights of the individual in contradistinction to the community— that, on the contrary, the attack was wholly directed against the form in which the community was represented. From the times of the Tarquins down to those of the Gracchi the cry of the party of progress in Rome was not for limitation of the power of the state, but for limitation of the power of the magistrates: nor amidst that cry was the truth ever forgotten, that the people ought not to govern, but to be governed.

This struggle was carried on within the burgess-body. Side by side with it another movement developed itself—the cry of the non-burgesses for equality of political privileges. Under this head are included the agitations of the plebeians, the Latins, the Italians, and the freedmen, all of whom—whether they may have borne the name of burgesses, as did the plebeians and the freedmen, or not, as was the case with the Latins and Italians—were destitute of, and desired, political equality.

A third distinction was one of a still more general nature; the distinction between the wealthy and the poor, especially such as had been dispossessed or were endangered in possession. The legal and political relations of Rome led to the rise of a numerous class of farmers—partly small proprietors who were dependent on the mercy of the capitalist, partly small temporary lessees who were dependent on the mercy of the landlord—and in many instances deprived individuals as well as whole communities of the lands which they held, without affecting their personal freedom. By these means the agricultural proletariate became at an early period so powerful as to have a material influence on the destinies of the community. The urban proletariate did not acquire political importance till a much later epoch.

On these distinctions hinged the internal history of Rome, and, as may be presumed, not less the history—totally lost to us—of the other Italian communities. The political movement within the fully-privileged burgess-body, the warfare between the excluded and excluding classes, and the social conflicts between the possessors and the non-possessors of land—variously as they crossed and interlaced, and singular as were the alliances they often produced —were nevertheless essentially and fundamentally distinct.

Abolition of the Life-Presidency of the Community

As the Servian reform, which placed the —metoikos— on a footing of equality in a military point of view with the burgess, appears to have originated from considerations of an administrative nature rather than from any political party-tendency, we may assume that the first of the movements which led to internal crises and changes of the constitution was that which sought to limit the magistracy. The earliest achievement of this, the most ancient opposition in Rome, consisted in the abolition of the life-tenure of the presidency of the community; in other words, in the abolition of the monarchy. How necessarily this was the result of the natural development of things, is most strikingly demonstrated by the fact, that the same change of constitution took place in an analogous manner through the whole circuit of the Italo-Grecian world. Not only in Rome, but likewise among the other Latins as well as among the Sabellians, Etruscans, and Apulians—and generally, in all the Italian communities, just as in those of Greece—we find the rulers for life of an earlier epoch superseded in after times by annual magistrates. In the case of the Lucanian canton there is evidence that it had a democratic government in time of peace, and it was only in the event of war that the magistrates appointed a king, that is, an official similar to the Roman dictator. The Sabellian civic communities, such as those of Capua and Pompeii, in like manner were in later times governed by a "community-manager" (-medix tuticus-) changed from year to year, and we may assume that similar institutions existed among the other national and civic communities of Italy. In this light the reasons which led to the substitution of consuls for kings in Rome need no explanation. The organism of the ancient Greek and Italian polity developed of itself by a sort of natural necessity the limitation of the life-presidency to a shortened, and for the most part an annual, term. Simple, however, as was the cause of this change, it might be brought about in various ways; a resolution might be adopted on the death of one life-ruler not to elect another—a course which the Roman senate is said to have attempted after the death of Romulus; or the ruler might voluntarily abdicate, as is alleged to have been the intention of king Servius Tullius; or the people might rise in rebellion against a tyrannical ruler, and expel him.

Expulsion of the Tarquins from Rome

It was in this latter way that the monarchy was terminated in Rome. For however much the history of the expulsion of the last Tarquinius, "the proud," may have been interwoven with anecdotes and spun out into a romance, it is not in its leading outlines to be called in question. Tradition credibly enough indicates as the causes of the revolt, that the king neglected to consult the senate and to complete its numbers; that he pronounced sentences of capital punishment and confiscation without advising with his counsellors; that he accumulated immense stores of grain in his granaries, and exacted from the burgesses military labour and task-work beyond what was due. The exasperation of the people is attested by the formal vow which they made man by man for themselves and for their posterity that thenceforth they would never tolerate a king; by the blind hatred with which the name of king was ever afterwards regarded in Rome; and above all by the enactment that the "king for offering sacrifice" (-rex sacrorum- or -sacrificulus-) —whom they considered it their duty to create that the gods might not miss their accustomed mediator—should be disqualified from holding any further office, so that this man became the foremost indeed, but also the most powerless in the Roman commonwealth. Along with the last king all the members of his clan were banished—a proof how close at that time gentile ties still were. The Tarquinii thereupon transferred themselves to Caere, perhaps their ancient home,(1) where their family tomb has recently been discovered. In the room of the one president holding office for life two annual rulers were now placed at the head of the Roman community.

This is all that can be looked upon as historically certain in reference to this important event.(2) It is conceivable that in a great community with extensive dominion like the Roman the royal power, particularly if it had been in the same family for several generations, would be more capable of resistance, and the struggle would thus be keener, than in the smaller states; but there is no certain indication of any interference by foreign states in the struggle. The great war with Etruria—which possibly, moreover, has been placed so close upon the expulsion of the Tarquins only in consequence of chronological confusion in the Roman annals—cannot be regarded as an intervention of Etruria in favour of a countryman who had been injured in Rome, for the very sufficient reason that the Etruscans notwithstanding their complete victory neither restored the Roman monarchy, nor even brought back the Tarquinian family.

Powers of the Consuls

If we are left in ignorance of the historical connections of this important event, we are fortunately in possession of clearer light as to the nature of the change which was made in the constitution. The royal power was by no means abolished, as is shown by the very fact that, when a vacancy occurred afterwards as before, an "interim king" (-interrex-) was nominated. The one life-king was simply replaced by two year-kings, who called themselves generals (-praetores-), or judges (-iudices-), or merely colleagues (consules).(3) The principles of collegiate tenure and of annual duration are those which distinguish the republic from the monarchy, and they first meet us here.

Collegiate Arrangement

The collegiate principle, from which the third and subsequently most current name of the annual kings was derived, assumed in their case an altogether peculiar form. The supreme power was not entrusted to the two magistrates conjointly, but each consul possessed and exercised it for himself as fully and wholly as it had been possessed and exercised by the king. This was carried so far that, instead of one of the two colleagues undertaking perhaps the administration of justice, and the other the command of the army, they both administered justice simultaneously in the city just as they both set out together to the army; in case of collision the matter was decided by a rotation measured by months or days. A certain partition of functions withal, at least in the supreme military command, might doubtless take place from the outset— the one consul for example taking the field against the Aequi, and the other against the Volsci—but it had in no wise binding force, and each of the colleagues was legally at liberty to interfere at any time in the province of the other. When,

9

therefore, supreme power confronted supreme power and the one colleague forbade what the other enjoined, the consular commands neutralized each other. This peculiarly Latin, if not peculiarly Roman, institution of co-ordinate supreme authorities—which in the Roman commonwealth on the whole approved itself as practicable, but to which it will be difficult to find a parallel in any other considerable state —manifestly sprang out of the endeavour to retain the regal power in legally undiminished fulness. They were thus led not to break up the royal office into parts or to transfer it from an individual to a college, but simply to double it and thereby, if necessary, to neutralize it through its own action.

Term of Office

As regards the termination of their tenure of office, the earlier -interregnum- of five days furnished a legal precedent. The ordinary presidents of the community were bound not to remain in office longer than a year reckoned from the day of their entering on their functions;(4) and they ceased -de jure- to be magistrates upon the expiry of the year, just as the interrex on the expiry of the five days. Through this set termination of the supreme office the practical irresponsibility of the king was lost in the case of the consul. It is true that the king was always in the Roman commonwealth subject, and not superior, to the law; but, as according to the Roman view the supreme judge could not be prosecuted at his own bar, the king might doubtless have committed a crime, but there was for him no tribunal and no punishment. The consul, again, if he had committed murder or treason, was protected by his office, but only so long as it lasted; on his retirement he was liable to the ordinary penal jurisdiction like any other burgess.

To these leading changes, affecting the principles of the constitution, other restrictions were added of a subordinate and more external character, some of which nevertheless produced a deep effect The privilege of the king to have his fields tilled by task-work of the burgesses, and the special relation of clientship in which the —-metoeci— as a body must have stood to the king, ceased of themselves with the life tenure of the office.

Right of Appeal

Hitherto in criminal processes as well as in fines and corporal punishments it had been the province of the king not only to investigate and decide the cause, but also to decide whether the person found guilty should or should not be allowed to appeal for pardon. The Valerian law now (in 245) enacted that the consul must allow the appeal of the condemned, where sentence of capital or corporal punishment had been pronounced otherwise than by martial law—a regulation which by a later law (of uncertain date, but passed before 303) was extended to heavy fines. In token of this right of appeal, when the consul appeared in the capacity of judge and not of general, the consular lictors laid aside the axes which they had previously carried by virtue of the penal jurisdiction belonging to their master. The law however threatened the magistrate, who did not allow due course to the -provocatio-, with no other penalty than infamy—which, as matters then stood, was essentially nothing but a moral stain, and at the utmost only had the effect of disqualifying the infamous person from giving testimony. Here too the course followed was based on the same view, that it was in law impossible to diminish the old regal powers, and that the checks imposed upon the holder of the supreme authority in consequence of the revolution had, strictly viewed, only a practical and moral value. When therefore the consul acted within the old regal jurisdiction, he might in so acting perpetrate an injustice, but he committed no crime and consequently was not amenable for what he did to the penal judge.

A limitation similar in its tendency took place in the civil jurisdiction; for probably there was taken from the consuls at the very outset the right of deciding at their discretion a legal dispute between private persons.

Restrictions on the Delegation of Powers

The remodelling of the criminal as of civil procedure stood in connection with a general arrangement respecting the transference of magisterial power to deputies or successors. While the king had been absolutely at liberty to nominate deputies but had never been compelled to do so, the consuls exercised the right of delegating power in an essentially different way. No doubt the rule that, if the supreme magistrate left the city, he had to appoint a warden there for the administration of justice,(5) remained in force also for the consuls, and the collegiate arrangement was not even extended to such delegation; on the contrary this appointment was laid on the consul who was the last to leave the city. But the right of delegation for the time when the consuls remained in the city was probably restricted, upon the very introduction of this office, by providing that delegation should be prescribed to the consul for definite cases, but should be prohibited for all cases in which it was not so prescribed. According to this principle, as we have said, the whole judicial system was organized. The consul could certainly exercise criminal jurisdiction also as to a capital process in the way of submitting his sentence to the community and having it thereupon confirmed or rejected; but he never, so far as we see, exercised this right, perhaps was soon not allowed to exercise it, and possibly pronounced a criminal judgment only in the case of appeal to the community being for any reason excluded. Direct conflict between the supreme magistrate of the community and the community itself was avoided, and the criminal procedure was organized really in such a way, that the supreme magistracy remained only in theory competent, but always acted through deputies who were necessary though appointed by himself. These were the two—not standing—pronouncers-of-judgment for revolt and high treason (-duoviri perduellionis-) and the two standing trackers of murder, the -quaestores parricidii-. Something similar may perhaps have occurred in the regal period, where the king had himself represented in such processes;(6) but the standing character of the latter institution, and the collegiate principle carried out in both, belong at any rate to the republic. The latter arrangement became of great importance also, in so far that thereby for the first time alongside of the two standing supreme magistrates were placed two assistants, whom each supreme magistrate nominated at his entrance on office, and who in due course also went out with him on his leaving it—whose position thus, like the supreme magistracy itself, was organized according to the principles of a standing office, of a collegiate form, and of an annual tenure. This was not indeed as yet the inferior magistracy itself, at least not in the sense which the republic associated with the magisterial position, inasmuch as the commissioners did not emanate from the choice of the community; but it doubtless became the starting-point for the institution of subordinate magistrates, which was afterwards developed in so manifold ways.

In a similar way the decision in civil procedure was withdrawn from the supreme magistracy, inasmuch as the right of the king to transfer an individual process for decision to a deputy was converted into the duty of the consul, after settling the legitimate title of the party and the object of the suit, to refer the disposal of it to a private man to be selected by him and furnished by him with instructions.

In like manner there was left to the consuls the important administration of the state-treasure and of the state-archives; nevertheless probably at once, or at least very early, there were associated with them standing assistants in that duty, namely, those quaestors who, doubtless, had in exercising this function absolutely to obey them, but without whose previous knowledge and co-operation the consuls could not act.

Where on the other hand such directions were not in existence, the president of the community in the capital had personally to intervene; as indeed, for example, at the introductory steps of a process he could not under any circumstances let himself be represented by deputy.

This double restriction of the consular right of delegation subsisted for the government of the city, and primarily for the administration of justice and of the state-chest. As commander-in-chief, on the other hand, the consul retained the right of handing over all or any of the duties devolving on him. This diversity in the treatment of civil and military delegation explains why in the government of the Roman community proper no delegated magisterial authority (-pro magistrate-) was possible, nor were purely urban magistrates ever represented by non-magistrates; and why, on the other hand, military deputies (-pro consuls-, -pro praetore-, -pro quaestore-) were excluded from all action within the community proper.

Nominating a Successor

The right of nominating a successor had not been possessed by the king, but only by the interrex.(7) The consul was in this respect placed on a like footing with the latter; nevertheless, in the event of his not having exercised the power, the interrex stepped in as before, and the necessary continuity of the office subsisted still undiminished under the republican government. The right of nomination, however, was materially restricted in favour of the burgesses, as the consul was bound to procure the assent of the burgesses for the successors designated by him, and, in the sequel, to nominate only those whom the community designated to him. Through this binding right of proposal the nomination of the ordinary supreme magistrates doubtless in a certain sense passed substantially into the hands of the community; practically, however, there still existed a very considerable distinction between that right of proposal and

12

the right of formal nomination. The consul conducting the election was by no means a mere returning officer; he could still, e. g. by virtue of his old royal prerogative reject particular candidates and disregard the votes tendered for them; at first he might even limit the choice to a list of candidates proposed by himself; and—what was of still more consequence—when the collegiate consulship was to be supplemented by the dictator, of whom we shall speak immediately, in so supplementing it the community was not consulted, but on the contrary the consul in that case appointed his colleague with the same freedom, wherewith the interrex had once appointed the king.

Change in the Nomination of Priests

The nomination of the priests, which had been a prerogative of the kings,(8) was not transferred to the consuls; but the colleges of priests filled up the vacancies in their own ranks, while the Vestals and single priests were nominated by the pontifical college, on which devolved also the exercise of the paternal jurisdiction, so to speak, of the community over the priestesses of Vesta. With a view to the performance of these acts, which could only be properly performed by a single individual, the college probably about this period first nominated a president, the -Pontifex maximus-. This separation of the supreme authority in things sacred from the civil power—while the already-mentioned "king for sacrifice" had neither the civil nor the sacred powers of the king, but simply the title, conferred upon him —and the semi-magisterial position of the new high priest, so decidedly contrasting with the character which otherwise marked the priesthood in Rome, form one of the most significant and important peculiarities of this state-revolution, the aim of which was to impose limits on the powers of the magistrates mainly in the interest of the aristocracy.

We have already mentioned that the outward state of the consul was far inferior to that of the regal office hedged round as it was with reverence and terror, that the regal name and the priestly consecration were withheld from him, and that the axe was taken away from his attendants. We have to add that, instead of the purple robe which the king had worn, the consul was distinguished from the ordinary burgess simply by the purple border of his toga, and that, while the king perhaps regularly appeared in public in his chariot, the consul was bound to accommodate himself to the general rule and like every other burgess to go within the city on foot.

The Dictator

These limitations, however, of the plenary power and of the insignia of the magistracy applied in the main only to the ordinary presidency of the community. In extraordinary cases, alongside of, and in a certain sense instead of, the two presidents chosen by the community there emerged a single one, the master of the army (-magister populi-) usually designated as the -dictator-. In the choice of dictator the community exercised no influence at all, but it proceeded solely from the free resolve of one of the consuls for the time being, whose action neither his colleague nor any other authority could hinder. There was no appeal from his sentence any more than from that of the king, unless he chose to allow it. As soon as he was nominated, all the other magistrates were by right subject to his authority. On the other hand the duration of the dictator's office was limited in two ways: first, as the official colleague of those consuls, one of whom had nominated him, he might not remain in office beyond their legal term; and secondly, a period of six months was fixed as the absolute maximum for the duration of his office. It was a further arrangement peculiar to the dictatorship, that the "master of the army" was bound to nominate for himself immediately a "master of horse" (-magister equitum-), who acted along with him as a dependent assistant somewhat as did the quaestor along with the consul, and with him retired from office—an arrangement undoubtedly connected with the fact that the dictator, presumably as being the leader of the infantry, was constitutionally prohibited from mounting on horseback. In the light of these regulations the dictatorship is doubtless to be conceived as an institution which arose at the same time with the consulship, and which was designed, especially in the event of war, to obviate for a time the disadvantages of divided power and to revive temporarily the regal authority; for in war more particularly the equality of rights in the consuls could not but appear fraught with danger; and not only positive testimonies, but above all the oldest names given to the magistrate himself and his assistant, as well as the limitation of the office to the duration of a summer campaign, and the exclusion of the -provocatio- attest the pre-eminently military design of the original dictatorship.

On the whole, therefore, the consuls continued to be, as the kings had been, the supreme administrators, judges, and generals; and even in a religious point of view it was not the -rex sacrorum- (who was only nominated that the name might be preserved), but the consul, who offered prayers and sacrifices for the community, and in its name ascertained the will of the gods with the aid of those skilled in sacred lore. Against cases of emergency, moreover, a power was retained of reviving at any moment, without previous consultation of the community, the full and unlimited regal authority, so as to set aside the limitations imposed by the collegiate arrangement and by the special curtailments of jurisdiction. In this way the problem of legally retaining and practically restricting the regal authority was solved in genuine Roman fashion with equal acuteness and simplicity by the nameless statesmen who worked out this revolution.

Centuries and Curies

The community thus acquired by the change of constitution rights of the greatest importance: the right of annually designating its presidents, and that of deciding in the last instance regarding the life or death of the burgess. But the body which acquired these rights could not possibly be the community as it had been hitherto constituted—the patriciate which had practically become an order of nobility. The strength of the nation lay in the "multitude" (-plebs-) which already comprehended in large numbers people of note and of wealth. The exclusion of this multitude from the public assembly, although it bore part of the public burdens, might be tolerated as long as that public assembly itself had no very material share in the working of the state machine, and as long as the royal power by the very fact of its high and free position remained almost equally formidable to the burgesses and to the —metoeci— and thereby maintained equality of legal redress in the nation. But when the community itself was called regularly to elect and to decide, and the president was practically reduced from its master to its commissioner for a set term, this relation could no longer be maintained as it stood; least of all when the state had to be remodelled on the morrow of a revolution, which could only have been carried out by the co-operation of the patricians and the —metoeci—. An extension of that community was inevitable; and it was accomplished in the most comprehensive manner, inasmuch as the collective plebeiate, that is, all the non-burgesses who were neither slaves nor citizens of extraneous communities living at Rome under the -ius hospitii-, were admitted into the burgess-body. The curiate assembly of the old burgesses, which hitherto had been legally and practically the first authority in the state, was almost totally deprived of its constitutional prerogatives. It was to retain its previous powers only in acts purely formal or in those which affected clan-relations —such as the vow of allegiance to be taken to the consul or to the dictator when they entered on office just as previously to the king,(9) and the legal dispensations requisite for an -arrogatio- or a testament—but it was not in future to perform any act of a properly political character. Soon even the plebeians were admitted to the right of voting also in the curies, and by that step the old burgess-body lost the right of meeting and of resolving at all. The curial organization was virtually rooted out, in so far as it was based on the clan-organization and this latter was to be found in its purity exclusively among the old burgesses. When the plebeians were admitted into the curies, they were certainly also allowed to constitute themselves -de jure- as—what in the earlier period they could only have been -de facto-(10)—families and clans; but it is distinctly recorded by tradition and in itself also very conceivable, that only a portion of the plebeians proceeded so far as to constitute -gentes-, and thus the new curiate assembly, in opposition to its original character, included numerous members who belonged to no clan.

All the political prerogatives of the public assembly—as well the decision on appeals in criminal causes, which indeed were essentially political processes, as the nomination of magistrates and the adoption or rejection of laws—were transferred to, or were now acquired by, the assembled levy of those bound to military service; so that the centuries now received the rights, as they had previously borne the burdens, of citizens. In this way the small initial movements made by the Servian constitution—such as, in particular, the handing over to the army the right of assenting to the declaration of an aggressive war(11)—attained such a development that the curies were completely and for ever cast into the shade by the assembly of the centuries, and people became accustomed to regard the latter as the sovereign people. In this assembly debate took place merely when the presiding magistrate chose himself to speak or bade others do so; of course in cases of appeal both parties had to be heard. A simple majority of the centuries was decisive.

As in the curiate assembly those who were entitled to vote at all were on a footing of entire equality, and therefore after the admission of all the plebeians into the curies the result would have been a complete democracy, it may be easily conceived that the decision of political questions continued to be withheld from the curies; the centuriate assembly placed the preponderating influence, not in the hands of the nobles certainly, but in those of the possessors of property, and the important privilege of priority in voting, which often practically decided the election, placed it in the hands of the -equites- or, in other words, of the rich.

Senate

The senate was not affected by the reform of the constitution in the same way as the community. The previously existing college of elders not only continued exclusively patrician, but retained also its essential prerogatives—the right of appointing the interrex, and of confirming or rejecting the resolutions adopted by the community as constitutional or unconstitutional. In fact these prerogatives were enhanced by the reform of the constitution, because the appointment of the magistrates also, which fell to be made by election of the community, was thenceforth subject to the confirmation or rejection of the patrician senate. In cases of appeal alone its confirmation, so far as we know, was never deemed requisite, because in these the matter at stake was the pardon of the guilty and, when this was granted by the sovereign assembly of the people, any cancelling of such an act was wholly out of the question.

But, although by the abolition of the monarchy the constitutional rights of the patrician senate were increased rather than diminished, there yet took place—and that, according to tradition, immediately on the abolition of the monarchy—so far as regards other affairs which fell to be discussed in the senate and admitted of a freer treatment, an enlargement of that body, which brought into it plebeians also, and which in its consequences led to a complete remodelling of the whole. From the earliest times the senate had acted also, although not solely or especially, as a state-council; and, while probably even in the time of the kings it was not regarded as unconstitutional for non-senators in this case to take part in the assembly,(12) it was now arranged that for such discussions there should be associated with the patrician senate (-patres-) a number of non-patricians "added to the roll" (-conscripti-). This did not at all put them on a footing of equality; the plebeians in the senate did not become senators, but remained members of the equestrian order, were not designated -patres-but were even now -conscripti-, and had no right to the badge of senatorial dignity, the red shoe.(13) Moreover, they not only remained absolutely excluded from the exercise of the magisterial prerogatives belonging to the senate (-auctoritas-), but were obliged, even where the question had reference merely to an advice (-consilium-), to rest content with the privilege of being present in silence while the question was put to the patricians in turn, and of only indicating their opinion by adding to the numbers when the division was taken—voting with the feet (-pedibus in sententiam ire-, -pedarii-) as the proud nobility expressed it. Nevertheless, the plebeians found their way through the new constitution not merely to the Forum, but also to the senate-house, and the first and most difficult step towards equality of rights was taken in this quarter also.

Otherwise there was no material change in the arrangements affecting the senate. Among the patrician members a distinction of rank soon came to be recognized, especially in putting the vote: those who were proximately designated for the supreme magistracy, or who had already administered it, were entered on the list and were called upon to vote before the rest; and the position of the first of them, the foreman of the senate (-princeps senatus-) soon became a highly coveted place of honour. The consul in office, on the other hand, no more ranked as a member of senate than did the king, and therefore in taking the votes did not include his own. The selection of the members—both of the narrower patrician senate and of those merely added to the roll—fell to be made by the consuls just as formerly by the kings; but the nature of the case implied that, while the king had still perhaps some measure of regard to the representation of the several clans in the senate, this consideration was of no account so far as concerned the plebeians, among whom the clan-organization was but imperfectly developed, and consequently the relation of the senate to that organization in general fell more and more into abeyance. We have no information that the electing consuls were restricted from admitting more than a definite number of plebeians to the senate; nor was there need for such a regulation, because the consuls themselves belonged to the nobility. On the other hand probably from the outset the consul was in virtue of his very position practically far less free, and far more bound by the opinions of his order and by custom, in the appointment of senators than the king. The rule in particular, that the holding of the consulship should necessarily be followed by admission to the senate for life, if, as was probably the case at this time, the consul was not yet a member of it at the time of his election, must have in all probability very early acquired consuetudinary force. In like manner it seems to have become early the custom not to fill up the senators' places immediately on their falling vacant, but to revise and complete the roll of the senate on occasion of the census, consequently, as a rule, every fourth year; which also involved a not unimportant restriction on the authority entrusted with the selection. The whole number of the senators remained as before, and in this the -conscripti- were also included; from which fact we are probably entitled to infer the numerical falling off of the patriciate.(14)

Conservative Character of the Revolution

We thus see that in the Roman commonwealth, even on the conversion of the monarchy into a republic, the old was as far as possible retained. So far as a revolution in a state can be conservative at all, this one was so; not one of the constituent elements of the commonwealth was really overthrown by it. This circumstance indicates the character of the whole movement. The expulsion of the Tarquins was not, as the pitiful and deeply falsified accounts of it represent, the work of a people carried away by sympathy and enthusiasm for liberty, but the work of two great political parties already engaged in conflict, and clearly aware that their conflict would steadily continue—the old burgesses and the —mctoeci— —who, like the English Whigs and Tories in 1688, were for a moment united by the common danger which threatened to convert the commonwealth into the arbitrary government of a despot, and differed again as soon as the danger was over. The old burgesses could not get rid of the monarchy without the cooperation of the new burgesses; but the new burgesses were far from being sufficiently strong to wrest the power out of the hands of the former at one blow. Compromises of this sort are necessarily limited to the smallest measure of mutual concessions obtained by tedious bargaining; and they leave the future to decide which of the constituent elements shall eventually preponderate, and whether they will work harmoniously together or counteract one another. To look therefore merely to the direct innovations, possibly to the mere change in the duration of the supreme magistracy, is altogether to mistake the broad import of the first Roman revolution: its indirect effects were by far the most important, and vaster doubtless than even its authors anticipated.

The New Community

This, in short, was the time when the Roman burgess-body in the later sense of the term originated. The plebeians had hitherto been —metoeci— who were subjected to their share of taxes and burdens, but who were nevertheless in the eye of the law really nothing but tolerated aliens, between whose position and that of foreigners proper it may have seemed hardly necessary to draw a definite line of distinction. They were now enrolled in the lists as burgesses liable to military service, and, although they were still far from being on a footing of legal equality—although the old burgesses still remained exclusively entitled to perform the acts of authority constitutionally pertaining to the council of elders, and exclusively eligible to the civil magistracies and priesthoods, nay even by preference entitled to participate in the usufructs of burgesses, such as the joint use of the public pasture—yet the first and most difficult step towards complete equalization was gained from the time when the plebeians no longer served merely in the common levy, but also voted in the common assembly and in the common council when its opinion was asked, and the head and back of the poorest —metoikos— were as well protected by the right of appeal as those of the noblest of the old burgesses.

One consequence of this amalgamation of the patricians and plebeians in a new corporation of Roman burgesses was the conversion of the old burgesses into a clan-nobility, which was incapable of receiving additions or even of filling up its own ranks, since the nobles no longer possessed the right of passing decrees in common assembly and the adoption of new families into the nobility by decree of the community appeared still less admissible. Under the kings the ranks of the Roman nobility had not been thus closed, and the admission of new clans was no very rare occurrence: now this genuine characteristic of patricianism made its appearance as the sure herald of the speedy loss of its political privileges and of its exclusive estimation in the community. The exclusion of the plebeians from all public magistracies and public priesthoods—while they were admissible to the position of officers and senators—and the maintenance, with perverse obstinacy, of the legal impossibility of marriage between old burgesses and plebeians, further impressed on the patriciate from the outset the stamp of an exclusive and wrongly privileged aristocracy.

A second consequence of the new union of the burgesses must have been a more definite regulation of the right of settlement, with reference both to the Latin confederates and to other states. It became necessary—not so much on account of the right of suffrage in the centuries (which indeed belonged only to the freeholder) as on account of the right of appeal, which was intended to be conceded to the

18

plebeian, but not to the foreigner dwelling for a time or even permanently in Rome—to express more precisely the conditions of the acquisition of plebeian rights, and to mark off the enlarged burgess-body in its turn from those who were now the non-burgesses. To thisepoch therefore we may trace back—in the views and feelings of the people—both the invidiousness of the distinction between patricians and plebeians, and the strict and haughty line of demarcation between -cives Romani- and aliens. But the former civic distinction was in its nature transient, while the latter political one was permanent; and the sense of political unity and rising greatness, which was thus implanted in the heart of the nation, was expansive enough first to undermine and then to carry away with its mighty current those paltry distinctions.

Law and Edict

It was at this period, moreover, that law and edict were separated. The distinction indeed had its foundation in the essential character of the Roman state; for even the regal power in Rome was subordinate, not superior, to the law of the land. But the profound and practical veneration, which the Romans, like every other people of political capacity, cherished for the principle of authority, gave birth to the remarkable rule of Roman constitutional and private law, that every command of the magistrate not based upon a law was at least valid during his tenure of office, although it expired with that tenure. It is evident that in this view, so long as the presidents were nominated for life, the distinction between law and edict must have practically been almost lost sight of, and the legislative activity of the public assembly could acquire no development. On the other hand it obtained a wide field of action after the presidents were changed annually; and the fact was now by no means void of practical importance, that, if the consul in deciding a process committed a legal informality, his successor could institute a fresh trial of the cause.

Civil and Military Authority

It was at this period, finally, that the provinces of civil and military authority were separated. In the former the law ruled, in the latter the axe: the former was governed by the constitutional checks of the right of appeal and of regulated delegation; in the latter the general held an absolute sway like the king.(15) It was an established principle, that the general and the army as such should not under ordinary circumstances enter the city proper. That organic and permanently operative enactments could only be made under the authority of the civil power, was implied in the spirit, if not in the letter, of the constitution. Instances indeed occasionally occurred where the general, disregarding this principle, convoked his forces in the camp as a burgess assembly, nor was a decree passed under such circumstances legally void; but custom disapproved of such a proceeding, and it soon fell into disuse as though it had been forbidden. The distinction between Quirites and soldiers became more and more deeply rooted in the minds of the burgesses.

Government of the Patriciate

Time however was required for the development of these consequences of the new republicanism; vividly as posterity felt its effects, the revolution probably appeared to the contemporary world at first in a different light. The non-burgesses indeed gained by it burgess-rights, and the new burgess-body acquired in the -comitia centuriata- comprehensive prerogatives; but the right of rejection on the part of the patrician senate, which in firm and serried ranks confronted the -comitia- as if it were an Upper House, legally hampered their freedom of movement precisely in the most important matters, and although not in a position to thwart the serious will of the collective body, could yet practically delay and cripple it. If the nobility in giving up their claim to be the sole embodiment of the community did not seem to have lost much, they had in other respects decidedly gained. The king, it is true, was a patrician as well as the consul, and the right of nominating the members of the senate belonged to the latter as to the former; but while his exceptional position raised the former no less above the patricians than above the plebeians, and while cases might easily occur in which he would be obliged to lean upon the support of the multitude even against the nobility, the consul—ruling for a brief term, but before and after that term simply one of the nobility, and obeying to-morrow the noble fellow-burgess whom he had commanded to-day—by no means occupied a position aloof from his order, and the spirit of the noble in him must have been far more powerful than that of the magistrate. Indeed, if at any time by way of exception a patrician disinclined to the rule of the nobility was called to the government, his official authority was paralyzed partly by the priestly colleges, which were pervaded by an intense aristocratic spirit, partly by his colleague, and was easily suspended by the dictatorship; and, what was of still more moment, he wanted the first element of political power, time. The president of a commonwealth, whatever plenary authority may be conceded to him, will never gain possession of political power, if he does not continue for some considerable time at the head of affairs; for a necessary condition of every dominion is duration. Consequently the senate appointed for life inevitably acquired—and that by virtue chiefly of its title to advise the magistrate in all points, so that we speak not of the narrower patrician, but of the enlarged patricio-plebeian, senate—so great an influence as contrasted with the annual rulers, that their legal relations became precisely inverted; the senate substantially assumed to itself the powers of government, and the former ruler sank into a president acting as its chairman and executing its decrees. In the case of every proposal to be submitted to the community for acceptance or rejection the practice of previously consulting the whole senate and obtaining its approval, while not constitutionally necessary, was consecrated by use and wont; and it was not lightly or willingly departed from. The same course was followed in the case of important state-treaties, of the management and distribution of the public lands, and generally of every act the effects of which extended beyond the official year; and nothing was left to the consul but the transaction of current business, the initial steps in civil processes, and the command in war. Especially important in its consequences was the change in virtue of which neither the consul, nor even the otherwise absolute dictator, was permitted to touch the public treasure except with the consent and by the will of the senate. The senate made it obligatory on the consuls to commit the administration of the public chest, which the king had managed or might at any rate have managed himself, to two standing subordinate magistrates, who were nominated no doubt by the consuls and had to obey them, but were, as may easily be conceived, much more dependent than the consuls themselves on the senate.(16) It thus drew into its own hands the management of finance; and this right of sanctioning the expenditure of money on the part of the Roman senate may be placed on a parallel in its effects with the right of sanctioning taxation in the constitutional monarchies of the present day.

The consequences followed as a matter of course. The first and most essential condition of all aristocratic government is, that the plenary power of the state be vested not in an individual but in a corporation. Now a preponderantly aristocratic corporation, the senate, had appropriated to itself the government, and at the same time the executive power not only remained in the hands of the nobility, but was also entirely subject to the governing corporation. It is true that a considerable number of men not belonging to the nobility sat in the senate; but as they were incapable of holding magistracies or even of taking part in the debates, and thus were excluded from all practical share in the government, they necessarily played a subordinate part in the senate, and were moreover kept in pecuniary dependence on the corporation through the economically important privilege of using the public pasture. The gradually recognized right of the patrician consuls to revise and modify the senatorial list at least every fourth year, ineffective as presumably it was over against the nobility, might very well be employed in their interest, and an obnoxious plebeian might by means of it be kept out of the senate or even be removed from its ranks.

The Plebeian Opposition

It is therefore quite true that the immediate effect of the revolution was to establish the aristocratic government. It is not, however, the whole truth. While the majority of contemporaries probably thought that the revolution had brought upon the plebeians only a more rigid despotism, we who come afterwards discern in that very revolution the germs of young liberty. What the patricians gained was gained at the expense not of the community, but of the magistrate's power. It is true that the community gained only a few narrowly restricted rights, which were far less practical and palpable than the acquisitions of the nobility, and which not one in a thousand probably had the wisdom to value; but they formed a pledge and earnest of the future. Hitherto the —metoeci— had been politically nothing, the old burgesses had been everything; now that the former were embraced in the community, the old burgesses were overcome; for, however much might still be wanting to full civil equality, it is the first breach, not the occupation of the last post, that decides the fall of the fortress. With justice therefore the Roman community dated its political existence from the beginning of the consulate.

While however the republican revolution may, notwithstanding the aristocratic rule which in the first instance it established, be justly called a victory of the former —metoeci— or the -plebs-, the revolution even in this respect bore by no means the character which we are accustomed in the present day to designate as democratic. Pure personal merit without the support of birth and wealth could perhaps gain influence and consideration more easily under the regal government than under that of the patriciate. Then admission to the patriciate was not in law foreclosed; now the highest object of plebeian ambition was to be admitted into the dumb appendage of the senate. The nature of the case implied that the governing aristocratic order, so far as it admitted plebeians at all, would grant the right of occupying seats in the senate not absolutely to the best men, but chiefly to the heads of the wealthy and notable plebeian families; and the families thus admitted jealously guarded the possession of the senatorial stalls. While a complete legal equality therefore had subsisted within the old burgess-body, the new burgess-body or former —metoeci— came to be in this way divided from the first into a number of privileged families and a multitude kept in a position of inferiority. But the power of the community now according to the centuriate organization came into the hands of that class which since the Servian reform of the army and of taxation had borne mainly the burdens of the state, namely the freeholders, and indeed not so much into the hands of the great proprietors or into those of the small cottagers, as into those of the intermediate class of farmers—an arrangement in which the seniors were still so far privileged that, although less numerous, they had as many voting-divisions as the juniors. While in this way the axe was laid to the root of the old burgess-body and their clan-nobility, and the basis of a new burgess-body was laid, the preponderance in the latter rested on the possession of land and on age, and the first beginnings were already visible of a new aristocracy based primarily on the actual consideration in which the families were held—the future nobility. There could be no clearer indication of the fundamentally conservative character of the Roman commonwealth than the fact, that the revolution which gave birth to the republic laid down at the same time the primary outlines of a new organization of the state, which was in like manner conservative and in like manner aristocratic.

Notes for Book II Chapter I

1. I. IX. The Tarquins

2. The well-known fable for the most part refutes itself. To a considerable extent it has been concocted for the explanation of surnames (-Brutus-, -Poplicola-, -Scaevola-). But even its apparently historical ingredients are found on closer examination to have been invented. Of this character is the statement that Brutus was captain of the horsemen (-tribunus celerum-) and in that capacity proposed the decree of the people as to the banishment of the Tarquins; for, according to the Roman constitution, it is quite impossible that a mere officer should have had the right to convoke the curies. The whole of this statement has evidently been invented with the view of furnishing a legal basis for the Roman republic; and very ill invented it is, for in its case the -tribunus celerum- is confounded with the entirely different -magister equitum- (V. Burdens Of The Burgesses f.), and then the right of convoking the centuries which pertained to the latter by virtue of his praetorian rank is made to apply to the assembly of the curies.

3. -Consules- are those who "leap or dance together," as -praesul- is one who "leaps before," -exsul-, one who "leaps out" (—o ekpeson—), -insula-, a "leap into," primarily applied to a mass of rock fallen into the sea.

4. The day of entering on office did not coincide with the beginning of the year (1st March), and was not at all fixed. The day of retiring was regulated by it, except when a consul was elected expressly in room of one who had dropped out (-consul suffectus-); in which case the substitute succeeded to the rights and consequently to the term of him whom he replaced. But these supplementary consuls in the earlier period only occurred when merely one of the consuls had dropped out: pairs of supplementary consuls are not found until the later ages of the republic. Ordinarily, therefore, the official year of a consul consisted of unequal portions of two civil years.

5. I. V. The King

6. I. XI. Crimes

7. I. V. Prerogatives of the Senate

8. I. V. The King

9. I. V. The King

10. I. VI. Dependents and Guests

11. I. VI. Political Effects of the Servian Military Organization

12. I. V. The Senate as State Council

13. I. V. Prerogatives of the Senate

14. That the first consuls admitted to the senate 164 plebeians, is hardly to be regarded as a historical fact, but rather as a proof that the later Roman archaeologists were unable to point out more than 136 -gentes- of the Roman nobility (Rom, Forsch. i. 121).

15. It may not be superfluous to remark, that the -iudicium legitimum-, as well as that -quod imperio continetur-, rested on the imperium of the directing magistrate, and the distinction only consisted in the circumstance that the -imperium- was in the former case limited by the -lex-, while in the latter it was free.

16. II. I. Restrictions on the Delegation of Powers

CHAPTER II

The Tribunate of the Plebs and the Decemvirate

Material Interests

Under the new organization of the commonwealth the old burgesses had attained by legal means to the full possession of political power. Governing through the magistracy which had been reduced to be their servant, preponderating in the Senate, in sole possession of all public offices and priesthoods, armed with exclusive cognizance of things human and divine and familiar with the whole routine of political procedure, influential in the public assembly through the large number of pliant adherents attached to the several families, and, lastly, entitled to examine and to reject every decree of the community,—the patricians might have long preserved their practical power, just because they had at the right time abandoned their claim to sole legal authority. It is true that the plebeians could not but be painfully sensible of their political disabilities; but undoubtedly in the first instance the nobility had not much to fear from a purely political opposition, if it understood the art of keeping the multitude, which desired nothing but equitable administration and protection of its material interests, aloof from political strife. In fact during the first period after the expulsion of the kings we meet with various measures which were intended, or at any rate seemed to be intended, to gain the favour of the commons for the government of the nobility especially on economic grounds. The port-dues were reduced; when the price of grain was high, large quantities of corn were purchased on account of the state, and the trade in salt was made a state-monopoly, in order to supply the citizens with corn and salt at reasonable prices; lastly, the national festival was prolonged for an additional day. Of the same character was the ordinance which we have already mentioned respecting property fines,(1) which was not merely intended in general to set limits to the dangerous fining-prerogative of the magistrates, but was also, in a significant manner, calculated for the especial protection of the man of small means. The magistrate was prohibited from fining the same man on the same day to an extent beyond two sheep or beyond thirty oxen, without granting leave to appeal; and the reason of these singular rates can only perhaps be found in the fact, that in the case of the man of small means possessing only a few sheep a different maximum appeared necessary from that fixed for the wealthy proprietor of herds of oxen —a considerate regard to the wealth or poverty of the person fined, from which modern legislators might take a lesson.

But these regulations were merely superficial; the main current flowed in the opposite direction. With the change in the constitution there was introduced a comprehensive revolution in the financial and economic relations of Rome, The government of the kings had probably abstained on principle from enhancing the power of capital, and had promoted as far as it could an increase in the number of farms. The new aristocratic government, again, appears to have aimed from the first at the destruction of the middle classes, particularly of the intermediate and smaller holdings of land, and at the development of a domination of landed and moneyed lords on the one hand, and of an agricultural proletariate on the other.

Rising Power of the Capitalists

The reduction of the port-dues, although upon the whole a popular measure, chiefly benefited the great merchant. But a much greater accession to the power of capital was supplied by the indirect system of finance-administration. It is difficult to say what were the remote causes that gave rise to it: but, while its origin may probably be referred to the regal period, after the introduction of the consulate the importance of the intervention of private agency must have been greatly increased, partly by the rapid succession of magistrates in Rome, partly by the extension of the financial action of the treasury to such matters as the purchase and sale of grain and salt; and thus the foundation must have been laid for that system of farming the finances, the development of which became so momentous and so pernicious for the Roman commonwealth. The state gradually put all its indirect revenues and all its more complicated payments and transactions into the hands of middlemen, who gave or received a round sum and then managed the matter for their own benefit. Of course only considerable capitalists and, as the state looked strictly to tangible security, in the main only large landholders, could enter into such engagements: and thus there grew up a class of tax-farmers and contractors, who, in the rapid growth of their wealth, in their power over the state to which they appeared to be servants, and in the absurd and sterile basis of their moneyed dominion, quite admit of comparison with the speculators on the stock exchange of the present day.

Public Land

The concentrated aspect assumed by the administration of finance showed itself first and most palpably in the treatment of the public lands, which tended almost directly to accomplish the material and moral annihilation of the middle classes. The use of the public pasture and of the state-domains generally was from its very nature a privilege of burgesses; formal law excluded the plebeian from the joint use of the common pasture. As however, apart from the conversion of the public land into private property or its assignation, Roman law knew no fixed rights of usufruct on the part of individual burgesses to be respected like those of property, it depended solely on the pleasure of the king, so long as the public land remained such, to grant and to define its joint enjoyment; and it is not to be doubted that he frequently made use of his right, or at least his power, as to this matter in favour of plebeians. But on the introduction of the republic the principle was again strictly insisted on, that the use of the common pasture belonged in law merely to the burgess of best right, or in other words to the patrician; and, though the senate still as before allowed exceptions in favour of the wealthy plebeian houses represented in it, the small plebeian landholders and the day-labourers, who stood most in need of the common pasture, had its joint enjoyment injuriously withheld from them. Moreover there had hitherto been paid for the cattle driven out on the common pasture a grazing-tax, which was moderate enough to make the right of using that pasture still be regarded as a privilege, and yet yielded no inconsiderable revenue to the public purse. The patrician quaestors were now remiss and indulgent in levying it, and gradually allowed it to fall into desuetude. Hitherto, particularly when new domains were acquired by conquest, allocations of land had been regularly arranged, in which all the poorer burgesses and —metoeci— were provided for; it was only the land which was not suitable for agriculture that was annexed to the common pasture. The ruling class did not venture wholly to give up such assignations, and still less to propose them merely in favour of the rich; but they became fewer and scantier, and were replaced by the pernicious system of occupation-that is to say, the cession of domain-lands, not in property or under formal lease for a definite term, but in special usufruct until further notice, to the first occupant and his heirs-at-law, so that the state was at any time entitled to resume them, and the occupier had to pay the tenth sheaf, or in oil and wine the fifth part of the produce, to the exchequer. This was simply the -precarium- already described(2) applied to the state-domains, and may have been already in use as to the public land at an earlier period, particularly as a temporary arrangement until its assignation should be carried out. Now, however, not only did this occupation-tenure become permanent, but, as was natural, none but privileged persons or their favourites participated, and the tenth and fifth were collected with the same negligence as the grazing-money. A threefold blow was thus struck at the intermediate and smaller landholders: they were deprived of the common usufructs of burgesses; the burden of taxation was increased in consequence of the domain revenues no longer flowing regularly into the public chest; and those land-allocations were stopped, which had provided a constant outlet for the agricultural proletariate somewhat as a great and well-regulated system of emigration would do at the present day. To these evils was added the farming on a large scale, which was probably already beginning to come into vogue, dispossessing the small agrarian clients, and in their stead cultivating the estates by rural slaves; a blow, which was more difficult to avert and perhaps more pernicious than all those political usurpations put together. The burdensome and partly unfortunate wars, and the exorbitant taxes and task-works to which these gave rise, filled up the measure of calamity, so as either to deprive the possessor directly of his farm and to make him the bondsman if not the slave of his creditor-lord, or to reduce him through encumbrances practically to the condition of a temporary lessee of his creditor. The capitalists, to whom a new field was here opened of lucrative speculation unattended by trouble or risk, sometimes augmented in this way their landed property; sometimes they left to the farmer, whose person and estate the law of debt placed in their hands, nominal proprietorship and actual possession. The latter course was probably the most common as well as the most pernicious; for while utter ruin might thereby be averted from the individual, this precarious position of the farmer, dependent at all times on the mercy of his creditor—a position in which he knew nothing of property but its burdens—threatened to demoralise and politically to annihilate the whole farmer-class. The intention of the legislator, when instead of mortgaging he prescribed the immediate transfer of the property to the creditor with a view to prevent insolvency and to devolve the burdens of the state on the real holders of the soil,(3) was evaded by the rigorous system of personal credit, which might be very suitable for merchants, but ruined the farmers. The free divisibility of the soil always involved the risk of an insolvent agricultural proletariate; and under such circumstances, when all burdens were increasing and all means of deliverance were foreclosed, distress and despair could not but spread with fearful rapidity among the agricultural middle class.

Relations of the Social Question to the Question between Orders

The distinction between rich and poor, which arose out of these relations, by no means coincided with that between the clans and the plebeians. If far the greater part

28

of the patricians were wealthy landholders, opulent and considerable families were, of course, not wanting among the plebeians; and as the senate, which even then perhaps consisted in greater part of plebeians, had assumed the superintendence of the finances to the exclusion even of the patrician magistrates, it was natural that all those economic advantages, for which the political privileges of the nobility were abused, should go to the benefit of the wealthy collectively; and the pressure fell the more heavily upon the commons, since those who were the ablest and the most capable of resistance were by their admission to the senate transferred from the class of the oppressed to the ranks of the oppressors.

But this state of things prevented the political position of the aristocracy from being permanently tenable. Had it possessed the self-control to govern justly and to protect the middle class—as individual consuls from its ranks endeavoured, but from the reduced position of the magistracy were unable effectually, to do—it might have long maintained itself in sole possession of the offices of state. Had it been willing to admit the wealthy and respectable plebeians to full equality of rights—possibly by connecting the acquisition of the patriciate with admission into the senate—both might long have governed and speculated with impunity. But neither of these courses was adopted; the narrowness of mind and short-sightedness, which are the proper and inalienable privileges of all genuine patricianism, were true to their character also in Rome, and rent the powerful commonwealth asunder in useless, aimless, and inglorious strife.

Secession to the Sacred Mount

The immediate crisis however proceeded not from those who felt the disabilities of their order, but from the distress of the farmers. The rectified annals place the political revolution in the year 244, the social in the years 259 and 260; they certainly appear to have followed close upon each other, but the interval was probably longer. The strict enforcement of the law of debt—so runs the story— excited the indignation of the farmers at large. When in the year 259 the levy was called forth for a dangerous war, the men bound to serve refused to obey the command. Thereupon the consul Publius Servilius suspended for a time the application of the debtor-laws, and gave orders to liberate the persons already imprisoned for debt as well as prohibited further arrests; so that the farmers took their places in the ranks and helped to secure the victory. On their return from the field of battle the peace, which had been achieved by their exertions, brought back their prison and their chains: with merciless rigour the second consul, Appius Claudius, enforced the debtor-laws and his colleague, to whom his former soldiers appealed for aid, dared not offer opposition. It seemed as if collegiate rule had been introduced not for the protection of the people, but to facilitate breach of faith and despotism; they endured, however, what could not be changed. But when in the following year the war was renewed, the word of the consul availed no longer. It was not till Manius Valerius was nominated dictator that the farmers submitted, partly from their awe of the higher magisterial authority, partly from their confidence in his friendly feeling to the popular cause—for the Valerii were one of those old patrician clans by whom government was esteemed a privilege and an honour, not a source of gain. The victory was again with the Roman standards; but when the victors came home and the dictator submitted his proposals of reform to the senate, they were thwarted by its obstinate opposition. The army still stood in its array, as usual, before the gates of the city. When the news arrived, the long threatening storm burst forth; the -esprit de corps- and the compact military organization carried even the timid and the indifferent along with the movement. The army abandoned its general and its encampment, and under the leadership of the commanders of the legions—the military tribunes, who were at least in great part plebeians—marched in martial order into the district of Crustumeria between the Tiber and the Anio, where it occupied a hill and threatened to establish in this most fertile part of the Roman territory a new plebeian city. This secession showed in a palpable manner even to the most obstinate of the oppressors that such a civil war must end with economic ruin to themselves; and the senate gave way. The dictator negotiated an agreement; the citizens returned within the city walls; unity was outwardly restored. The people gave Manius Valerius thenceforth the name of "the great" (-maximus-)—and called the mount beyond the Anio "the sacred mount." There was something mighty and elevating in such a revolution, undertaken by the multitude itself without definite guidance under generals whom accident supplied, and accomplished without bloodshed; and with pleasure and pride the citizens recalled its memory. Its consequences were felt for many centuries: it was the origin of the tribunate of the plebs.

Plebian Tribunes and Plebian Aediles

In addition to temporary enactments, particularly for remedying the most urgent distress occasioned by debt, and for providing for a number of the rural population by the founding of various colonies, the dictator carried in constitutional form a law, which he moreover —doubtless in order to secure amnesty to the burgesses for the breach of their military oath—caused every individual member of the community to swear to, and then had it deposited in a temple under the charge and custody of two magistrates specially appointed from the plebs for the purpose, the two "house-masters" (-aediles-). This law placed by the side of the two patrician consuls two plebeian tribunes, who were to be elected by the plebeians assembled in curies. The power of the tribunes was of no avail in opposition to the military -imperium-, that is, in opposition to the authority of the dictator everywhere or to that of the consuls beyond the city; but it confronted, on a footing of independence and equality, the ordinary civil powers which the consuls exercised. There was, however, no partition of powers. The tribunes obtained the right which pertained to the consul against his fellow-consul and all the more against an inferior magistrate,(4) namely, the right to cancel any command issued by a magistrate, as to which the burgess whom it affected held himself aggrieved and lodged a complaint, through their protest timeously and personally interposed, and likewise of hindering or cancelling at discretion any proposal made by a magistrate to the burgesses, in other words, the right of intercession or the so-called tribunician veto.

Intercession

The power of the tribunes, therefore, primarily involved the right of putting a stop to administration and to judicial action at their pleasure, of enabling a person bound to military service to withhold himself from the levy with impunity, of preventing or cancelling the raising of an action and legal execution against the debtor, the initiation of a criminal process and the arrest of the accused while the investigation was pending, and other powers of the same sort. That this legal help might not be frustrated by the absence of the helpers, it was further ordained that the tribune should not spend a night out of the city, and that his door must stand open day and night. Moreover, it lay in the power of the tribunate of the people through a single word of a single tribune to restrain the adoption of a resolution by the community, which otherwise by virtue of its sovereign right might have without ceremony recalled the privileges conferred by it on the plebs.

But these rights would have been ineffective, if there had not belonged to the tribune of the people an instantaneously operative and irresistible power of enforcing them against him who did not regard them, and especially against the magistrate contravening them. This was conferred in such a form that the acting in opposition to the tribune when making use of his right, above all things the laying hands on his person, which at the Sacred Mount every plebeian, man by man for himself and his descendants, had sworn to protect now and in all time to come from all harm, should be a capital crime; and the exercise of this criminal justice was committed not to the magistrates of the community but to those of the plebs. The tribune might in virtue of this his judicial office call to account any burgess, especially the consul in office, have him seized if he should not voluntarily submit, place him under arrest during investigation or allow him to find bail, and then sentence him to death or to a fine. For this purpose the two plebeian aediles appointed at the same time were attached to the tribunes as their servants and assistants, primarily to effect arrest, on which account the same inviolable character was assured to them also by the collective oath of the plebeians. Moreover the aediles themselves had judicial powers like the tribunes, but only for the minor causes that might be settled by fines. If an appeal was lodged against the decision of tribune or aedile, it was addressed not to the whole body of the burgesses, with which the officials of the plebs were not entitled at all to transact business, but to the whole body of the plebeians, which in this case met by curies and finally decided by majority of votes.

This procedure certainly savoured of violence rather than of justice, especially when it was adopted against a non-plebeian, as must in fact have been ordinarily the case. It was not to be reconciled either with the letter or the spirit of the constitution that a patrician should be called to account by authorities who presided not over the body of burgesses, but over an association formed within it, and that he should be compelled to appeal, not to the burgesses, but to this very association. This was originally without question Lynch justice; but the self-help was doubtless carried into effect from early times in form of law, and was after the legal recognition of the tribunate of the plebs regarded as lawfully admissible.

In point of intention this new jurisdiction of the tribunes and the aediles, and the appellate decision of the plebeian assembly therein originating, were beyond doubt just as much bound to the laws as the jurisdiction of the consuls and quaestors and the judgment of the centuries on appeal; the legal conceptions of crime against the community(5) and of offences against order(6) were transferred from the community and its magistrates to the plebs and its champions. But these conceptions were themselves so little fixed, and their statutory definition was so difficult and indeed impossible, that the administration of justice under these categories from its very nature bore almost inevitably the stamp of arbitrariness. And now when the very idea of right had become obscured amidst the struggles of the orders, and when the legal party—leaders on both sides were furnished with a co-ordinate jurisdiction, this jurisdiction must have more and more approximated to a mere arbitrary police. It affected in particular the magistrate. Hitherto the latter according to Roman state law, so long as he was a magistrate, was amenable to no jurisdiction at all, and, although after demitting his office he might have been legally made responsible for each of his acts, the exercise of this right lay withal in the hands of the members of his own order and ultimately of the collective community, to which these likewise belonged. Now in the tribunician jurisdiction there emerged a new power, which on the one hand might interfere against the supreme magistrate even during his tenure of office, and on the other hand was wielded against the noble burgesses exclusively by the non-noble, and which was the more oppressive that neither the crime nor its punishment was formally defined by law. In reality through the co-ordinate jurisdiction of the plebs and the community the estates, limbs, and lives of the burgesses were abandoned to the arbitrary pleasure of the party assemblies.

In civil jurisdiction the plebeian institutions interfered only so far, that in the processes affecting freedom, which were so important for the plebs, the nomination of jurymen was withdrawn from the consuls, and the decisions in such cases were pronounced by the "ten-men-judges" destined specially for that purpose (-iudices-, -decemviri-, afterwards -decemviri litibus iudicandis-).

Legislation

With this co-ordinate jurisdiction there was further associated a co-ordinate initiative in legislation. The right of assembling the members and of procuring decrees on their part already pertained to the tribunes, in so far as no association at all can be conceived without such a right. But it was conferred upon them, in a marked way, by legally securing that the autonomous right of the plebs to assemble and pass resolutions should not be interfered with on the part of the magistrates of the community or, in fact, of the community itself. At all events it was the necessary preliminary to the legal recognition of the plebs generally, that the tribunes could not be hindered from having their successors elected by the assembly of the plebs and from procuring the confirmation of their criminal sentences by the same body; and this right accordingly was further specially guaranteed to them by the Icilian law (262), which threatened with severe punishment any one who should interrupt the tribune while speaking, or should bid the assembly disperse. It is evident that under such circumstances the tribune could not well be prevented from taking a vote on other proposals than the choice of his successor and the confirmation of his sentences. Such "resolves of the multitude" (-plebi scita-) were not indeed strictly valid decrees of the people; on the contrary, they were at first little more than are the resolutions of our modern public meetings; but, as the distinction between the comitia of the people and the councils of the multitude was of a formal nature rather than aught else, the validity of these resolves as autonomous determinations of the community was at once claimed at least on the part of the plebeians, and the Icilian law for instance was immediately carried in this way. Thus was the tribune of the people appointed as a shield and protection for the individual, and as leader and manager for all, provided with unlimited judicial power in criminal proceedings, that in this way he might give emphasis to his command, and lastly even pronounced to be in his person inviolable (-sacrosanctus-), inasmuch as whoever laid hands upon him or his servant was not merely regarded as incurring the vengeance of the gods, but was also among men accounted as if, after legally proven crime, deserving of death.

Relation of the Tribune to the Consul

The tribunes of the multitude (-tribuni plebis-) arose out of the military tribunes and derived from them their name; but constitutionally they had no further relation to them. On the contrary, in respect of powers the tribunes of the plebs stood on a level with the consuls. The appeal from the consul to the tribune, and the tribune's right of intercession in opposition to the consul, were, as has been already said, precisely of the same nature with the appeal from consul to consul and the intercession of the one consul in opposition to the other; and both cases were simply applications of the general principle of law that, where two equal authorities differ, the veto prevails over the command. Moreover the original number (which indeed was soon augmented), and the annual duration of the magistracy, which in the case of the tribunes changed its occupants on the 10th of December, were common to the tribunes and the consuls. They shared also the peculiar collegiate arrangement, which placed the full powers of the office in the hands of each individual consul and of each individual tribune, and, when collisions occurred within the college, did not count the votes, but gave the Nay precedence over the Yea; for which reason, when a tribune forbade, the veto of the individual was sufficient notwithstanding the opposition of his colleagues, while on the other hand, when he brought an accusation, he could be thwarted by any one of those colleagues. Both consuls and tribunes had full and co-ordinate criminal jurisdiction, although the former exercised it indirectly, and the latter directly; as the two quaestors were attached to the former, the two aediles were associated with the latter.(7) The consuls were necessarily patricians, the tribunes necessarily plebeians. The former had the ampler power, the latter the more unlimited, for the consul submitted to the prohibition and the judgment of the tribunes, but the tribune did not submit himself to the consul. Thus the tribunician power was a copy of the consular; but it was none the less a contrast to it. The power of the consuls was essentially positive, that of the tribunes essentially negative. The consuls alone were magistrates of the Roman people, not the tribunes; for the former were elected by the whole burgesses, the latter only by the plebeian association. In token of this the consul appeared in public with the apparel and retinue pertaining to state-officials; the tribunes sat on a stool instead of the "chariot seat," and lacked the official attendants, the purple border, and generally all the insignia of magistracy: even in the senate the tribune had neither presidency nor so much as a seat. Thus in this remarkable institution absolute prohibition was in the most stern and abrupt fashion opposed to absolute command; the quarrel was settled by legally recognizing and regulating the discord between rich and poor.

Political Value of the Tribunate

But what was gained by a measure which broke up the unity of the state; which subjected the magistrates to a controlling authority unsteady in its action and dependent on all the passions of the moment; which in the hour of peril might have brought the administration to a dead-lock at the bidding of any one of the opposition chiefs elevated to the rival throne; and which, by investing all the magistrates with co-ordinate jurisdiction in the administration of criminal law, as it were formally transferred that administration from the domain of law to that of politics and corrupted it for all time coming? It is true indeed that the tribunate, if it did not directly contribute to the political equalization of the orders, served as a powerful weapon in the hands of the plebeians when these soon afterwards desired admission to the offices of state. But this was not the real design of the tribunate. It was a concession wrung not from the politically privileged order, but from the rich landlords and capitalists; it was designed to ensure to the commons equitable administration of law, and to promote a more judicious administration of finance. This design it did not, and could not, fulfil. The tribune might put a stop to particular iniquities, to individual instances of crying hardship; but the fault lay not in the unfair working of a righteous law, but in a law which was itself unrighteous, and how could the tribune regularly obstruct the ordinary course of justice? Could he have done so, it would have served little to remedy the evil, unless the sources of impoverishment were stopped—the perverse taxation, the wretched system of credit, and the pernicious occupation of the domain-lands. But such measures were not attempted, evidently because the wealthy plebeians themselves had no less interest in these abuses than the patricians. So this singular magistracy was instituted, which presented to the commons an obvious and available aid, and yet could not possibly carry out the necessary economic reform. It was no proof of political wisdom, but a wretched compromise between the wealthy aristocracy and the leaderless multitude. It has been affirmed that the tribune of the people preserved Rome from tyranny. Were it true, it would be of little moment: a change in the form of the state is not in itself an evil for a people; on the contrary, it was a misfortune for the Romans that monarchy was introduced too late, after the physical and mental energies of the nation were exhausted. But the assertion is not even correct; as is shown by the circumstance that the Italian states remained as regularly free from tyrants as the Hellenic states regularly witnessed their emergence. The reason lies simply in the fact that tyranny is everywhere the result of universal suffrage, and that the Italians excluded the burgesses who had no land from their public assemblies longer than the Greeks did: when Rome departed from this course, monarchy did not fail to emerge, and was in fact associated with this very tribunician orifice. That the tribunate had its use, in pointing out legitimate paths of opposition and averting many a wrong, no one will fail to acknowledge; but it is equally evident that, where it did prove useful, it was employed for very different objects from those for which it had been established. The bold experiment of allowing the leaders of the opposition a constitutional veto, and of investing them with power to assert it regardless of the consequences, proved to be an expedient by which the state was politically unhinged; and social evils were prolonged by the application of useless palliatives.

Further Dissensions

Now that civil war was organized, it pursued its course. The parties stood face to face as if drawn up for battle, each under its leaders. Restriction of the consular and extension of the tribunician power were the objects contended for on the one side; the annihilation of the tribunate was sought on the other. Legal impunity secured for insubordination, refusal to enter the ranks for the defence of the land, impeachments involving fines and penalties directed specially against magistrates who had violated the rights of the commons or who had simply provoked their displeasure, were the weapons of the plebeians; and to these the patricians opposed violence, concert with the public foes, and occasionally also the dagger of the assassin. Hand-to-hand conflicts took place in the streets, and on both sides the sacredness of the magistrate's person was violated. Many families of burgesses are said to have migrated, and to have sought more peaceful abodes in neighbouring communities; and we may well believe it. The strong patriotism of the people is obvious from the fact, not that they adopted this constitution, but that they endured it, and that the community, notwithstanding the most vehement convulsions, still held together.

Coriolanus

The best-known incident in these conflicts of the orders is the history of Gnaeus Marcius, a brave aristocrat, who derived his surname from the storming of Corioli. Indignant at the refusal of the centuries to entrust to him the consulate in the year 263, he is reported to have proposed, according to one version, the suspension of the sales of corn from the state-stores, till the hungry people should give up the tribunate; according to another version, the direct abolition of the tribunate itself. Impeached by the tribunes so that his life was in peril, it is said that he left the city, but only to return at the head of a Volscian army; that when he was on the point of conquering the city of his fathers for the public foe, the earnest appeal of his mother touched his conscience; and that thus he expiated his first treason by a second, and both by death. How much of this is true cannot be determined; but the story, over which the naïve misrepresentations of the Roman annalists have shed a patriotic glory, affords a glimpse of the deep moral and political disgrace of these conflicts between the orders. Of a similar stamp was the surprise of the Capitol by a band of political refugees, led by a Sabine chief, Appius Herdonius, in the year 294; they summoned the slaves to arms, and it was only after a violent conflict, and by the aid of the Tusculans who hastened to render help, that the Roman burgess-force overcame the Catilinarian band. The same character of fanatical exasperation marks other events of this epoch, the historical significance of which can no longer be apprehended in the lying family narratives; such as the predominance of the Fabian clan which furnished one of the two consuls from 269 to 275, and the reaction against it, the emigration of the Fabii from Rome, and their annihilation by the Etruscans on the Cremera (277). Still more odious was the murder of the tribune of the people, Gnaeus Genucius, who had ventured to call two consulars to account, and who on the morning of the day fixed for the impeachment was found dead in bed (281). The immediate effect of this misdeed was the Publilian law (283), one of the most momentous in its consequences with which Roman history has to deal. Two of the most important arrangements—the introduction of the plebeian assembly of tribes, and the placing of the -plebiscitum- on a level, although conditionally, with the formal law sanctioned by the whole community—are to be referred, the former certainly, the latter probably, to the proposal of Volero Publilius the tribune of the people in 283. The plebs had hitherto adopted its resolutions by curies; accordingly in these its separate assemblies, on the one hand, the voting had been by mere number without distinction of wealth or of freehold property, and, on the other hand, in consequence of that standing side by side on the part of the clansmen, which was implied in the very nature of the curial assembly, the clients of the great patrician families had voted with one another in the assembly of the plebeians. These two circumstances had given to the nobility various opportunities of exercising influence on that assembly, and especially of managing the election of tribunes according to their views; and both were henceforth done away by means of the new method of voting according to tribes. Of these, four had been formed under the Servian constitution for the purposes of the levy, embracing town and country alike;(8) subsequently-perhaps in the year 259—the Roman territory had been divided into twenty districts, of which the first four embraced the city and its immediate environs, while the other sixteen were formed out of the rural territory on the basis of the clan-cantons of the earliest Roman domain.(9) To these was added—probably only in consequence of the Publilian law, and with a view to bring about the inequality, which was desirable for voting purposes, in the total number of the divisions—as a twenty-first tribe the Crustuminian, which derived its name from the place where the plebs had constituted itself as such and had established the tribunate;(10) and thenceforth the special assemblies of the plebs took place, no longer by curies, but by tribes. In these divisions, which were based throughout on the possession of land, the voters were exclusively freeholders: but they voted without distinction as to the size of their possession, and just as they dwelt together in villages and hamlets. Consequently, this assembly of the tribes, which otherwise was externally modelled on that of the curies, was in reality an assembly of the independent middle class, from which, on the one hand, the great majority of freedmen and clients were excluded as not being freeholders, and in which, on the other hand, the larger landholders had no such preponderance as in the centuries. This "meeting of the multitude" (-concilium plebis-) was even less a general assembly of the burgesses than the plebeian assembly by curies had been, for it not only, like the latter, excluded all the patricians, but also the plebeians who had no land; but the multitude was powerful enough to carry the point that its decree should have equal legal validity with that adopted by the centuries, in the event of its having been previously approved by the whole senate. That this last regulation had the force of established law before the issuing of the Twelve Tables, is certain; whether it was directly introduced on occasion of the Publilian -plebiscitum-, or whether it had already been called into existence by some other—now forgotten—statute, and was only applied to the Publilian -plebiscitum- cannot be any longer ascertained. In like manner it remains uncertain whether the number of tribunes was raised by this law from two to four, or whether that increase had taken place previously.

More sagacious in plan than all these party steps was the attempt of Spurius Cassius to break down the financial omnipotence of the rich, and so to put a stop to the true source of the evil. He was a patrician, and none in his order surpassed him in rank and renown. After two triumphs, in his third consulate (268), he submitted to the burgesses a proposal to have the public domain measured and to lease part of it for the benefit of the public treasury, while a further portion was to be distributed among the necessitous. In other words, he attempted to wrest the control of the public lands from the senate, and, with the support of the burgesses, to put an end to the selfish system of occupation. He probably imagined that his personal distinction, and the equity and wisdom of the measure, might carry it even amidst that stormy sea of passion and of weakness. But he was mistaken. The nobles rose as one man; the rich plebeians took part with them; the commons were displeased because Spurius Cassius desired, in accordance with federal rights and equity, to give to the Latin confederates their share in the assignation. Cassius had to die. There is some truth in the charge that he had usurped regal power, for he had indeed endeavoured like the kings to protect the free commons against his own order. His law was buried along with him; but its spectre thenceforward incessantly haunted the eyes of the rich, and again and again it rose from the tomb against them, until amidst the conflicts to which it led the commonwealth perished.

Decemvirs

A further attempt was made to get rid of the tribunician power by securing to the plebeians equality of rights in a more regular and more effectual way. The tribune of the people, Gaius Terentilius Arsa, proposed in 292 the nomination of a commission of five men to prepare a general code of law by which the consuls should in future be bound in exercising their judicial powers. But the senate refused to sanction this proposal, and ten years elapsed ere it was carried into effect—years of vehement strife between the orders, and variously agitated moreover by wars and internal troubles. With equal obstinacy the party of the nobles hindered the concession of the law in the senate, and the plebs nominated again and again the same men as tribunes. Attempts were made to obviate the attack by other concessions. In the year 297 an increase of the tribunes from four to ten was sanctioned—a very dubious gain; and in the following year, by an Icilian -plebiscitum- which was admitted among the sworn privileges of the plebs, the Aventine, which had hitherto been a temple-grove and uninhabited, was distributed among the poorer burgesses as sites for buildings in heritable occupancy. The plebs took what was offered to them, but never ceased to insist in their demand for a legal code. At length, in the year 300, a compromise was effected; the senate in substance gave way. The preparation of a legal code was resolved upon; for that purpose, as an extraordinary measure, the centuries were to choose ten men who were at the same time to act as supreme magistrates in room of the consuls (-decemviri consulari imperio legibus scribundls-), and to this office not merely patricians, but plebeians also might be elected. These were here for the first time designated as eligible, though only for an extraordinary office. This was a great step in the progress towards full political equality; and it was not too dearly purchased, when the tribunate of the people as well as the right of appeal were suspended while the decemvirate lasted, and the decemvirs were simply bound not to infringe the sworn liberties of the community. Previously however an embassy was sent to Greece to bring home the laws of Solon and other Greek laws; and it was only on its return that the decemvirs were chosen for the year 303. Although they were at liberty to elect plebeians, the choice fell on patricians alone— so powerful was the nobility still—and it was only when a second election became necessary for 304, that some plebeians were chosen—the first non-patrician magistrates that the Roman community had.

Taking a connected view of these measures, we can scarcely attribute to them any other design than that of substituting for tribunician intercession a limitation of the consular powers by written law. On both sides there must have been a conviction that things could not remain as they were, and the perpetuation of anarchy, while it ruined the commonwealth, was in reality of no benefit to any one. People in earnest could not but discern that the interference of the tribunes in administration and their action as prosecutors had an absolutely pernicious effect; and the only real gain which the tribunate brought to the plebeians was the protection which it afforded against a partial administration of justice, by operating as a sort of court of cassation to check the caprice of the magistrate. Beyond doubt, when the plebeians desired a written code, the patricians replied that in that event the legal protection of tribunes would be superfluous; and upon this there appears to have been concession by both sides. Perhaps there was never anything definitely expressed as to what was to be done after the drawing up of the code; but that the plebs definitely renounced the tribunate is not to be doubted, since it was brought by the decemvirate into such a position that it could not get back the tribunate otherwise than by illegal means. The promise given to the plebs that its sworn liberties should not be touched, may be referred to the rights of the plebeians independent of the tribunate, such as the - provocatio- and the possession of the Aventine. The intention seems to have been that the decemvirs should, on their retiring, propose to the people to re-elect the consuls who should now judge no longer according to their arbitrary pleasure but according to written law.

Legislation of the Twelve Tables

The plan, if it should stand, was a wise one; all depended on whether men's minds exasperated on either side with passion would accept that peaceful adjustment. The decemvirs of the year 303 submitted their law to the people, and it was confirmed by them, engraven on ten tables of copper, and affixed in the Forum to the rostra in front of the senate-house. But as a supplement appeared necessary, decemvirs were again nominated in the year 304, who added two more tables. Thus originated the first and only Roman code, the law of the Twelve Tables. It proceeded from a compromise between parties, and for that very reason could not well have contained any changes in the existing law of a comprehensive nature, going beyond the regulation of secondary matters and of the mere adaptation of means and ends. Even in the system of credit no further alleviation was introduced than the establishment of a—probably low—maximum of interest (10 per cent) and the threatening of heavy penalties against the usurer-penalties, characteristically enough, far heavier than those of the thief; the harsh procedure in actions of debt remained at least in its leading features unaltered. Still less, as may easily be conceived, were changes contemplated in the rights of the orders. On the contrary the legal distinction between burgesses liable to be taxed and those who were without estate, and the invalidity of marriage between patricians and plebeians, were confirmed anew in the law of the city. In like manner, with a view to restrict the caprice of the magistrate and to protect the burgess, it was expressly enacted that the later law should uniformly have precedence over the earlier, and that no decree of the people should be issued against a single burgess. The most remarkable feature was the exclusion of appeal to the -comitia tributa- in capital causes, while the privilege of appeal to the centuries was guaranteed; which admits of explanation from the circumstance that the penal jurisdiction was in fact usurped by the plebs and its presidents,(11) and with the tribunate there necessarily fell the tribunician capital process, while it was perhaps the intention to retain the aedilician process of fine (-multa-). The essential political significance of the measure resided far less in the contents of the legislation than in the formal obligation now laid upon the consuls to administer justice according to these forms of process and these rules of law, and in the public exhibition of the code, by which the administration of justice was subjected to the control of publicity and the consul was compelled to dispense equal and truly common justice to all.

Fall of the Decemvirs

The end of the decemvirate is involved in much obscurity. It only remained—so runs the story—for the decemvirs to publish the last two tables, and then to give place to the ordinary magistracy. But they delayed to do so: under the pretext that the laws were not yet ready, they themselves prolonged their magistracy after the expiry of their official year—which was so far possible, as under Roman constitutional law the magistracy called in an extraordinary way to the revision of the constitution could not become legally bound by the term set for its ending. The moderate section of the aristocracy, with the Valerii and Horatii at their head, are said to have attempted in the senate to compel the abdication of the decemvirate; but the head of the decemvirs Appius Claudius, originally a rigid aristocrat, but now changing into a demagogue and a tyrant, gained the ascendancy in the senate, and the people submitted. The levy of two armies was accomplished without opposition, and war was begun against the Volscians as well as against the Sabines. Thereupon the former tribune of the people, Lucius Siccius Dentatus, the bravest man in Rome, who had fought in a hundred and twenty battles and had forty-five honourable scars to show, was found dead in front of the camp, foully murdered, as it was said, at the instigation of the decemvirs. A revolution was fermenting in men's minds; and its outbreak was hastened by the unjust sentence pronounced by Appius in the process as to the freedom of the daughter of the centurion Lucius Verginius, the bride of the former tribune of the people Lucius Icilius—a sentence which wrested the maiden from her relatives with a view to make her non-free and beyond the pale of the law, and induced her father himself to plunge his knife into the heart of his daughter in the open Forum, to rescue her from certain shame. While the people in amazement at the unprecedented deed surrounded the dead body of the fair maiden, the decemvir commanded his lictors to bring the father and then the bridegroom before his tribunal, in order to render to him, from whose decision there lay no appeal, immediate account for their rebellion against his authority. The cup was now full. Protected by the furious multitude, the father and the bridegroom of the maiden made their escape from the lictors of the despot, and while the senate trembled and wavered in Rome, the pair presented themselves, with numerous witnesses of the fearful deed, in the two camps. The unparalleled tale was told; the eyes of all were opened to the gap which the absence of tribunician protection had made in the security of law; and what the fathers had done their sons repeated. Once more the armies abandoned their leaders: they marched in warlike order through the city, and proceeded once more to the Sacred Mount, where they again nominated their own tribunes. Still the decemvirs refused to lay down their power; then the army with its tribunes appeared in the city, and encamped on the Aventine. Now at length, when civil war was imminent and the conflict in the streets might hourly begin, the decemvirs renounced their usurped and dishonoured power; and the consuls Lucius Valerius and Marcus Horatius negotiated a second compromise, by which the tribunate of the plebs was again established. The impeachment of the decemvirs terminated in the two most guilty, Appius Claudius and Spurius Oppius, committing suicide in prison, while the other eight went into exile and the state confiscated their property. The prudent and moderate tribune of the plebs, Marcus Duilius, prevented further judicial prosecutions by a seasonable use of his veto.

So runs the story as recorded by the pen of the Roman aristocrats; but, even leaving out of view the accessory circumstances, the great crisis out of which the Twelve Tables arose cannot possibly have ended in such romantic adventures, and in political issues so incomprehensible. The decemvirate was, after the abolition of the monarchy and the institution of the tribunate of the people, the third great victory of the plebs; and the exasperation of the opposite party against the institution and against its head Appius Claudius is sufficiently intelligible. The plebeians had through its means secured the right of eligibility to the highest magistracy of the community and a general code of law; and it was not they that had reason to rebel against the new magistracy, and to restore the purely patrician consular government by force of arms. This end can only have been pursued by the party of the nobility, and if the patricio-plebeian decemvirs made the attempt to maintain themselves in office beyond their time, the nobility were certainly the first to enter the lists against them; on which occasion doubtless the nobles would not neglect to urge that the stipulated rights of the plebs should be curtailed and the tribunate, in particular, should be taken from it. If the nobility thereupon succeeded in setting aside the decemvirs, it is certainly conceivable that after their fall the plebs should once more assemble in arms with a view to secure the results both of the earlier revolution of 260 and of the latest movement; and the Valerio-Horatian laws of 305 can only be understood as forming a compromise in this conflict.

The Valerio-Horatian Laws

The compromise, as was natural, proved very favourable to the plebeians, and again imposed severely felt restrictions on the power of the nobility. As a matter of course the tribunate of the people was restored, the code of law wrung from the aristocracy was definitively retained, and the consuls were obliged to judge according to it. Through the code indeed the tribes lost their usurped jurisdiction in capital causes; but the tribunes got it back, as a way was found by which it was possible for them to transact business as to such cases with the centuries. Besides they retained, in the right to award fines without limitation and to submit this sentence to the -comitia tributa-, a sufficient means of putting an end to the civic existence of a patrician opponent. Further, it was on the proposition of the consuls decreed by the centuries that in future every magistrate—and therefore the dictator among the rest—should be bound at his nomination to allow the right of appeal: any one who should nominate a magistrate on other terms was to expiate the offence with his life. In other respects the dictator retained his former powers; and in particular his official acts could not, like those of the consuls, be cancelled by a tribune.

The plenitude of the consular power was further restricted in so far as the administration of the military chest was committed to two paymasters (-quaestores-) chosen by the community, who were nominated for the first time in 307. The nomination as well of the two new paymasters for war as of the two administering the city-chest now passed over to the community; the consul retained merely the conduct of the election instead of the election itself. The assembly in which the paymasters were elected was that of the whole patricio-plebeian freeholders, and voted by districts; an arrangement which likewise involved a concession to the plebeian farmers, who had far more command of these assemblies than of the centuriate -comitia-.

A concession of still greater consequence was that which allowed the tribunes to share in the discussions of the senate. To admit the tribunes to the hall where the senate sat, appeared to that body beneath its dignity; so a bench was placed for them at the door that they might from that spot follow its proceedings. The tribunician right of intercession had extended also to the decrees of the senate as a collective body, after the latter had become not merely a deliberative but a decretory board, which probably occurred at first in the case of a -plebiscitum- that was meant to be binding for the whole community;(12) it was natural that there should thenceforth be conceded to the tribunes a certain participation in the discussions of the senate-house. In order also to secure the decrees of the senate— with the validity of which indeed that of the most important -plebiscita- was bound up—from being tampered with or forged, it was enacted that in future they should be deposited not merely under charge of the patrician -quaestores urbani- in the temple of Saturn, but also under that of the plebian aediles in the temple of Ceres. Thus this struggle, which was begun in order to get rid of the tribunician power, terminated in the renewed and now definitive sanctioning of its right to annul not only particular acts of administration on the appeal of the person aggrieved, but also any resolution of the constituent powers of the state at pleasure. The persons of the tribunes, and the uninterrupted maintenance of the college at its full number, were once more secured by the most sacred oaths and by every element of reverence that religion could present, and not less by the most formal laws. No attempt to abolish this magistracy was ever from this time forward made in Rome.

Notes for Book II Chapter II

1. II. I. Right of Appeal

2. I. XIII. Landed proprietors

3. I. VI. Character of the Roman Law

4. II. I. Collegiate Arrangement

5. I. XI. Property

6. I. XI. Punishment of Offenses against Order

7. That the plebeian aediles were formed after the model of the patrician quaestors in the same way as the plebeian tribunes after the model of the patrician consuls, is evident both as regards their criminal functions (in which the distinction between the two magistracies seems to have lain in their tendencies only, not in their powers) and as regards their charge of the archives. The temple of Ceres was to the aediles what the temple of Saturn was to the quaestors, and from the former they derived their name. Significant in this respect is the enactment of the law of 305 (Liv. iii. 55), that the decrees of the senate should be delivered over to the aediles there (p. 369), whereas, as is well known, according to the ancient —and subsequently after the settlement of the struggles between the orders, again preponderant—practice those decrees were committed to the quaestors for preservation in the temple of Saturn.

8. I. VI. Levy Districts

9. I. III. Clan-Villages

10. II. II. Secession to the Sacred mount

11. II. II. Intercession

12. II. II. Legislation

CHAPTER III

The Equalization of the Orders, and the New Aristocracy

Union of the Plebians

The tribunician movements appear to have mainly originated in social rather than political discontent, and there is good reason to suppose that some of the wealthy plebeians admitted to the senate were no less opposed to these movements than the patricians. For they too benefited by the privileges against which the agitation was mainly directed; and although in other respects they found themselves treated as inferior, it probably seemed to them by no means an appropriate time for asserting their claim to participate in the magistracies, when the exclusive financial power of the whole senate was assailed. This explains why during the first fifty years of the republic no step was taken aiming directly at the political equalization of the orders.

But this league between the patricians and the wealthy plebeians by no means bore within itself any guarantee of permanence. Beyond doubt from the very first a portion of the leading plebeian families had attached themselves to the movement-party, partly from a sense of what was due to the fellow-members of their order, partly in consequence of the natural bond which unites all who are treated as inferior, and partly because they perceived that concessions to the multitude were inevitable in the issue, and that, if turned to due account, they would result in the abrogation of the exclusive rights of the patriciate and would thereby give to the plebeian aristocracy a decisive preponderance in the state. Should this conviction become —-as was inevitable—more and more prevalent, and should the plebeian aristocracy at the head of its order take up the struggle with the patrician nobility, it would wield in the tribunate a legalized instrument of civil warfare, and it might, with the weapon of social distress, so fight its battles as to dictate to the nobility the terms of peace and, in the position of mediator between the two parties, compel its own admission to the offices of state.

Such a crisis in the position of parties occurred after the fall of the decemvirate. It had now become perfectly clear that the tribunate of the plebs could never be set aside; the plebeian aristocracy could not do better than seize this powerful lever and employ it for the removal of the political disabilities of their order.

Throwing Open of Marriage and of Magistracies—
Military Tribunes with Consular Powers

Nothing shows so clearly the defencelessness of the clan-nobility when opposed to the united plebs, as the fact that the fundamental principle of the exclusive party—-the invalidity of marriage between patricians and plebeians—fell at the first blow scarcely four years after the decemviral revolution. In the year 309 it was enacted by the Canuleian plebiscite, that a marriage between a patrician and a plebeian should be valid as a true Roman marriage, and that the children begotten of such a marriage should follow the rank of the father. At the same time it was further carried that, in place of consuls, military tribunes—of these there were at that time, before the division of the army into legions, six, and the number of these magistrates was adjusted accordingly-with consular powers(1) and consular duration of office should be elected by the centuries. The proximate cause was of a military nature, as the various wars required a greater number of generals in chief command than the consular constitution allowed; but the change came to be of essential importance for the conflicts of the orders, and it may be that that military object was rather the pretext than the reason for this arrangement. According to the ancient law every burgess or —metoikos— liable to service might attain the post of an officer,(2) and in virtue of that principle the supreme magistracy, after having been temporarily opened up to the plebeians in the decemvirate, was now after a more comprehensive fashion rendered equally accessible to all freeborn burgesses. The question naturally occurs, what interest the aristocracy could have—now that it was under the necessity of abandoning its exclusive possession of the supreme magistracy and of yielding in the matter—in refusing to the plebeians the title, and conceding to them the consulate under this singular form?(3) But, in the first place, there were associated with the holding of the supreme magistracy various honorary rights, partly personal, partly hereditary; thus the honour of a triumph was regarded as legally dependent on the occupancy of the supreme magistracy, and was never given to an officer who had not administered the latter office in person; and the descendants of a curule magistrate were at liberty to set up the image of such an ancestor in the family hall and to exhibit it in public on fitting occasions, while this was not allowed in the case of other ancestors.(4) It is as easy to be explained as it is difficult to be vindicated, that the governing aristocratic order should have allowed the government itself to be wrested from their hands far sooner than the honorary rights associated with it, especially such as were hereditary; and therefore, when it was obliged to share the former with the plebeians, it gave to the actual supreme magistrate the legal standing not of the holder of a curule chair, but of a simple staff-officer, whose distinction was one purely personal. Of greater political importance, however, than the refusal of the -ius imaginum- and of the honour of a triumph was the circumstance, that the exclusion of the plebeians sitting in the senate from debate necessarily ceased in respect to those of their number who, as designated or former consuls, ranked among the senators whose opinion had to be asked before the rest; so far it was certainly of great importance for the nobility to admit the plebeian only to a consular office, and not to the consulate itself.

Opposition of the Patriciate

But notwithstanding these vexatious disabilities the privileges of the clans, so far as they had a political value, were legally superseded by the new institution; and, had the Roman nobility been worthy of its name, it must now have given up the struggle. But it did not. Though a rational and legal resistance was thenceforth impossible, spiteful opposition still found a wide field of petty expedients, of chicanery and intrigue; and, far from honourable or politically prudent as such resistance was, it was still in a certain sense fruitful of results. It certainly procured at length for the commons concessions which could not easily have been wrung from the united Roman aristocracy; but it also prolonged civil war for another century and enabled the nobility, in defiance of those laws, practically to retain the government in their exclusive possession for several generations longer.

Their Expedients

The expedients of which the nobility availed themselves were as various as political paltriness could suggest. Instead of deciding at once the question as to the admission or exclusion of the plebeians at the elections, they conceded what they were compelled to concede only with reference to the elections immediately impending. The vain struggle was thus annually renewed whether patrician consuls or military tribunes from both orders with consular powers should be nominated; and among the weapons of the aristocracy this mode of conquering an opponent by wearying and annoying him proved by no means the least effective.

Subdivision of the Magistracy—
Censorship

Moreover they broke up the supreme power which had hitherto been undivided, in order to delay their inevitable defeat by multiplying the points to be assailed. Thus the adjustment of the budget and of the burgess—and taxation-rolls, which ordinarily took place every fourth year and had hitherto been managed by the consuls, was entrusted as early as the year 319 to two valuators (-censores-), nominated by the centuries from among the nobles for a period, at the most, of eighteen months. The new office gradually became the palladium of the aristocratic party, not so much on account of its financial influence as on account of the right annexed to it of filling up the vacancies in the senate and in the equites, and of removing individuals from the lists of the senate, equites, and burgesses on occasion of their adjustment. At this epoch, however, the censorship by no means possessed the great importance and moral supremacy which afterwards were associated with it.

Quaestorship

But the important change made in the year 333 in respect to the quaestorship amply compensated for this success of the patrician party. The patricio-plebeian assembly of the tribes—perhaps taking up the ground that at least the two military paymasters were in fact officers rather than civil functionaries, and that so far the plebeian appeared as well entitled to the quaestorship as to the military tribuneship—carried the point that plebeian candidates also were admitted for the quaestorial elections, and thereby acquired for the first time the privilege of eligibility as well as the right of election for one of the ordinary magistracies. With justice it was felt on the one side as a great victory, on the other as a severe defeat, that thenceforth patrician and plebeian were equally capable of electing and being elected to the military as well as to the urban quaestorship.

Attempts at Counterrevolution

The nobility, in spite of the most obstinate resistance, only sustained loss after loss; and their exasperation increased as their power decreased. Attempts were doubtless still made directly to assail the rights secured by agreement to the commons; but such attempts were not so much the well-calculated manoeuvres of party as the acts of an impotent thirst for vengeance. Such in particular was the process against Maelius as reported by the tradition—certainly not very trustworthy—that has come down to us. Spurius Maelius, a wealthy plebeian, during a severe dearth (315) sold corn at such prices as to put to shame and annoy the patrician store-president (-praefectus annonae-) Gaius Minucius. The latter accused him of aspiring to kingly power; with what amount of reason we cannot decide, but it is scarcely credible that a man who had not even filled the tribunate should have seriously thought of sovereignty. Nevertheless the authorities took up the matter in earnest, and the cry of "King" always produced on the multitude in Rome an effect similar to that of the cry of "Pope" on the masses in England. Titus Quinctius Capitolinus, who was for the sixth time consul, nominated Lucius Quinctius Cincinnatus, who was eighty years of age, as dictator without appeal, in open violation of the solemnly sworn laws.(5) Maelius, summoned before him, seemed disposed to disregard the summons; and the dictator's master of the horse, Gaius Servilius Ahala, slew him with his own hand. The house of the murdered man was pulled down, the corn from his granaries was distributed gratuitously to the people, and those who threatened to avenge his death were secretly made away with. This disgraceful judicial murder—a disgrace even more to the credulous and blind people than to the malignant party of young patricians—passed unpunished; but if that party had hoped by such means to undermine the right of appeal, it violated the laws and shed innocent blood in vain.

Intrigues of the Nobility

Electioneering intrigues and priestly trickery proved in the hands of the nobility more efficient than any other weapons. The extent to which the former must have prevailed is best seen in the fact that in 322 it appeared necessary to issue a special law against electioneering practices, which of course was of little avail. When the voters could not be influenced by corruption or threatening, the presiding magistrates stretched their powers—admitting, for example, so many plebeian candidates that the votes of the opposition were thrown away amongst them, or omitting from the list of candidates those whom the majority were disposed to choose. If in spite of all this an obnoxious election was carried, the priests were consulted whether no vitiating circumstance had occurred in the auspices or other religious ceremonies on the occasion; and some such flaw they seldom failed to discover. Taking no thought as to the consequences and unmindful of the wise example of their ancestors, the people allowed the principle to be established that the opinion of the skilled colleges of priests as to omens of birds, portents, and the like was legally binding on the magistrate, and thus put it into their power to cancel any state-act—whether the consecration of a temple or any other act of administration, whether law or election—on the ground of religious informality. In this way it became possible that, although the eligibility of plebeians had been established by law already in 333 for the quaestorship and thenceforward continued to be legally recognized, it was only in 345 that the first plebeian attained the quaestorship; in like manner patricians almost exclusively held the military tribunate with consular powers down to 354. It was apparent that the legal abolition of the privileges of the nobles had by no means really and practically placed the plebeian aristocracy on a footing of equality with the clan-nobility. Many causes contributed to this result: the tenacious opposition of the nobility far more easily allowed itself to be theoretically superseded in a moment of excitement, than to be permanently kept down in the annually recurring elections; but the main cause was the inward disunion between the chiefs of the plebeian aristocracy and the mass of the farmers. The middle class, whose votes were decisive in the comitia, did not feel itself specially called on to advance the interests of genteel non-patricians, so long as its own demands were disregarded by the plebeian no less than by the patrician aristocracy.

The Suffering Farmers

During these political struggles social questions had lain on the whole dormant, or were discussed at any rate with less energy. After the plebeian aristocracy had gained possession of the tribunate for its own ends, no serious notice was taken either of the question of the domains or of a reform in the system of credit; although there was no lack either of newly acquired lands or of impoverished or decaying farmers. Instances indeed of assignations took place, particularly in the recently conquered border-territories, such as those of the domain of Ardea in 312, of Labici in 336, and of Veii in 361—more however on military grounds than for the relief of the farmer, and by no means to an adequate extent. Individual tribunes doubtless attempted to revive the law of Cassius—for instance Spurius Maecilius and Spurius Metilius instituted in the year 337 a proposal for the distribution of the whole state-lands—but they were thwarted, in a manner characteristic of the existing state of parties, by the opposition of their own colleagues or in other words of the plebeian aristocracy. Some of the patricians also attempted to remedy the common distress; but with no better success than had formerly attended Spurius Cassius. A patrician like Cassius and like him distinguished by military renown and personal valour, Marcus Manlius, the saviour of the Capitol during the Gallic siege, is said to have come forward as the champion of the oppressed people, with whom he was connected by the ties of comradeship in war and of bitter hatred towards his rival, the celebrated general and leader of the optimate party, Marcus Furius Camillus. When a brave officer was about to be led away to a debtor's prison, Manlius interceded for him and released him with his own money; at the same time he offered his lands to sale, declaring loudly that, as long as he possessed a foot's breadth of land, such iniquities should not occur. This was more than enough to unite the whole government party, patricians as well as plebeians, against the dangerous innovator. The trial for high treason, the charge of having meditated a renewal of the monarchy, wrought on the blind multitude with the insidious charm which belongs to stereotyped party-phrases. They themselves condemned him to death, and his renown availed him nothing save that it was deemed expedient to assemble the people for the bloody assize at a spot whence the voters could not see the rock of the citadel—the dumb monitor which might remind them how their fatherland had been saved from the extremity of danger by the hands of the very man whom they were now consigning to the executioner (370).

While the attempts at reformation were thus arrested in the bud, the social disorders became still more crying; for on the one hand the domain-possessions were ever extending in consequence of successful wars, and on the other hand debt and impoverishment were ever spreading more widely among the farmers, particularly from the effects of the severe war with Veii (348-358) and of the burning of the capital in the Gallic invasion (364). It is true that, when in the Veientine war it became necessary to prolong the term of service of the soldiers and to keep them under arms not—as hitherto at the utmost—only during summer, but also throughout the winter, and when the farmers, foreseeing their utter economic ruin, were on the point of refusing their consent to the declaration of war, the senate resolved on making an important concession. It charged the pay, which hitherto the tribes had defrayed by contribution, on the state-chest, or in other words, on the produce of the indirect revenues and the domains (348). It was only in the event of the state-chest being at the moment empty that a general contribution (-tributum-) was imposed on account of the pay; and in that case it was considered as a forced loan and was afterwards repaid by the community. The arrangement was equitable and wise; but, as it was not placed upon the essential foundation of turning the domains to proper account for the benefit of the exchequer, there were added to the increased burden of service frequent contributions, which were none the less ruinous to the man of small means that they were officially regarded not as taxes but as advances.

Combination of the Plebian Aristocracy and the Farmers against the
Nobility—
Licinio-Sextian Laws

Under such circumstances, when the plebeian aristocracy saw itself practically excluded by the opposition of the nobility and the indifference of the commons from equality of political rights, and the suffering farmers were powerless as opposed to the close aristocracy, it was natural that they should help each other by a compromise. With this view the tribunes of the people, Gaius Licinius and Lucius Sextius, submitted to the commons proposals to the following effect: first, to abolish the consular tribunate; secondly, to lay it down as a rule that at least one of the consuls should be a plebeian; thirdly, to open up to the plebeians admission to one of the three great colleges of priests—that of the custodiers of oracles, whose number was to be increased to ten (-duoviri-, afterwards -decemviri sacris faciundis-(6)); fourthly, as respected the domains, to allow no burgess to maintain upon the common pasture more than a hundred oxen and five hundred sheep, or to hold more than five hundred -jugera- (about 300 acres) of the domain lands left free for occupation; fifthly, to oblige the landlords to employ in the labours of the field a number of free labourers proportioned to that of their rural slaves; and lastly, to procure alleviation for debtors by deduction of the interest which had been paid from the capital, and by the arrangement of set terms for the payment of arrears.

The tendency of these enactments is obvious. They were designed to deprive the nobles of their exclusive possession of the curule magistracies and of the hereditary distinctions of nobility therewith associated; which, it was characteristically conceived, could only be accomplished by the legal exclusion of the nobles from the place of second consul. They were designed, as a consequence, to emancipate the plebeian members of the senate from the subordinate position which they occupied as silent by-sitters,(7) in so far as those of them at least who had filled the consulate thereby acquired a title to deliver their opinion with the patrician consulars before the other patrician senators.(8) They were intended, moreover, to withdraw from the nobles the exclusive possession of spiritual dignities; and in carrying out this purpose for reasons sufficiently obvious the old Latin priesthoods of the augurs and Pontifices were left to the old burgesses, but these were obliged to open up to the new burgesses the third great college of more recent origin and belonging to a worship that was originally foreign. They were intended, in fine, to procure a share in the common usufructs of burgesses for the poorer commons, alleviation for the suffering debtors, and employment for the day-labourers that were destitute of work. Abolition of privileges, civil equality, social reform—these were the three great ideas, of which it was the design of this movement to secure the recognition. Vainly the patricians exerted all the means at their command in opposition to these legislative proposals; even the dictatorship and the old military hero Camillus were able only to delay, not to avert their accomplishment. Willingly would the people have separated the proposals; of what moment to it were the consulate and custodiership of oracles, if only the burden of debt were lightened and the public lands were free! But it was not for nothing that the plebeian nobility had adopted the popular cause; it included the proposals in one single project of law, and after a long struggle—it is said of eleven years—the senate at length gave its consent and they passed in the year 387.

Political Abolition of the Patriciate

With the election of the first non-patrician consul—the choice fell on one of the authors of this reform, the late tribune of the people, Lucius Sextius Lateranus—the clan-aristocracy ceased both in fact and in law to be numbered among the political institutions of Rome. When after the final passing of these laws the former champion of the clans, Marcus Furius Camillus, founded a sanctuary of Concord at the foot of the Capitol—upon an elevated platform, where the senate was wont frequently to meet, above the old meeting-place of the burgesses, the Comitium—we gladly cherish the belief that he recognized in the legislation thus completed the close of a dissension only too long continued. The religious consecration of the new concord of the community was the last public act of the old warrior and statesman, and a worthy termination of his long and glorious career. He was not wholly mistaken; the more judicious portion of the clans evidently from this time forward looked upon their exclusive political privileges as lost, and were content to share the government with the plebeian aristocracy. In the majority, however, the patrician spirit proved true to its incorrigible character. On the strength of the privilege which the champions of legitimacy have at all times claimed of obeying the laws only when these coincide with their party interests, the Roman nobles on various occasions ventured, in open violation of the stipulated arrangement, to nominate two patrician consuls. But, when by way of answer to an election of that sort for the year 411 the community in the year following formally resolved to allow both consular positions to be filled by non-patricians, they understood the implied threat, and still doubtless desired, but never again ventured, to touch the second consular place.

Praetorship—
Curule Aedileship—
Complete Opening Up of Magistracies and Priesthoods

In like manner the aristocracy simply injured itself by the attempt which it made, on the passing of the Licinian laws, to save at least some remnant of its ancient privileges by means of a system of political clipping and paring. Under the pretext that the nobility were exclusively cognizant of law, the administration of justice was detached from the consulate when the latter had to be thrown open to the plebeians; and for this purpose there was nominated a special third consul, or, as he was commonly called, a praetor. In like manner the supervision of the market and the judicial police-duties connected with it, as well as the celebration of the city-festival, were assigned to two newly nominated aediles, who—by way of distinction from the plebeian aediles—were named from their standing jurisdiction "aediles of the judgment seat" (-aediles curules-). But the curule aedileship became immediately so far accessible to the plebeians, that it was held by patricians and plebeians alternately. Moreover the dictatorship was thrown open to plebeians in 398, as the mastership of the horse had already been in the year before the Licinian laws (386); both the censorships were thrown open in 403, and the praetorship in 417; and about the same time (415) the nobility were by law excluded from one of the censorships, as they had previously been from one of the consulships. It was to no purpose that once more a patrician augur detected secret flaws, hidden from the eyes of the uninitiated, in the election of a plebeian dictator (427), and that the patrician censor did not up to the close of our present period (474) permit his colleague to present the solemn sacrifice with which the census closed; such chicanery served merely to show the ill humour of patricianism. Of as little avail were the complaints which the patrician presidents of the senate would not fail to raise regarding the participation of the plebeians in its debates; it became a settled rule that no longer the patrician members, but those who had attained to one of the three supreme ordinary magistracies—the consulship, praetorship, and curule aedileship —should be summoned to give their opinion in this order and without distinction of class, while the senators who had held none of these offices still even now took part merely in the division. The right, in fine, of the patrician senate to reject a decree of the community as unconstitutional—a right, however, which in all probability it rarely ventured to exercise—was withdrawn from it by the Publilian law of 415 and by the Maenian law which was not passed before the middle of the fifth century, in so far that it had to bring forward its constitutional objections, if it had any such, when the list of candidates was exhibited or the project of law was brought in; which practically amounted to a regular announcement of its consent beforehand. In this character, as a purely formal right, the confirmation of the decrees of the people still continued in the hands of the nobility down to the last age of the republic.

The clans retained, as may naturally be conceived, their religious privileges longer. Indeed, several of these, which were destitute of political importance, were never interfered with, such as their exclusive eligibility to the offices of the three supreme - flamines-and that of -rex sacrorum- as well as to the membership of the colleges of Salii. On the other hand the two colleges of Pontifices and of augurs, with which a considerable influence over the courts and the comitia were associated, were too important to remain in the exclusive possession of the patricians. The Ogulnian law of 454 accordingly threw these also open to plebeians, by increasing the number both of the pontifices and of the augurs from six to nine, and equally distributing the stalls in the two colleges between patricians and plebeians.

Equivalence of Law and Plebiscitum

The two hundred years' strife was brought at length to: a close by the law of the dictator Q. Hortensius (465, 468) which was occasioned by a dangerous popular insurrection, and which declared that the decrees of the plebs should stand on an absolute footing of equality—instead of their earlier conditional equivalence—with those of the whole community. So greatly had the state of things been changed that that portion of the burgesses which had once possessed exclusively the right of voting was thenceforth, under the usual form of taking votes binding for the whole burgess-body, no longer so much as asked the question.

The Later Patricianism

The struggle between the Roman clans and commons was thus substantially at an end. While the nobility still preserved out of its comprehensive privileges the -de facto- possession of one of the consulships and one of the censorships, it was excluded by law from the tribunate, the plebeian aedileship, the second consulship and censorship, and from participation in the votes of the plebs which were legally equivalent to votes of the whole body of burgesses. As a righteous retribution for its perverse and stubborn resistance, the patriciate had seen its former privileges converted into so many disabilities. The Roman clan-nobility, however, by no means disappeared because it had become an empty name. The less the significance and power of the nobility, the more purely and exclusively the patrician spirit developed itself. The haughtiness of the "Ramnians" survived the last of their class-privileges for centuries; after they had steadfastly striven "to rescue the consulate from the plebeian filth" and had at length become reluctantly convinced of the impossibility of such an achievement, they continued at least rudely and spitefully to display their aristocratic spirit. To understand rightly the history of Rome in the fifth and sixth centuries, we must never overlook this sulking patricianism; it could indeed do little more than irritate itself and others, but this it did to the best of its ability. Some years after the passing of the Ogulnian law (458) a characteristic instance of this sort occurred. A patrician matron, who was married to a leading plebeian that had attained to the highest dignities of the state, was on account of this misalliance expelled from the circle of noble dames and was refused admission to the common festival of Chastity; and in consequence of that exclusion separate patrician and plebeian goddesses of Chastity were thenceforward worshipped in Rome. Doubtless caprices of this sort were of very little moment, and the better portion of the clans kept themselves entirely aloof from this miserable policy of peevishness; but it left behind on both sides a feeling of discontent, and, while the struggle of the commons against the clans was in itself a political and even moral necessity, these convulsive efforts to prolong the strife—the aimless combats of the rear-guard after the battle had been decided, as well as the empty squabbles as to rank and standing—needlessly irritated and disturbed the public and private life of the Roman community.

The Social Distress, and the Attempt to Relieve It

Nevertheless one object of the compromise concluded by the two portions of the plebs in 387, the abolition of the patriciate, had in all material points been completely attained. The question next arises, how far the same can be affirmed of the two positive objects aimed at in the compromise?—whether the new order of things in reality checked social distress and established political equality? The two were intimately connected; for, if economic embarrassments ruined the middle class and broke up the burgesses into a minority of rich men and a suffering proletariate, such a state of things would at once annihilate civil equality and in reality destroy the republican commonwealth. The preservation and increase of the middle class, and in particular of the farmers, formed therefore for every patriotic statesman of Rome a problem not merely important, but the most important of all. The plebeians, moreover, recently called to take part in the government, greatly indebted as they were for their new political rights to the proletariate which was suffering and expecting help at their hands, were politically and morally under special obligation to attempt its relief by means of government measures, so far as relief was by such means at all attainable.

The Licinian Agrarian Laws

Let us first consider how far any real relief was contained in that part of the legislation of 387 which bore upon the question. That the enactment in favour of the free day-labourers could not possibly accomplish its object—namely, to check the system of farming on a large scale and by means of slaves, and to secure to the free proletarians at least a share of work—is self-evident. In this matter legislation could afford no relief, without shaking the foundations of the civil organization of the period in a way that would reach far beyond its immediate horizon. In the question of the domains, on the other hand, it was quite possible for legislation to effect a change; but what was done was manifestly inadequate. The new domain-arrangement, by granting the right of driving very considerable flocks and herds upon the public pastures, and that of occupying domain-land not laid out in pasture up to a maximum fixed on a high scale, conceded to the wealthy an important and perhaps even disproportionate prior share in the produce of the domains; and by the latter regulation conferred upon the domain-tenure, although it remained in law liable to pay a tenth and revocable at pleasure, as well as upon the system of occupation itself, somewhat of a legal sanction. It was a circumstance still more suspicious, that the new legislation neither supplemented the existing and manifestly unsatisfactory provisions for the collection of the pasture-money and the tenth by compulsory measures of a more effective kind, nor prescribed any thorough revision of the domanial possessions, nor appointed a magistracy charged with the carrying of the new laws into effect. The distribution of the existing occupied domain-land partly among the holders up to a fair maximum, partly among the plebeians who had no property, in both cases in full ownership; the abolition in future of the system of occupation; and the institution of an authority empowered to make immediate distribution of any future acquisitions of territory, were so clearly demanded by the circumstances of the case, that it certainly was not through want of discernment that these comprehensive measures were neglected. We cannot fail to recollect that it was the plebeian aristocracy, in other words, a portion of the very class that was practically privileged in respect to the usufructs of the domains, which proposed the new arrangement, and that one of its very authors, Gaius Licinius Stolo, was among the first to be condemned for having exceeded the agrarian maximum; and we cannot but ask whether the legislators dealt altogether honourably, and whether they did not on the contrary designedly evade a solution, really tending to the common benefit, of the unhappy question of the domains. We do not mean, however, to express any doubt that the regulations of the Licinian laws, such as they were, might and did substantially benefit the small farmer and the day-labourer. It must, moreover, be acknowledged that in the period immediately succeeding the passing of the law the authorities watched with at least comparative strictness over the observance of its rules as to the maximum, and frequently condemned the possessors of large herds and the occupiers of the domains to heavy fines.

Laws Imposing Taxes—
Laws of Credit

In the system of taxation and of credit also efforts were made with greater energy at this period than at any before or subsequent to it to remedy the evils of the national economy, so far as legal measures could do so. The duty levied in 397 of five per cent on the value of slaves that were to be manumitted was—irrespective of the fact that it imposed a check on the undesirable multiplication of freedmen—the first tax in Rome that was really laid upon the rich. In like manner efforts were made to remedy the system of credit. The usury laws, which the Twelve Tables had established,(9) were renewed and gradually rendered more stringent, so that the maximum of interest was successively lowered from 10 per cent (enforced in 397) to 5 per cent (in 407) for the year of twelve months, and at length (412) the taking of interest was altogether forbidden. The latter foolish law remained formally in force, but, of course, it was practically inoperative; the standard rate of interest afterwards usual, *viz.* 1 per cent per month, or 12 per cent for the civil common year—which, according to the value of money in antiquity, was probably at that time nearly the same as, according to its modern value, a rate of 5 or 6 per cent—must have been already about this period established as the maximum of appropriate interest. Any action at law for higher rates must have been refused, perhaps even judicial claims for repayment may have been allowed; moreover notorious usurers were not unfrequently summoned before the bar of the people and readily condemned by the tribes to heavy fines. Still more important was the alteration of the procedure in cases of debt by the Poetelian law (428 or 441). On the one hand it allowed every debtor who declared on oath his solvency to save his personal freedom by the cession of his property; on the other hand it abolished the former summary proceedings in execution on a loan-debt, and laid down the rule that no Roman burgess could be led away to bondage except upon the sentence of jurymen.

Continued Distress

It is plain that all these expedients might perhaps in some respects mitigate, but could not remove, the existing economic disorders. The continuance of the distress is shown by the appointment of a bank-commission to regulate the relations of credit and to provide advances from the state-chest in 402, by the fixing of legal payment by instalments in 407, and above all by the dangerous popular insurrection about 467, when the people, unable to obtain new facilities for the payment of debts, marched out to the Janiculum, and nothing but a seasonable attack by external enemies, and the concessions contained in the Hortensian law,(10) restored peace to the community. It is, however, very unjust to reproach these earnest attempts to check the impoverishment of the middle class with their inadequacy. The belief that it is useless to employ partial and palliative means against radical evils, because they only remedy them in part, is an article of faith never preached unsuccessfully by baseness to simplicity, but it is none the less absurd. On the contrary, we may ask whether the vile spirit of demagogism had not even thus early laid hold of this matter, and whether expedients were really needed so violent and dangerous as, for example, the deduction of the interest paid from the capital. Our documents do not enable us to decide the question of right or wrong in the case. But we recognize clearly enough that the middle class of freeholders still continued economically in a perilous and critical position; that various endeavours were made by those in power to remedy it by prohibitory laws and by respites, but of course in vain; and that the aristocratic ruling class continued to be too weak in point of control over its members, and too much entangled in the selfish interests of its order, to relieve the middle class by the only effectual means at the disposal of the government—the entire and unreserved abolition of the system of occupying the state-lands—and by that course to free the government from the reproach of turning to its own advantage the oppressed position of the governed.

Influence of the Extension of the Roman Dominion in Elevating the Farmer-Class

A more effectual relief than any which the government was willing or able to give was derived by the middle classes from the political successes of the Roman community and the gradual consolidation of the Roman sovereignty over Italy. The numerous and large colonies which it was necessary to found for the securing of that sovereignty, the greater part of which were sent forth in the fifth century, furnished a portion of the agricultural proletariate with farms of their own, while the efflux gave relief to such as remained at home. The increase of the indirect and extraordinary sources of revenue, and the flourishing condition of the Roman finances in general, rendered it but seldom necessary to levy any contribution from the farmers in the form of a forced loan. While the earlier small holdings were probably lost beyond recovery, the rising average of Roman prosperity must have converted the former larger landholders into farmers, and in so far added new members to the middle class. People of rank sought principally to secure the large newly-acquired districts for occupation; the mass of wealth which flowed to Rome through war and commerce must have reduced the rate of interest; the increase in the population of the capital benefited the farmer throughout Latium; a wise system of incorporation united a number of neighbouring and formerly subject communities with the Roman state, and thereby strengthened especially the middle class; finally, the glorious victories and their mighty results silenced faction. If the distress of the farmers was by no means removed and still less were its sources stopped, it yet admits of no doubt that at the close of this period the Roman middle class was on the whole in a far less oppressed condition than in the first century after the expulsion of the kings.

Civic Equality

Lastly civic equality was in a certain sense undoubtedly attained or rather restored by the reform of 387, and the development of its legitimate consequences. As formerly, when the patricians still in fact formed the burgesses, these had stood upon a footing of absolute equality in rights and duties, so now in the enlarged burgess-body there existed in the eye of the law no arbitrary distinctions. The gradations to which differences of age, sagacity, cultivation, and wealth necessarily give rise in civil society, naturally also pervaded the sphere of public life; but the spirit animating the burgesses and the policy of the government uniformly operated so as to render these differences as little conspicuous as possible. The whole system of Rome tended to train up her burgesses on an average as sound and capable, but not to bring into prominence the gifts of genius. The growth of culture among the Romans did not at all keep pace with the development of the power of their community, and it was instinctively repressed rather than promoted by those in power. That there should be rich and poor, could not be prevented; but (as in a genuine community of farmers) the farmer as well as the day-labourer personally guided the plough, and even for the rich the good economic rule held good that they should live with uniform frugality and above all should hoard no unproductive capital at home—excepting the salt-cellar and the sacrificial ladle, no silver articles were at this period seen in any Roman house. Nor was this of little moment. In the mighty successes which the Roman community externally achieved during the century from the last Veientine down to the Pyrrhic war we perceive that the patriciate has now given place to the farmers; that the fall of the highborn Fabian would have been not more and not less lamented by the whole community than the fall of the plebeian Decian was lamented alike by plebeians and patricians; that the consulate did not of itself fall even to the wealthiest aristocrat; and that a poor husbandman from Sabina, Manius Curius, could conquer king Pyrrhus in the field of battle and chase him out of Italy, without ceasing to be a simple Sabine farmer and to cultivate in person his own bread-corn.

New Aristocracy

In regard however to this imposing republican equality we must not overlook the fact that it was to a considerable extent only formal, and that an aristocracy of a very decided stamp grew out of it or rather was contained in it from the very first. The non-patrician families of wealth and consideration had long ago separated from the plebs, and leagued themselves with the patriciate in the participation of senatorial rights and in the prosecution of a policy distinct from that of the plebs and very often counteracting it. The Licinian laws abrogated the legal distinctions within the ranks of the aristocracy, and changed the character of the barrier which excluded the plebeian from the government, so that it was no longer a hindrance unalterable in law, but one, not indeed insurmountable, but yet difficult to be surmounted in practice. In both ways fresh blood was mingled with the ruling order in Rome; but in itself the government still remained, as before, aristocratic. In this respect the Roman community was a genuine farmer-commonwealth, in which the rich holder of a whole hide was little distinguished externally from the poor cottager and held intercourse with him on equal terms, but aristocracy nevertheless exercised so all-powerful a sway that a man without means far sooner rose to be master of the burgesses in the city than mayor in his own village. It was a very great and valuable gain, that under the new legislation even the poorest burgess might fill the highest office of the state; nevertheless it was a rare exception when a man from the lower ranks of the population reached such a position,(11) and not only so, but probably it was, at least towards the close of this period, possible only by means of an election carried by the opposition.

New Opposition

Every aristocratic government of itself calls forth a corresponding opposition party; and as the formal equalization of the orders only modified the aristocracy, and the new ruling order not only succeeded the old patriciate but engrafted itself on it and intimately coalesced with it, the opposition also continued to exist and in all respects pursued a similar course. As it was now no longer the plebeian burgesses as such, but the common people, that were treated as inferior, the new opposition professed from the first to be the representative of the lower classes and particularly of the small farmers; and as the new aristocracy attached itself to the patriciate, so the first movements of this new opposition were interwoven with the final struggles against the privileges of the patricians. The first names in the series of these new Roman popular leaders were Manius Curius (consul 464, 479, 480; censor 481) and Gaius Fabricius (consul 472, 476, 481; censor 479); both of them men without ancestral lineage and without wealth, both summoned—in opposition to the aristocratic principle of restricting re-election to the highest office of the state—thrice by the votes of the burgesses to the chief magistracy, both, as tribunes, consuls, and censors, opponents of patrician privileges and defenders of the small farmer-class against the incipient arrogance of the leading houses. The future parties were already marked out; but the interests of party were still suspended on both sides in presence of the interests of the commonweal. The patrician Appius Claudius and the farmer Manius Curius—vehement in their personal antagonism—jointly by wise counsel and vigorous action conquered king Pyrrhus; and while Gaius Fabricius as censor inflicted penalties on Publius Cornelius Rufinus for his aristocratic sentiments and aristocratic habits, this did not prevent him from supporting the claim of Rufinus to a second consulate on account of his recognized ability as a general. The breach was already formed; but the adversaries still shook hands across it.

The New Government

The termination of the struggles between the old and new burgesses, the various and comparatively successful endeavours to relieve the middle class, and the germs—already making their appearance amidst the newly acquired civic equality—of the formation of a new aristocratic and a new democratic party, have thus been passed in review. It remains that we describe the shape which the new government assumed amidst these changes, and the positions in which after the political abolition of the nobility the three elements of the republican commonwealth—the burgesses, the magistrates, and the senate—stood towards each other.

The Burgess-Body—
Its Composition

The burgesses in their ordinary assemblies continued as hitherto to be the highest authority in the commonwealth and the legal sovereign. But it was settled by law that—apart from the matters committed once for all to the decision of the centuries, such as the election of consuls and censors—voting by districts should be just as valid as voting by centuries: a regulation introduced as regards the patricio-plebeian assembly by the Valerio-Horatian law of 305(12) and extended by the Publilian law of 415, but enacted as regards the plebeian separate assembly by the Hortensian law about 467.(13) We have already noticed that the same individuals, on the whole, were entitled to vote in both assemblies, but that—apart from the exclusion of the patricians from the plebeian separate assembly—in the general assembly of the districts all entitled to vote were on a footing of equality, while in the centuriate comitia the working of the suffrage was graduated with reference to the means of the voters, and in so far, therefore, the change was certainly a levelling and democratic innovation. It was a circumstance of far greater importance that, towards the end of this period, the primitive freehold basis of the right of suffrage began for the first time to be called in question. Appius Claudius, the boldest innovator known in Roman history, in his censorship in 442 without consulting the senate or people so adjusted the burgess-roll, that a man who had no land was received into whatever tribe he chose and then according to his means into the corresponding century. But this alteration was too far in advance of the spirit of the age to obtain full acceptance. One of the immediate successors of Appius, Quintus Fabius Rullianus, the famous conqueror of the Samnites, undertook in his censorship of 450 not to set it aside entirely, but to confine it within such limits that the real power in the burgess-assemblies should continue to be vested in the holders of land and of wealth. He assigned those who had no land collectively to the four city tribes, which were now made to rank not as the first but as the last. The rural tribes, on the other hand, the number of which gradually increased between 367 and 513 from seventeen to thirty-one—thus forming a majority, greatly preponderating from the first and ever increasing in preponderance, of the voting-divisions—were reserved by law for the whole of the burgesses who were freeholders. In the centuries the equalization of the freeholders and non-freeholders remained as Appius had introduced it. In this manner provision was made for the preponderance of the freeholders in the comitia of the tribes, while for the centuriate comitia in themselves the wealthy already turned the scale. By this wise and moderate arrangement on the part of a man who for his warlike feats and still more for this peaceful achievement justly received the surname of the Great (-Maximus-), on the one hand the duty of bearing arms was extended, as was fitting, also to the non-freehold burgesses; on the other hand care was taken that their influence, especially that of those who had once been slaves and who were for the most part without property in land, should be subjected to that check which is unfortunately, in a state allowing slavery, an indispensable necessity. A peculiar moral jurisdiction, moreover, which gradually came to be associated with the census and the making up of the burgess-roll, excluded from the burgess-body all individuals notoriously unworthy, and guarded the full moral and political purity of citizenship.

Increasing Powers of the Burgesses

The powers of the comitia exhibited during this period a tendency to enlarge their range, but in a manner very gradual. The increase in the number of magistrates to be elected by the people falls, to some extent, under this head; it is an especially significant fact that from 392 the military tribunes of one legion, and from 443 four tribunes in each of the first four legions respectively, were nominated no longer by the general, but by the burgesses. During this period the burgesses did not on the whole interfere in administration; only their right of declaring war was, as was reasonable, emphatically maintained, and held to extend also to cases in which a prolonged armistice concluded instead of a peace expired and what was not in law but in fact a new war began (327). In other instances a question of administration was hardly submitted to the people except when the governing authorities fell into collision and one of them referred the matter to the people—as when the leaders of the moderate party among the nobility, Lucius Valerius and Marcus Horatius, in 305, and the first plebeian dictator, Gaius Marcius Rutilus, in 398, were not allowed by the senate to receive the triumphs they had earned; when the consuls of 459 could not agree as to their respective provinces of jurisdiction; and when the senate, in 364, resolved to give up to the Gauls an ambassador who had forgotten his duty, and a consular tribune carried the matter to the community. This was the first occasion on which a decree of the senate was annulled by the people; and heavily the community atoned for it. Sometimes in difficult cases the government left the decision to the people, as first, when Caere sued for peace, after the people had declared war against it but before war had actually begun (401); and at a subsequent period, when the senate hesitated to reject unceremoniously the humble entreaty of the Samnites for peace (436). It is not till towards the close of this epoch that we find a considerably extended intervention of the -comitia tributa- in affairs of administration, particularly through the practice of consulting it as to the conclusion of peace and of alliances: this extension probably dates from the Hortensian law of 467.

Decreasing Importance of the Burgess-Body

But notwithstanding these enlargements of the powers of the burgess-assemblies, their practical influence on state affairs began, particularly towards the close of this period, to wane. First of all, the extension of the bounds of Rome deprived her primary assembly of its true basis. As an assembly of the freeholders of the community, it formerly might very well meet in sufficiently full numbers, and might very well know its own wishes, even without discussion; but the Roman burgess-body had now become less a civic community than a state. The fact that those dwelling together voted also with each other, no doubt, introduced into the Roman comitia, at least when the voting was by tribes, a sort of inward connection and into the voting now and then energy and independence; but under ordinary circumstances the composition of the comitia and their decision were left dependent on the person who presided or on accident, or were committed to the hands of the burgesses domiciled in the capital. It is, therefore, quite easy to understand how the assemblies of the burgesses, which had great practical importance during the first two centuries of the republic, gradually became a mere instrument in the hands of the presiding magistrate, and in truth a very dangerous instrument, because the magistrates called to preside were so numerous, and every resolution of the community was regarded as the ultimate legal expression of the will of the people. But the enlargement of the constitutional rights of the burgesses was not of much moment, inasmuch as these were less than formerly capable of a will and action of their own, and there was as yet no demagogism, in the proper sense of that term, in Rome. Had any such demagogic spirit existed, it would have attempted not to extend the powers of the burgesses, but to remove the restrictions on political debate in their presence; whereas throughout this whole period there was undeviating acquiescence in the old maxims, that the magistrate alone could convoke the burgesses, and that he was entitled to exclude all debate and all proposal of amendments. At the time this incipient breaking up of the constitution made itself felt chiefly in the circumstance that the primary assemblies assumed an essentially passive attitude, and did not on the whole interfere in government either to help or to hinder it.

The Magistrates. Partition and Weakening of the Consular Powers

As regards the power of the magistrates, its diminution, although not the direct design of the struggles between the old and new burgesses, was doubtless one of their most important results. At the beginning of the struggle between the orders or, in other words, of the strife for the possession of the consular power, the consulate was still the one and indivisible, essentially regal, magistracy; and the consul, like the king in former times, still had the appointment of all subordinate functionaries left to his own free choice. At the termination of that contest its most important functions —jurisdiction, street-police, election of senators and equites, the census and financial administration —were separated from the consulship and transferred to magistrates, who like the consul were nominated by the community and occupied a position far more co-ordinate than subordinate. The consulate, formerly the single ordinary magistracy of the state, was now no longer even absolutely the first. In the new arrangement as to the ranking and usual order of succession of the public offices the consulate stood indeed above the praetorship, aedileship, and quaestorship, but beneath the censorship, which—in addition to the most important financial duties —- was charged with the adjustment of the rolls of burgesses, equites, and senators, and thereby wielded a wholly arbitrary moral control over the entire community and every individual burgess, the humblest as well as the most prominent. The conception of limited magisterial power or special function, which seemed to the original Roman state-law irreconcilable with the conception of supreme office, gradually gained a footing and mutilated and destroyed the earlier idea of the one and indivisible -imperium-. A first step was already taken in this direction by the institution of the standing collateral offices, particularly the quaestorship;(14) it was completely carried out by the Licinian laws (387), which prescribed the functions of the three supreme magistrates, and assigned administration and the conduct of war to the two first, and the management of justice to the third. But the change did not stop here. The consuls, although they were in law wholly and everywhere co-ordinate, naturally from the earliest times divided between them in practice the different departments of duty (-provinciae-). Originally this was done simply by mutual concert, or in default of it by casting lots; but by degrees the other constituent authorities in the commonwealth interfered with this practical definition of functions. It became usual for the senate to define annually the spheres of duty; and, while it did not directly distribute them among the co-ordinate magistrates, it exercised decided influence on the personal distribution by advice and request. In an extreme case the senate doubtless obtained a decree of the community, definitively to settle the question of distribution;(15) the government, however, very seldom employed this dangerous expedient. Further, the most important affairs, such as the concluding of peace, were withdrawn from the consuls, and they were in such matters obliged to have recourse to the senate and to act according to its instructions. Lastly, in cases of extremity the senate could at any time suspend the consuls from office; for, according to an usage never established by law but never violated in practice, the creation of a dictatorship depended simply upon the resolution of the senate, and the fixing of the person to be nominated, although constitutionally vested in the nominating consul, really under ordinary circumstances lay with the senate.

Limitation of the Dictatorship

The old unity and plenary legal power of the -imperium- were retained longer in the case of the dictatorship than in that of the consulship. Although of course as an extraordinary magistracy it had in reality from the first its special functions, it had in law far less of a special character than the consulate. But it also was gradually affected by the new idea of definite powers and functions introduced into the legal life of Rome. In 391 we first meet with a dictator expressly nominated from theological scruples for the mere accomplishment of a religious ceremony; and though that dictator himself, doubtless in formal accordance with the constitution, treated the restriction of his powers as null and took the command of the army in spite of it, such an opposition on the part of the magistrate was not repeated on occasion of the subsequent similarly restricted nominations, which occurred in 403 and thenceforward very frequently. On the contrary, the dictators thenceforth accounted themselves bound by their powers as specially defined.

Restriction as to the Accumulation and the Reoccupation of Offices

Lastly, further seriously felt restrictions of the magistracy were involved in the prohibition issued in 412 against the accumulation of the ordinary curule offices, and in the enactment of the same date, that the same person should not again administer the same office under ordinary circumstances before an interval of ten years had elapsed, as well as in the subsequent regulation that the office which practically was the highest, the censorship, should not be held a second time at all (489). But the government was still strong enough not to be afraid of its instruments or to desist purposely on that account from employing those who were the most serviceable. Brave officers were very frequently released from these rules,(16) and cases still occurred like those of Quintus Fabius Rullianus, who was five times consul in twenty-eight years, and of Marcus Valerius Corvus (384-483) who, after he had filled six consulships, the first in his twenty-third, the last in his seventy-second year, and had been throughout three generations the protector of his countrymen and the terror of the foe, descended to the grave at the age of a hundred.

While the Roman magistrate was thus more and more completely and definitely transformed from the absolute lord into the limited commissioner and administrator of the community, the old counter-magistracy, the tribunate of the people, was undergoing at the same time a similar transformation internal rather than external. It served a double purpose in the commonwealth. It had been from the beginning intended to protect the humble and the weak by a somewhat revolutionary assistance (-auxilium-) against the overbearing violence of the magistrates; it had subsequently been employed to get rid of the legal disabilities of the commons and the privileges of the gentile nobility. The latter end was attained. The original object was not only in itself a democratic ideal rather than a political possibility, but it was also quite as obnoxious to the plebeian aristocracy into whose hands the tribunate necessarily fell, and quite as incompatible with the new organization which originated in the equalization of the orders and had if possible a still more decided aristocratic hue than that which preceded it, as it was obnoxious to the gentile nobility and incompatible with the patrician consular constitution. But instead of abolishing the tribunate, they preferred to convert it from a weapon of opposition into an instrument of government, and now introduced the tribunes of the people, who were originally excluded from all share in administration and were neither magistrates nor members of the senate, into the class of governing authorities.

While in jurisdiction they stood from the beginning on an equality with the consuls and in the early stages of the conflicts between the orders acquired like the consuls the right of initiating legislation, they now received—we know not exactly when, but presumably at or soon after the final equalization of the orders—a position of equality with the consuls as confronting the practically governing authority, the senate. Hitherto they had been present at the proceedings of the senate, sitting on a bench at the door; now they obtained, like the other magistrates and by their side, a place in the senate itself and the right to interpose their word in its discussions. If they were precluded from the right of voting, this was simply an application of the general principle of Roman state-law, that those only should give counsel who were not called to act; in accordance with which the whole of the acting magistrates possessed during their year of office only a seat, not a vote, in the council of the state.(17) But concession did not rest here. The tribunes received the distinctive prerogative of supreme magistracy, which among the ordinary magistrates belonged only to the consuls and praetors besides—the right of convoking the senate, of consulting it, and of procuring decrees from it.(18) This was only as it should be; the heads of the plebeian aristocracy could not but be placed on an equality with those of the patrician aristocracy in the senate, when once the government had passed from the clan-nobility to the united aristocracy. Now that this opposition-college, originally excluded from all share in the public administration, became—particularly with reference to strictly urban affairs—a second supreme executive and one of the most usual and most serviceable instruments of the government, or in other words of the senate, for managing the burgesses and especially for checking the excesses of the magistrates, it was certainly, as respected its original character, absorbed and politically annihilated; but this course was really enjoined by necessity. Clearly as the defects of the Roman aristocracy were apparent, and decidedly as the steady growth of aristocratic ascendency was connected with the practical setting aside of the tribunate, none can fail to see that government could not be long carried on with an authority which was not only aimless and virtually calculated to put off the suffering proletariate with a deceitful prospect of relief, but was at the same time decidedly revolutionary and possessed of a—strictly speaking —anarchical prerogative of obstruction to the authority of the magistrates and even of the state itself. But that faith in an ideal, which is the foundation of all the power and of all the impotence of democracy, had come to be closely associated in the minds of the Romans with the tribunate of the plebs; and we do not need to recall the case of Cola Rienzi in order to perceive that, however unsubstantial might be the advantage thence arising to the multitude, it could not be abolished without a formidable convulsion of the state. Accordingly with genuine political prudence they contented themselves with reducing it to a nullity under forms that should attract as little attention as possible. The mere name of this essentially revolutionary magistracy was still retained within the aristocratically governed commonwealth—an incongruity for the present, and for the future, in the hands of a coming revolutionary party, a sharp and dangerous weapon. For the moment, however, and for a long time to come the aristocracy was so absolutely powerful and so completely possessed control over the tribunate, that no trace at all is to be met with of a collegiate opposition on the part of the tribunes to the senate; and the government overcame the forlorn movements of opposition that now and then proceeded from individual tribunes, always without difficulty, and ordinarily by means of the tribunate itself.

The Senate. Its Composition

In reality it was the senate that governed the commonwealth, and did so almost without opposition after the equalization of the orders. Its very composition had undergone a change. The free prerogative of the chief magistrates in this matter, as it had been exercised after the setting aside of the old clan-representation,(19) had been already subjected to very material restrictions on the abolition of the presidency for life.(20)

A further step towards the emancipation of the senate from the power of the magistrates took place, when the adjustment of the senatorial lists was transferred from the supreme magistrates to subordinate functionaries—from the consuls to the censors.(21) Certainly, whether immediately at that time or soon afterwards, the right of the magistrate entrusted with the preparation of the list to omit from it individual senators on account of a stain attaching to them and thereby to exclude them from the senate was, if not introduced, at least more precisely defined,(22) and in this way the foundations were laid of that peculiar jurisdiction over morals on which the high repute of the censors was chiefly based.(23) But censures of that sort—especially since the two censors had to be at one on the matter —might doubtless serve to remove particular persons who did not contribute to the credit of the assembly or were hostile to the spirit prevailing there, but could not bring the body itself into dependence on the magistracy.

But the right of the magistrates to constitute the senate according to their judgment was decidedly restricted by the Ovinian law, which was passed about the middle of this period, probably soon after the Licinian laws. That law at once conferred a seat and vote in the senate provisionally on every one who had been curule aedile, praetor, or consul, and bound the next censors either formally to inscribe these expectants in the senatorial roll, or at any rate to exclude them from the roll only for such reasons as sufficed for the rejection of an actual senator. The number of those, however, who had been magistrates was far from sufficing to keep the senate up to the normal number of three hundred; and below that point it could not be allowed to fall, especially as the list of senators was at the same time that of jurymen. Considerable room was thus always left for the exercise of the censorial right of election; but those senators who were chosen not in consequence of having held office, but by selection on the part of the censor—frequently burgesses who had filled a non-curule public office, or distinguished themselves by personal valour, who had killed an enemy in battle or saved the life of a burgess—took part in voting, but not in debate.(24) The main body of the senate, and that portion of it into whose hands government and administration were concentrated, was thus according to the Ovinian law substantially based no longer on the arbitrary will of a magistrate, but indirectly on election by the people. The Roman state in this way made some approach to, although it did not reach, the great institution of modern times, representative popular government, while the aggregate of the non-debating senators furnished—what it is so necessary and yet so difficult to get in governing corporations—a compact mass of members capable of forming and entitled to pronounce an opinion, but voting in silence.

Powers of the Senate

The powers of the senate underwent scarcely any change in form. The senate carefully avoided giving a handle to opposition or to ambition by unpopular changes, or manifest violations, of the constitution; it permitted, though it did nor promote, the enlargement in a democratic direction of the power of the burgesses. But while the burgesses acquired the semblance, the senate acquired the substance of power —a decisive influence over legislation and the official elections, and the whole control of the state.

Its Influence in Legislation

Every new project of law was subjected to a preliminary deliberation in the senate, and scarcely ever did a magistrate venture to lay a proposal before the community without or in opposition to the senate's opinion. If he did so, the senate had—in the intercessory powers of the magistrates and the annulling powers of the priests—an ample set of means at hand to nip in the bud, or subsequently to get rid of, obnoxious proposals; and in case of extremity it had in its hands as the supreme administrative authority not only the executing, but the power of refusing to execute, the decrees of the community. The senate further with tacit consent of the community claimed the right in urgent cases of absolving from the laws, under the reservation that the community should ratify the proceeding—a reservation which from the first was of little moment, and became by degrees so entirely a form that in later times they did not even take the trouble to propose the ratifying decree.

Influence on the Elections

As to the elections, they passed, so far as they depended on the magistrates and were of political importance, practically into the hands of the senate. In this way it acquired, as has been mentioned already,(25) the right to appoint the dictator. Great regard had certainly to be shown to the community; the right of bestowing the public magistracies could not be withdrawn from it; but, as has likewise been already observed, care was taken that this election of magistrates should not be constructed into the conferring of definite functions, especially of the posts of supreme command when war was imminent. Moreover the newly introduced idea of special functions on the one hand, and on the other the right practically conceded to the senate of dispensation from the laws, gave to it an important share in official appointments. Of the influence which the senate exercised in settling the official spheres of the consuls in particular, we have already spoken.(26) One of the most important applications of the dispensing right was the dispensation of the magistrate from the legal term of his tenure of office—a dispensation which, as contrary to the fundamental laws of the community, might not according to Roman state-law be granted in the precincts of the city proper, but beyond these was at least so far valid that the consul or praetor, whose term was prolonged, continued after its expiry to discharge his functions "in a consul's or praetor's stead" (-pro consule- -pro praetore-). Of course this important right of extending the term of office —- essentially on a par with the right of nomination—belonged by law to the community alone, and at the beginning was in fact exercised by it; but in 447, and regularly thenceforward, the command of the commander-in-chief was prolonged by mere decree of the senate. To this was added, in fine, the preponderating and skilfully concerted influence of the aristocracy over the elections, which guided them ordinarily, although not always, to the choice of candidates agreeable to the government.

Senatorial Government

Finally as regards administration, war, peace and alliances, the founding of colonies, the assignation of lands, building, in fact every matter of permanent and general importance, and in particular the whole system of finance, depended absolutely on the senate. It was the senate which annually issued general instructions to the magistrates, settling their spheres of duty and limiting the troops and moneys to be placed at the disposal of each; and recourse was had to its counsel in every case of importance. The keepers of the state-chest could make no payment to any magistrate with the exception of the consul, or to any private person, unless authorized by a previous decree of the senate. In the management, however, of current affairs and in the details of judicial and military administration the supreme governing corporation did not interfere; the Roman aristocracy had too much political judgment and tact to desire to convert the control of the commonwealth into a guardianship over the individual official, or to turn the instrument into a machine.

That this new government of the senate amidst all its retention of existing forms involved a complete revolutionizing of the old commonwealth, is clear. That the free action of the burgesses should be arrested and benumbed; that the magistrates should be reduced to be the presidents of its sittings and its executive commissioners; that a corporation for the mere tendering of advice should seize the inheritance of both the authorities sanctioned by the constitution and should become, although under very modest forms, the central government of the state—these were steps of revolution and usurpation. Nevertheless, if any revolution or any usurpation appears justified before the bar of history by exclusive ability to govern, even its rigorous judgment must acknowledge that this corporation timeously comprehended and worthily fulfilled its great task. Called to power not by the empty accident of birth, but substantially by the free choice of the nation; confirmed every fifth year by the stern moral judgment of the worthiest men; holding office for life, and so not dependent on the expiration of its commission or on the varying opinion of the people; having its ranks close and united ever after the equalization of the orders; embracing in it all the political intelligence and practical statesmanship that the people possessed; absolute in dealing with all financial questions and in the guidance of foreign policy; having complete power over the executive by virtue of its brief duration and of the tribunician intercession which was at the service of the senate after the termination of the quarrels between the orders—the Roman senate was the noblest organ of the nation, and in consistency and political sagacity, in unanimity and patriotism, in grasp of power and unwavering courage, the foremost political corporation of all times—still even now an "assembly of kings," which knew well how to combine despotic energy with republican self-devotion. Never was a state represented in its external relations more firmly and worthily than Rome in its best times by its senate. In matters of internal administration it certainly cannot be concealed that the moneyed and landed aristocracy, which was especially represented in the senate, acted with partiality in affairs that bore upon its peculiar interests, and that the sagacity and energy of the body were often in such cases employed far from beneficially to the state. Nevertheless the great principle established amidst severe conflicts, that all Roman burgesses were equal in the eye of the law as respected rights and duties, and the opening up of a political career (or in other words, of admission to the senate) to every one, which was the result of that principle, concurred with the brilliance of military and political successes in preserving the harmony of the state and of the nation, and relieved the distinction of classes from that bitterness and malignity which marked the struggle of the patricians and plebeians. And, as the fortunate turn taken by external politics had the effect of giving the rich for more than a century ample space for themselves and rendered it unnecessary that they should oppress the middle class, the Roman people was enabled by means of its senate to carry out for a longer term than is usually granted to a people the grandest of all human undertakings—a wise and happy self-government.

Notes for Book II Chapter III

1. The hypothesis that legally the full -imperium- belonged to the patrician, and only the military -imperium- to the plebeian, consular tribunes, not only provokes various questions to which there is no answer—as to the course followed, for example, in the event of the election falling, as was by law quite possible, wholly on plebeians —but specially conflicts with the fundamental principle of Roman constitutional law, that the -imperium-, that is to say, the right of commanding the burgess in name of the community, was functionally indivisible and capable of no other limitation at all than a territorial one. There was a province of urban law and a province of military law, in the latter of which the -provocatio- and other regulations of urban law were not applicable; there were magistrates, such as the proconsuls, who were empowered to discharge functions simply in the latter; but there were, in the strict sense of law, no magistrates with merely jurisdictional, as there were none with merely military, -imperium-. The proconsul was in his province, just like the consul, at once commander-in-chief and supreme judge, and was entitled to send to trial actions not only between non-burgesses and soldiers, but also between one burgess and another. Even when, on the institution of the praetorship, the idea rose of apportioning special functions to the -magistratus maiores-, this division of powers had more of a practical than of a strictly legal force; the -praetor urbanus- was primarily indeed the supreme judge, but he could also convoke the centuries, at least for certain cases, and could command an army; the consul in the city held primarily the supreme administration and the supreme command, but he too acted as a judge in cases of emancipation and adoption—the functional indivisibility of the supreme magistracy was therefore, even in these instances, very strictly adhered to on both sides. Thus the military as well as jurisdictional authority, or, laying aside these abstractions foreign to the Roman law of this period, the absolute magisterial power, must have virtually pertained to the plebeian consular tribunes as well as to the patrician. But it may well be, as Becker supposes (Handb. ii. 2, 137), that, for the same reasons, for which at a subsequent period there was placed alongside of the consulship common to both orders the praetorship actually reserved for a considerable time for the patricians, even during the consular tribunate the plebeian members of the college were -de facto- kept aloof from jurisdiction, and so far the consular tribunate prepared the way for the subsequent actual division of jurisdiction between consuls and praetors.

2. I. VI. Political Effects of the Servian Military Organization

3. The defence, that the aristocracy clung to the exclusion of the plebeians from religious prejudice, mistakes the fundamental character of the Roman religion, and imports into antiquity the modern distinction between church and state. The admittance of a non-burgess to a religious ceremony of the citizens could not indeed but appear sinful to the orthodox Roman; but even the most rigid orthodoxy never doubted that admittance to civic communion, which absolutely and solely depended on the state, involved also full religious equality. All such scruples of conscience, the honesty of which in themselves we do not mean to doubt, were precluded, when once they granted to the plebeians -en masse- at the right time the patriciate. This

only may perhaps be alleged by way of excuse for the nobility, that after it had neglected the right moment for this purpose at the abolition of the monarchy, it was no longer in a position subsequently of itself to retrieve the neglect (*ii*. I. The New Community).

4. Whether this distinction between these "curule houses" and the other families embraced within the patriciate was ever of serious political importance, cannot with certainty be either affirmed or denied; and as little do we know whether at this epoch there really was any considerable number of patrician families that were not yet curule.

5. II. II. The Valerio-Horatian Laws

6. I. XII. Foreign Worships

7. II. I. Senate,

8. II. I. Senate, *ii*. III. Opposition of the Patriciate

9. II. II. Legislation of the Twelve Tables

10. II. III. Equivalence Law and Plebiscitum

11. The statements as to the poverty of the consulars of this period, which play so great a part in the moral anecdote-books of a later age, mainly rest on a misunderstanding on the one hand of the old frugal economy—which might very well consist with considerable prosperity —and on the other hand of the beautiful old custom of burying men who had deserved well of the state from the proceeds of penny collections —which was far from being a pauper burial. The method also of explaining surnames by etymological guess-work, which has imported so many absurdities into Roman history, has furnished its quota to this belief (-Serranus-).

12. II. II. The Valerio-Horatian Laws

13. II. III. Equivalence Law and Plebiscitum

14. II. I. Restrictions on the Delegation of Powers

15. II. III. Increasing Powers of the Burgesses

16. Any one who compares the consular Fasti before and after 412 will have no doubt as to the existence of the above-mentioned law respecting re-election to the consulate; for, while before that year a return to office, especially after three or four years, was a common occurrence, afterwards intervals of ten years and more were as frequent. Exceptions, however, occur in very great numbers, particularly during the

severe years of war 434-443. On the other hand, the principle of not allowing a plurality of offices was strictly adhered to. There is no certain instance of the combination of two of the three ordinary curule (Liv. xxxix. 39, 4) offices (the consulate, praetorship, and curule aedileship), but instances occur of other combinations, such as of the curule aedileship and the office of master of the horse (Liv. xxiii. 24, 30); of the praetorship and censorship (Fast. Cap. a. 501); of the praetorship and the dictatorship (Liv. viii. 12); of the consulate and the dictatorship (Liv. viii. 12).

17. II. I. Senate

18. Hence despatches intended for the senate were addressed to Consuls, Praetors, Tribunes of the Plebs, and Senate (Cicero, ad Fam. xv. 2, *et al.*)

19. I. V. The Senate

20. II. I. Senate

21. II. III. Censorship

22. This prerogative and the similar ones with reference to the equestrian and burgess-lists were perhaps not formally and legally assigned to the censors, but were always practically implied in their powers. It was the community, not the censor, that conferred burgess-rights; but the person, to whom the latter in making up the list of persons entitled to vote did not assign a place or assigned an inferior one, did not lose his burgess-right, but could not exercise the privileges of a burgess, or could only exercise them in the inferior place, till the preparation of a new list. The same was the case with the senate; the person omitted by the censor from his list ceased to attend the senate, as long as the list in question remained valid—unless the presiding magistrate should reject it and reinstate the earlier list. Evidently therefore the important question in this respect was not so much what was the legal liberty of the censors, as how far their authority availed with those magistrates who had to summon according to their lists. Hence it is easy to understand how this prerogative gradually rose in importance, and how with the increasing consolidation of the nobility such erasures assumed virtually the form of judicial decisions and were virtually respected as such. As to the adjustment of the senatorial list undoubtedly the enactment of the Ovinian -plebiscitum- exercised a material share of influence—-that the censors should admit to the senate "the best men out of all classes."

23. II. III. The Burgess-Body. Its Composition

24. II. III. Complete Opening Up of Magistracies and Priesthoods

25. II. III. Restrictions as to the Accumulation and the Reoccupation of Offices

26. II. III. Partition and Weakening of Consular Powers

CHAPTER IV

Fall of the Etruscan Power-the Celts

Etrusco-Carthaginian Maritime Supremacy

In the previous chapters we have presented an outline of the development of the Roman constitution during the first two centuries of the republic; we now recur to the commencement of that epoch for the purpose of tracing the external history of Rome and of Italy. About the time of the expulsion of the Tarquins from Rome the Etruscan power had reached its height. The Tuscans, and the Carthaginians who were in close alliance with them, possessed undisputed supremacy on the Tyrrhene Sea. Although Massilia amidst continual and severe struggles maintained her independence, the seaports of Campania and of the Volscian land, and after the battle of Alalia Corsica also,(1) were in the possession of the Etruscans. In Sardinia the sons of the Carthaginian general Mago laid the foundation of the greatness both of their house and of their city by the complete conquest of the island (about 260); and in Sicily, while the Hellenic colonies were occupied with their internal feuds, the Phoenicians retained possession of the western half without material opposition. The vessels of the Etruscans were no less dominant in the Adriatic; and their pirates were dreaded even in the more eastern waters.

Subjugation of Latium by Etruria

By land also their power seemed to be on the increase. To acquire possession of Latium was of the most decisive importance to Etruria, which was separated by the Latins alone from the Volscian towns that were dependent on it and from its possessions in Campania. Hitherto the firm bulwark of the Roman power had sufficiently protected Latium, and had successfully maintained against Etruria the frontier line of the Tiber. But now, when the whole Tuscan league, taking advantage of the confusion and the weakness of the Roman state after the expulsion of the Tarquins, renewed its attack more energetically than before under the king Lars Porsena of Clusium, it no longer encountered the wonted resistance. Rome surrendered, and in the peace (assigned to 247) not only ceded all her possessions on the right bank of the Tiber to the adjacent Tuscan communities and thus abandoned her exclusive command of the river, but also delivered to the conqueror all her weapons of war and promised to make use of iron thenceforth only for the ploughshare. It seemed as if the union of Italy under Tuscan supremacy was not far distant.

Etruscans Driven Back from Latium—
Fall of the Etrusco-Carthaginian Maritime Supremacy—
Victories of Salamis and Himera, and Their Effects

But the subjugation, with which the coalition of the Etruscan and Carthaginian nations had threatened both Greeks and Italians, was fortunately averted by the combination of peoples drawn towards each other by family affinity as well as by common peril. The Etruscan army, which after the fall of Rome had penetrated into Latium, had its victorious career checked in the first instance before the walls of Aricia by the well-timed intervention of the Cumaeans who had hastened to the succour of the Aricines (248). We know not how the war ended, nor, in particular, whether Rome even at that time tore up the ruinous and disgraceful peace. This much only is certain, that on this occasion also the Tuscans were unable to maintain their ground permanently on the left bank of the Tiber.

Soon the Hellenic nation was forced to engage in a still more comprehensive and still more decisive conflict with the barbarians both of the west and of the east. It was about the time of the Persian wars. The relation in which the Tyrians stood to the great king led Carthage also to follow in the wake of Persian policy —there exists a credible tradition even as to an alliance between the Carthaginians and Xerxes—and, along with the Carthaginians, the Etruscans. It was one of the grandest of political combinations which simultaneously directed the Asiatic hosts against Greece, and the Phoenician hosts against Sicily, to extirpate at a blow liberty and civilization from the face of the earth. The victory remained with the Hellenes. The battle of Salamis (274) saved and avenged Hellas proper; and on the same day—so runs the story—the rulers of Syracuse and Agrigentum, Gelon and Theron, vanquished the immense army of the Carthaginian general Hamilcar, son of Mago, at Himera so completely, that the war was thereby terminated, and the Phoenicians, who by no means cherished at that time the project of subduing the whole of Sicily on their own account, returned to their previous defensive policy. Some of the large silver pieces are still preserved which were coined for this campaign from the ornaments of Damareta, the wife of Gelon, and other noble Syracusan dames: and the latest times gratefully remembered the gentle and brave king of Syracuse and the glorious victory whose praises Simonides sang.

The immediate effect of the humiliation of Carthage was the fall of the maritime supremacy of her Etruscan allies. Anaxilas, ruler of Rhegium and Zancle, had already closed the Sicilian straits against their privateers by means of a standing fleet (about 272); soon afterwards (280) the Cumaeans and Hiero of Syracuse achieved a decisive victory near Cumae over the Tyrrhene fleet, to which the Carthaginians vainly attempted to render aid. This is the victory which Pindar celebrates in his first Pythian ode; and there is still extant an Etruscan helmet, which Hiero sent to Olympia, with the inscription: "Hiaron son of Deinomenes and the Syrakosians to Zeus, Tyrrhane spoil from Kyma."(2)

Maritime Supremacy of the Tarentines and Syracusans—
Dionysius of Syracuse

While these extraordinary successes against the Carthaginians and Etruscans placed Syracuse at the head of the Greek cities in Sicily, the Doric Tarentum rose to undisputed pre-eminence among the Italian Hellenes, after the Achaean Sybaris had fallen about the time of the expulsion of the kings from Rome (243). The terrible defeat of the Tarentines by the Iapygians (280), the most severe disaster which a Greek army had hitherto sustained, served only, like the Persian invasion of Hellas, to unshackle the whole might of the national spirit in the development of an energetic democracy. Thenceforth the Carthaginians and the Etruscans were no longer paramount in the Italian waters; the Tarentines predominated in the Adriatic and Ionic, the Massiliots and Syracusans in the Tyrrhene, seas. The latter in particular restricted more and more the range of Etruscan piracy. After the victory at Cumae, Hiero had occupied the island of Aenaria (Ischia), and by that means interrupted the communication between the Campanian and the northern Etruscans. About the year 302, with a view thoroughly to check Tuscan piracy, Syracuse sent forth a special expedition, which ravaged the island of Corsica and the Etruscan coast and occupied the island of Aethalia (Elba). Although Etrusco-Carthaginian piracy was not wholly repressed—Antium, for example, having apparently continued a haunt of privateering down to the beginning of the fifth century of Rome—the powerful Syracuse formed a strong bulwark against the allied Tuscans and Phoenicians. For a moment, indeed, it seemed as if the Syracusan power must be broken by the attack of the Athenians, whose naval expedition against Syracuse in the course of the Peloponnesian war (339-341) was supported by the Etruscans, old commercial friends of Athens, with three fifty-oared galleys. But the victory remained, as is well known, both in the west and in the east with the Dorians. After the ignominious failure of the Attic expedition, Syracuse became so indisputably the first Greek maritime power that the men, who were there at the head of the state, aspired to the sovereignty of Sicily and Lower Italy, and of both the Italian seas; while on the other hand the Carthaginians, who saw their dominion in Sicily now seriously in danger, were on their part also obliged to make, and made, the subjugation of the Syracusans and the reduction of the whole island the aim of their policy. We cannot here narrate the decline of the intermediate Sicilian states, and the increase of the Carthaginian power in the island, which were the immediate results of these struggles; we notice their effect only so far as Etruria is concerned. The new ruler of Syracuse, Dionysius (who reigned 348-387), inflicted on Etruria blows which were severely felt. The far-scheming king laid the foundation of his new colonial power especially in the sea to the east of Italy, the more northern waters of which now became, for the first time, subject to a Greek maritime power. About the year 367, Dionysius occupied and colonized the port of Lissus and island of Issa on the Illyrian coast, and the ports of Ancona, Numana, and Atria, on the coast of Italy. The memory of the Syracusan dominion in this remote region is preserved not only by the "trenches of Philistus," a canal constructed at the mouth of the Po beyond doubt by the well-known historian and friend of Dionysius who spent the years of his exile (368 et seq.) at Atria, but also by the alteration in the name of the Italian eastern sea itself, which from this time forth, instead of its earlier designation of the "Ionic Gulf",(3) received the appellation still current at the present day, and probably referable to these events, of the sea "of Hadria."(4) But not content with these attacks on the possessions and commercial communications of the Etruscans in the eastern sea, Dionysius assailed the very heart of the Etruscan power by storming and plundering Pyrgi, the rich seaport of Caere (369). From this blow it never recovered. When the internal disturbances that followed the death of Dionysius in Syracuse gave the Carthaginians freer scope, and their fleet resumed in the Tyrrhene sea that ascendency which with but slight interruptions they thenceforth maintained, it proved a burden no less grievous to Etruscans than to Greeks; so that, when Agathocles of Syracuse in 444 was making preparations for war with Carthage, he was even joined by eighteen Tuscan vessels of war. The Etruscans perhaps had their fears in regard to Corsica, which they probably still at that time retained. The old Etrusco-Phoenician symmachy, which still existed in the time of Aristotle (370-432), was thus broken up; but the Etruscans never recovered their maritime strength.

The Romans Opposed to the Etruscans in Veii

This rapid collapse of the Etruscan maritime power would be inexplicable but for the circumstance that, at the very time when the Sicilian Greeks were attacking them by sea, the Etruscans found themselves assailed with the severest blows oil every side by land. About the time of the battles of Salamis, Himera, and Cumae a furious war raged for many years, according to the accounts of the Roman annals, between Rome and Veii (271-280). The Romans suffered in its course severe defeats. Tradition especially preserved the memory of the catastrophe of the Fabii (277), who had in consequence of internal commotions voluntarily banished themselves from the capital(4) and had undertaken the defence of the frontier against Etruria, and who were slain to the last man capable of bearing arms at the brook Cremera. But the armistice for 400 months, which in room of a peace terminated the war, was so far favourable to the Romans that it at least restored the -status quo- of the regal period; the Etruscans gave up Fidenae and the district won by them on the right bank of the Tiber. We cannot ascertain how far this Romano-Etruscan war was connected directly with the war between the Hellenes and the Persians, and with that between the Sicilians and Carthaginians; but whether the Romans were or were not allies of the victors of Salamis and of Himera, there was at any rate a coincidence of interests as well as of results.

The Samnites Opposed to the Etruscans in Campania

The Samnites as well as the Latins threw themselves upon the Etruscans; and hardly had their Campanian settlement been cut off from the motherland in consequence of the battle of Cumae, when it found itself no longer able to resist the assaults of the Sabellian mountain tribes. Capua, the capital, fell in 330; and the Tuscan population there was soon after the conquest extirpated or expelled by the Samnites. It is true that the Campanian Greeks also, isolated and weakened, suffered severely from the same invasion: Cumae itself was conquered by the Sabellians in 334. But the Hellenes maintained their ground at Neapolis especially, perhaps with the aid of the Syracusans, while the Etruscan name in Campania disappeared from history —- excepting some detached Etruscan communities, which prolonged a pitiful and forlorn existence there.

Events still more momentous, however, occurred about the same time in Northern Italy. A new nation was knocking at the gates of the Alps: it was the Celts; and their first pressure fell on the Etruscans.

The Celtic, Galatian, or Gallic nation received from the common mother endowments different from those of its Italian, Germanic, and Hellenic sisters. With various solid qualities and still more that were brilliant, it was deficient in those deeper moral and political qualifications which lie at the root of all that is good and great in human development. It was reckoned disgraceful, Cicero tells us, for the free Celts to till their fields with their own hands. They preferred a pastoral life to agriculture; and even in the fertile plains of the Po they chiefly practised the rearing of swine, feeding on the flesh of their herds, and staying with them in the oak forests day and night. Attachment to their native soil, such as characterized the Italians and the Germans, was wanting in the Celts; while on the other hand they delighted to congregate in towns and villages, which accordingly acquired magnitude and importance among the Celts earlier apparently than in Italy. Their political constitution was imperfect. Not only was the national unity recognized but feebly as a bond of connection—as is, in fact, the case with all nations at first—but the individual communities were deficient in concord and firm control, in earnest public spirit and consistency of aim. The only organization for which they were fitted was a military one, where the bonds of discipline relieved the individual from the troublesome task of self-control. "The prominent qualities of the Celtic race," says their historian Thierry, "were personal bravery, in which they excelled all nations; an open impetuous temperament, accessible to every impression; much intelligence, but at the same time extreme mobility, want of perseverance, aversion to discipline and order, ostentation and perpetual discord—the result of boundless vanity." Cato the Elder more briefly describes them, nearly to the same effect; "the Celts devote themselves mainly to two things—fighting and -esprit-."(6) Such qualities—those of good soldiers but of bad citizens—explain the historical fact, that the Celts have shaken all states and have founded none. Everywhere we find them ready to rove or, in other words, to march; preferring moveable property to landed estate, and gold to everything else; following the profession of arms as a system of organized pillage or even as a trade for hire, and with such success at all events that even the Roman historian Sallust acknowledges that the Celts bore off the prize from the Romans in feats of arms. They were the true soldiers-of-fortune of antiquity, as figures and descriptions represent them: with big but not sinewy bodies, with shaggy hair and long mustaches—quite a contrast to the Greeks and Romans, who shaved the head and upper lip; in variegated embroidered dresses, which in combat were not unfrequently thrown off; with a broad gold ring round the neck; wearing no helmets and without missile weapons of any sort, but furnished instead with an immense shield, a long ill-tempered sword, a dagger and a lance—all ornamented with gold, for they were not unskilful at working in metals. Everything was made subservient to ostentation, even wounds, which were often subsequently enlarged for the purpose of boasting a broader scar. Usually they fought on foot, but certain tribes on horseback, in which case every freeman was followed by two attendants likewise mounted; war-chariots were early in use, as they were among the Libyans and the Hellenes in the earliest times. Various traits remind us of the chivalry of the Middle Ages; particularly the custom of single combat, which was foreign to the Greeks and Romans. Not only were they accustomed during war to challenge a single enemy to fight, after having previously insulted him by words and gestures; during peace also they fought with each other in splendid suits of armour, as for life or death. After such feats carousals followed as a matter of course. In this way they led, whether under their own or a foreign banner, a restless soldier-life; they were dispersed from Ireland and Spain to Asia Minor, constantly occupied in fighting and so-called feats of heroism. But all their enterprises melted away like snow in spring; and nowhere did they create a great state or develop a distinctive culture of their own.

Celtic Migrations—
The Celts Assail the Etruscans in Northern Italy

Such is the description which the ancients give us of this nation. Its origin can only be conjectured. Sprung from the same cradle from which the Hellenic, Italian, and Germanic peoples issued,(7) the Celts doubtless like these migrated from their eastern motherland into Europe, where at a very early period they reached the western ocean and established their headquarters in what is now France, crossing to settle in the British isles on the north, and on the south passing the Pyrénées and contending with the Iberian tribes for the possession of the peninsula. This, their first great migration, flowed past the Alps, and it was from the lands to the westward that they first began those movements of smaller masses in the opposite direction—movements which carried them over the Alps and the Haemus and even over the Bosporus, and by means of which they became and for many centuries continued to be the terror of the whole civilized nations of antiquity, till the victories of Cæsar and the frontier defence organized by Augustus for ever broke their power.

The native legend of their migrations, which has been preserved to us mainly by Livy, relates the story of these later retrograde movements as follows.(8) The Gallic confederacy, which was headed then as in the time of Cæsar by the canton of the Bituriges (around Bourges), sent forth in the days of king Ambiatus two great hosts led by the two nephews of the king. One of these nephews, Sigovesus, crossed the Rhine and advanced in the direction of the Black Forest, while the second, Bellovesus, crossed the Graian Alps (the Little St. Bernard) and descended into the valley of the Po. From the former proceeded the Gallic settlement on the middle Danube; from the latter the oldest Celtic settlement in the modern Lombardy, the canton of the Insubres with Mediolanum (Milan) as its capital. Another host soon followed, which founded the canton of the Cenomani with the towns of Brixia (Brescia) and Verona. Ceaseless streams thenceforth poured over the Alps into the beautiful plain; the Celtic tribes with the Ligurians whom they dislodged and swept along with them wrested place after place from the Etruscans, till the whole left bank of the Po was in their hands. After the fall of the rich Etruscan town Melpum (presumably in the district of Milan), for the subjugation of which the Celts already settled in the basin of the Po had united with newly arrived tribes (358?), these latter crossed to the right bank of the river and began to press upon the Umbrians and Etruscans in their original abodes. Those who did so were chiefly the Boii, who are alleged to have penetrated into Italy by another route, over the Poenine Alps (the Great St. Bernard): they settled in the modern Romagna, where the old Etruscan town Felsina, with its name changed by its new masters to Bononia, became their capital. Finally came the Senones, the last of the larger Celtic tribes which made their way over the Alps; they took up their abode along the coast of the Adriatic from Rimini to Ancona. But isolated bands of Celtic settlers must have advanced even far in the direction of Umbria, and up to the border of Etruria proper; for stone-inscriptions in the Celtic language have been found even at Todi on the upper Tiber. The limits of Etruria on the north and east became more and more contracted, and about the middle of the fourth century the Tuscan nation found themselves substantially restricted to the territory which thenceforth bore and still bears their name.

Attack on Etruria by the Romans

Subjected to these simultaneous and, as it were, concerted assaults on the part of very different peoples—the Syracusans, Latins, Samnites, and above all the Celts—-the Etruscan nation, that had just acquired so vast and sudden an ascendency in Latium and Campania and on both the Italian seas, underwent a still more rapid and violent collapse. The loss of their maritime supremacy and the subjugation of the Campanian Etruscans belong to the same epoch as the settlement of the Insubres and Cenomani on the Po; and about this same period the Roman burgesses, who had not very many years before been humbled to the utmost and almost reduced to bondage by Porsena, first assumed an attitude of aggression towards Etruria. By the armistice with Veii in 280 Rome had recovered its ground, and the two nations were restored in the main to the state in which they had stood in the time of the kings. When it expired in the year 309, the warfare began afresh; but it took the form of border frays and pillaging excursions which led to no material result on either side. Etruria was still too powerful for Rome to be able seriously to attack it. At length the revolt of the Fidenates, who expelled the Roman garrison, murdered the Roman envoys, and submitted to Lars Tolumnius, king of the Veientes, gave rise to a more considerable war, which ended favourably for the Romans; the king Tolumnius fell in combat by the hand of the Roman consul Aulus Cornelius Cossus (326?), Fidenae was taken, and a new armistice for 200 months was concluded in 329. During this truce the troubles of Etruria became more and more aggravated, and the Celtic arms were already approaching the settlements that hitherto had been spared on the right bank of the Po. When the armistice expired in the end of 346, the Romans on their part resolved to undertake a war of conquest against Etruria; and on this occasion the war was carried on not merely to vanquish Veii, but to crush it.

Conquest of Veii

The history of the war against the Veientes, Capenates, and Falisci, and of the siege of Veii, which is said, like that of Troy, to have lasted ten years, rests on evidence far from trustworthy. Legend and poetry have taken possession of these events as their own, and with reason; for the struggle in this case was waged, with unprecedented exertions, for an unprecedented prize. It was the first occasion on which a Roman army remained in the field summer and winter, year after year, till its object was attained. It was the first occasion on which the community paid the levy from the resources of the state. But it was also the first occasion on which the Romans attempted to subdue a nation of alien stock, and carried their arms beyond the ancient northern boundary of the Latin land. The struggle was vehement, but the issue was scarcely doubtful. The Romans were supported by the Latins and Hernici, to whom the overthrow of their dreaded neighbour was productive of scarcely less satisfaction and advantage than to the Romans themselves; whereas Veii was abandoned by its own nation, and only the adjacent towns of Capena and Falerii, along with Tarquinii, furnished contingents to its help. The contemporary attacks of the Celts would alone suffice to explain the nonintervention of the northern communities; it is affirmed however, and there is no reason to doubt, that this inaction of the other Etruscans was primarily occasioned by internal factions in the league of the Etruscan cities, and particularly by the opposition which the regal form of government retained or restored by the Veientes encountered from the aristocratic governments of the other cities. Had the Etruscan nation been able or willing to take part in the conflict, the

Roman community would hardly have been able —undeveloped as was the art of besieging at that time—to accomplish the gigantic task of subduing a large and strong city. But isolated and forsaken as Veii was, it succumbed (358) after a valiant resistance to the persevering and heroic spirit of Marcus Furius Camillus, who first opened up to his countrymen the brilliant and perilous career of foreign conquest. The joy which this great success excited in Rome had its echo in the Roman custom, continued down to a late age, of concluding the festal games with a "sale of Veientes," at which, among the mock spoils submitted to auction, the most wretched old cripple who could be procured wound up the sport in a purple mantle and ornaments of gold as "king of the Veientes." The city was destroyed, and the soil was doomed to perpetual desolation. Falerii and Capena hastened to make peace; the powerful Volsinii, which with federal indecision had remained quiet during the agony of Veii and took up arms after its capture, likewise after a few years (363) consented to peace. The statement that the two bulwarks of the Etruscan nation, Melpum and Veii, yielded on the same day, the former to the Celts, the latter to the Romans, may be merely a melancholy legend; but it at any rate involves a deep historical truth. The double assault from the north and from the south, and the fall of the two frontier strongholds, were the beginning of the end of the great Etruscan nation.

The Celts Attack Rome—
Battle on the Allia—
Capture of Rome

For a moment, however, it seemed as if the two peoples, through whose co-operation Etruria saw her very existence put in jeopardy, were about to destroy each other, and the reviving power of Rome was to be trodden under foot by foreign barbarians. This turn of things, so contrary to what might naturally have been expected, the Romans brought upon themselves by their own arrogance and shortsightedness.

The Celtic swarms, which had crossed the river after the fall of Melpum, rapidly overflowed northern Italy—not merely the open country on the right bank of the Po and along the shore of the Adriatic, but also Etruria proper to the south of the Apennines. A few years afterwards (363) Clusium situated in the heart of Etruria (Chiusi, on the borders of Tuscany and the Papal State) was besieged by the Celtic Senones; and so humbled were the Etruscans that the Tuscan city in its straits invoked aid from the destroyers of Veii. Perhaps it would have been wise to grant it and to reduce at once the Gauls by arms, and the Etruscans by according to them protection, to a state of dependence on Rome; but an intervention with aims so extensive, which would have compelled the Romans to undertake a serious struggle on the northern Tuscan frontier, lay beyond the horizon of the Roman policy at that time. No course was therefore left but to refrain from all interference. Foolishly, however, while declining to send auxiliary troops, they despatched envoys. With still greater folly these sought to impose upon the Celts by haughty language, and, when this failed, they conceived that they might with impunity violate the law of nations in dealing with barbarians; in the ranks of the Clusines they took part in a skirmish, and in the course of it one of them stabbed and dismounted a Gallic officer. The barbarians acted in this case with moderation and prudence. They sent in the first instance to the Roman community to demand the surrender of those who had outraged the law of nations, and the senate was ready to comply with the reasonable request. But with the multitude compassion for their countrymen outweighed justice towards the foreigners; satisfaction was refused by the burgesses; and according to some accounts they even nominated the brave champions of their fatherland as consular tribunes for the year 364,(9) which was to be so fatal in the Roman annals. Then the Brennus or, in other words, the "king of the army" of the Gauls broke up the siege of Clusium, and the whole Celtic host—the numbers of which are stated at 70,000 men—turned against Rome. Such expeditions into unknown land distant regions were not unusual for the Gauls, who marched as bands of armed emigrants, troubling themselves little as to the means of cover or of retreat; but it was evident that none in Rome anticipated the dangers involved in so sudden and so mighty an invasion. It was not till the Gauls were marching upon Rome that a Roman military force crossed the Tiber and sought to bar their way. Not twelve miles from the gates, opposite to the confluence of the rivulet Allia with the Tiber, the armies met, and a battle took place on the 18th July, 364. Even now they went into battle—not as against an army, but as against freebooters—with arrogance and foolhardiness and under inexperienced leaders, Camillus having in consequence of the dissensions of the orders withdrawn from taking part in affairs. Those against whom they were to fight were but barbarians; what need was there of a camp, or of securing a retreat? These barbarians, however, were men whose courage despised death, and their mode of fighting was to the Italians as novel as it was terrible; sword in hand the Celts precipitated themselves with furious onset on the Roman phalanx, and shattered it at the first shock. The overthrow was complete; of the Romans, who had fought with the river in their rear, a large portion met their death in the attempt to cross it; such as escaped threw themselves by a flank movement into the neighbouring Veii. The victorious Celts stood between the remnant of the beaten army and the capital. The latter was irretrievably abandoned to the enemy; the small force that was left behind, or that had fled thither, was not sufficient to garrison the walls, and three days after the battle the victors marched through the open gates into Rome. Had they done so at first, as they might have done, not only the city, but the state also must have been lost; the brief interval gave opportunity to carry away or to bury the sacred objects, and, what was more important, to occupy the citadel and to furnish it with provisions for the exigency. No one was admitted to the citadel who was incapable of bearing arms—there was not food for all. The mass of the defenceless dispersed among the neighbouring towns; but many, and in particular a number of old men of high standing, would not survive the downfall of the city and awaited death in their houses by the sword of the barbarians. They came, murdered all they met with, plundered whatever property they found, and at length set the city on fire on all sides before the eyes of the Roman garrison in the Capitol. But they had no knowledge of the art of besieging, and the blockade of the steep citadel rock was tedious and difficult, because subsistence for the great host could only be procured by armed foraging parties, and the citizens of the neighbouring Latin cities, the Ardeates in particular, frequently attacked the foragers with courage and success. Nevertheless the Celts persevered, with an energy which in their circumstances was unparalleled, for seven months beneath the rock, and the garrison, which had escaped a surprise on a dark night only in consequence of the cackling of the sacred geese in the Capitoline temple and the accidental awaking of the brave Marcus Manlius, already found its provisions beginning to fail, when the Celts received information as to the Veneti having invaded the Senonian territory recently acquired on the Po, and were thus induced to accept the ransom money that was offered to procure their withdrawal. The scornful throwing down of the Gallic sword, that it might be outweighed by Roman gold, indicated very truly how matters stood. The iron of the barbarians had conquered, but they sold their victory and by selling lost it.

Fruitlessness of the Celtic Victory

The fearful catastrophe of the defeat and the conflagration, the 18th of July and the rivulet of the Allia, the spot where the sacred objects were buried, and the spot where the surprise of the citadel had been repulsed—all the details of this unparalleled event—were transferred from the recollection of contemporaries to the imagination of posterity; and we can scarcely realize the fact that two thousand years have actually elapsed since those world-renowned geese showed greater vigilance than the sentinels at their posts. And yet —although there was an enactment in Rome that in future, on occasion of a Celtic invasion no legal privilege should give exemption from military service; although dates were reckoned by the years from the conquest of the city; although the event resounded throughout the whole of the then civilized world and found its way even into the Grecian annals—the battle of the Allia and its results can scarcely be numbered among those historical events that are fruitful of consequences. It made no alteration at all in political relations. When the Gauls had marched off again with their gold—which only a legend of late and wretched invention represents the hero Camillus as having recovered for Rome—and when the fugitives had again made their way home, the foolish idea suggested by some faint-hearted prudential politicians, that the citizens should migrate to Veii, was set aside by a spirited speech of Camillus; houses arose out of the ruins hastily and irregularly—the narrow and crooked streets of Rome owed their origin to this epoch; and Rome again stood in her old commanding position. Indeed it is not improbable that this occurrence contributed materially, though not just at the moment, to diminish the antagonism between Rome and Etruria, and above all to knit more closely the ties of union between Latium and Rome. The conflict between the Gauls and the Romans was not, like that between Rome and Etruria or between Rome and Samnium, a collision of two political powers which affect and modify each other; it may be compared to those catastrophes of nature, after which the organism, if it is not destroyed, immediately resumes its equilibrium. The Gauls often returned to Latium: as in the year 387, when Camillus defeated them at Alba—the last victory of the aged hero, who had been six times military tribune with consular powers, and five times dictator, and had four times marched in triumph to the Capitol; in the year 393, when the dictator Titus Quinctius Pennus encamped opposite to them not five miles from the city at the bridge of the Anio, but before any encounter took place the Gallic host marched onward to Campania; in the year 394, when the dictator Quintus Servilius Ahala fought in front of the Colline gate with the hordes returning from Campania; in the year 396, when the dictator Gaius Sulpicius Peticus inflicted on them a signal defeat; in the year 404, when they even spent the winter encamped upon the Alban mount and joined with the Greek pirates along the coast for plunder, till Lucius Furius Camillus, the son of the celebrated general, in the following year dislodged them—an incident which came to the ears of Aristotle who was contemporary (370-432) in Athens. But these predatory expeditions, formidable and troublesome as they may have been, were rather incidental misfortunes than events of political significance; and their most essential result was, that the Romans were more and more regarded by themselves and by foreigners as the bulwark of the civilized nations of Italy against the onset of the dreaded barbarians—a view which tended more than is usually supposed to further their subsequent claim to universal empire.

Further Conquests of Rome in Etruria—
South Etruria Roman

The Tuscans, who had taken advantage of the Celtic attack on Rome to assail Veii, had accomplished nothing, because they had appeared in insufficient force; the barbarians had scarcely departed, when the heavy arm of Latium descended on the Tuscans with undiminished weight. After the Etruscans had been repeatedly defeated, the whole of southern Etruria as far as the Ciminian hills remained in the hands of the Romans, who formed four new tribes in the territories of Veii, Capena, and Falerii (367), and secured the northern boundary by establishing the fortresses of Sutrium (371) and Nepete (381). With rapid steps this fertile region, covered with Roman colonists, became completely Romanized. About 396 the nearest Etruscan towns, Tarquinii, Caere, and Falerii, attempted to revolt against the Roman encroachments, and the deep exasperation which these had aroused in Etruria was shown by the slaughter of the whole of the Roman prisoners taken in the first campaign, three hundred and seven in number, in the market-place of Tarquinii; but it was the exasperation of impotence. In the peace (403) Caere, which as situated nearest to the Romans suffered the heaviest retribution, was compelled to cede half its territory to Rome, and with the diminished domain which was left to it to withdraw from the Etruscan league, and to enter into the relationship of subjects to Rome which had in the meanwhile been constituted primarily for individual Latin communities. It seemed, however, not advisable to leave to this more remote community alien in race from the Roman such communal independence as was still retained by the subject communities of Latium; the Caerite community received the Roman franchise not merely without the privilege of electing or of being elected at Rome, but also subject to the withholding of self-administration, so that the place of magistrates of its own was as regards justice and the census taken by those of Rome, and a representative (-praefectus-) of the Roman praetor conducted the administration on the spot—a form of subjection, which in state-law first meets us here, whereby a state which had hitherto been independent became converted into a community continuing to subsist -de jure-, but deprived of all power of movement on its own part. Not long afterwards (411) Falerii, which had preserved its original Latin nationality even under Tuscan rule, abandoned the Etruscan league and entered into perpetual alliance with Rome; and thereby the whole of southern Etruria became in one form or other subject to Roman supremacy. In the case of Tarquinii and perhaps of northern Etruria generally, the Romans were content with restraining them for a lengthened period by a treaty of peace for 400 months (403).

In northern Italy likewise the peoples that had come into collision and conflict gradually settled on a permanent footing and within more defined limits. The migrations over the Alps ceased, partly perhaps in consequence of the desperate defence which the Etruscans made in their more restricted home, and of the serious resistance of the powerful Romans, partly perhaps also in consequence of changes unknown to us on the north of the Alps. Between the Alps and the Apennines, as far south as the Abruzzi, the Celts were now generally the ruling nation, and they were masters more especially of the plains and rich pastures; but from the lax and superficial nature of their settlement their dominion took no deep root in the newly acquired land and by no means assumed the shape of exclusive possession. How matters stood in the Alps, and to what extent Celtic settlers became mingled there with earlier Etruscan or other stocks, our unsatisfactory information as to the nationality of the later Alpine peoples does not permit us to ascertain; only the Raeti in the modern Grisons and Tyrol may be described as a probably Etruscan stock. The Umbrians retained the valleys of the Apennines, and the Veneti, speaking a different language, kept possession of the north-eastern portion of the valley of the Po. Ligurian tribes maintained their footing in the western mountains, dwelling as far south as Pisa and Arezzo, and separating the Celt-land proper from Etruria. The Celts dwelt only in the intermediate flat country, the Insubres and Cenomani to the north of the Po, the Boii to the south, and—not to mention smaller tribes —the Senones on the coast of the Adriatic, from Ariminum to Ancona, in the so-called "country of the Gauls" (-ager Gallicus-). But even there Etruscan settlements must have continued partially at least to subsist, somewhat as Ephesus and Miletus remained Greek under the supremacy of the Persians. Mantua at any rate, which was protected by its insular position, was a Tuscan city even in the time of the empire, and Atria on the Po also, where numerous discoveries of vases have been made, appears to have retained its Etruscan character; the description of the coasts that goes under the name of Scylax, composed about 418, calls the district of Atria and Spina Tuscan land. This alone, moreover, explains how Etruscan corsairs could render the Adriatic unsafe till far into the fifth century, and why not only Dionysius of Syracuse covered its coasts with colonies, but even Athens, as a remarkable document recently discovered informs us, resolved about 429 to establish a colony in the Adriatic for the protection of seafarers against the Tyrrhene pirates.

But while more or less of an Etruscan character continued to mark these regions, it was confined to isolated remnants and fragments of their earlier power; the Etruscan nation no longer reaped the benefit of such gains as were still acquired there by individuals in peaceful commerce or in maritime war. On the other hand it was probably from these half-free Etruscans that the germs proceeded of such civilization as we subsequently find among the Celts and Alpine peoples in general.(10) The very fact that the Celtic hordes in the plains of Lombardy, to use the language of the so-called Scylax, abandoned their warrior-life and took to permanent settlement, must in part be ascribed to this influence; the rudiments moreover of handicrafts and arts and the alphabet came to the Celts in Lombardy, and in fact to the Alpine peoples as far as the modern Styria, through the medium of the Etruscans.

Thus the Etruscans, after the loss of their possessions in Campania and of the whole district to the north of the Apennines and to the south of the Ciminian Forest, remained restricted to very narrow bounds; their season of power and of aspiration had for ever passed away. The closest reciprocal relations subsisted between this external decline and the internal decay of the nation, the seeds of which indeed were doubtless already deposited at a far earlier period. The Greek authors of this age are full of descriptions of the unbounded luxury of Etruscan life: poets of Lower Italy in the fifth century of the city celebrate the Tyrrhenian wine, and the contemporary historians Timaeus and Theopompus delineate pictures of Etruscan unchastity and of Etruscan banquets, such as fall nothing short of the worst Byzantine or French demoralization. Unattested as may be the details in these accounts, the statement at least appears to be well founded, that the detestable amusement of gladiatorial combats—the gangrene of the later Rome and of the last epoch of antiquity generally—first came into vogue among the Etruscans. At any rate on the whole they leave no doubt as to the deep degeneracy of the nation. It pervaded even its political condition. As far as our scanty information reaches, we find aristocratic tendencies prevailing, in the same way as they did at the same period in Rome, but more harshly and more perniciously. The abolition of royalty, which appears to have been carried out in all the cities of Etruria about the time of the siege of Veii, called into existence in the several cities a patrician government, which experienced but slight restraint from the laxity of the federal bond. That bond but seldom succeeded in combining all the Etruscan cities even for the defence of the land, and the nominal hegemony of Volsinii does not admit of the most remote comparison with the energetic vigour which the leadership of Rome communicated to the Latin nation. The struggle against the exclusive claim put forward by the old burgesses to all public offices and to all public usufructs, which must have destroyed even the Roman state, had not its external successes enabled it in some measure to satisfy the demands of the oppressed proletariate at the expense of foreign nations and to open up other paths to ambition—that struggle against the exclusive rule and (what was specially prominent in Etruria) the priestly monopoly of the clan-nobility—must have ruined Etruria politically, economically, and morally. Enormous wealth, particularly in landed property, became concentrated in the hands of a few nobles, while the masses were impoverished; the social revolutions which thence arose increased the distress which they sought to remedy; and, in consequence of the impotence of the central power, no course at last remained to the distressed aristocrats— e. g. in Arretium in 453, and in Volsinii in 488—but to call in the aid of the Romans, who accordingly put an end to the disorder but at the same time extinguished the remnant of independence. The energies of the nation were broken from the day of Veii and Melpum. Earnest attempts were still once or twice made to escape from the Roman supremacy, but in such instances the stimulus was communicated to the Etruscans from without—from another Italian stock, the Samnites.

Notes for Book II Chapter IV

1. I. X. Phoenicians and Italians in Opposition to the Hellenes

2. —Fiaron o Deinomeneos kai toi Surakosioi toi Di Turan apo Kumas.—

3. I. X. Home of the Greek Immigrants

4. Hecataeus (after 257 u. c.) and Herodotus also (270-after 345) only know Hatrias as the delta of the Po and the sea that washes its shores (O. Muller, Etrusker, i. p. 140; Geogr. Graeci min. ed. C. Muller, i. p. 23). The appellation of Adriatic sea, in its more extended sense, first occurs in the so-called Scylax about 418 U. C.

5. II. II. Coriolanus

6. -Pleraque Gallia duas res industriosissime persequitur: rem militarem et argute loqui- (Cato, Orig, l. ii. fr. 2. Jordan).

7. It has recently been maintained by expert philologists that there is a closer affinity between the Celts and Italians than there is even between the latter and the Hellenes. In other words they hold that the branch of the great tree, from which the peoples of Indo-Germanic extraction in the west and south of Europe have sprung, divided itself in the first instance into Greeks and Italo-Celts, and that the latter at a considerably later period became subdivided into Italians and Celts. This hypothesis commends itself much to acceptance in a geographical point of view, and the facts which history presents may perhaps be likewise brought into harmony with it, because what has hitherto been regarded as Graeco-Italian civilization may very well have been Graeco-Celto-Italian—in fact we know nothing of the earliest stage of Celtic culture. Linguistic investigation, however, seems not to have made as yet such progress as to warrant the insertion of its results in the primitive history of the peoples.

8. The legend is related by Livy, v. 34, and Justin, xxiv. 4, and Cæsar also has had it in view (B. G. vi. 24). But the association of the migration of Bellovesus with the founding of Massilia, by which the former is chronologically fixed down to the middle of the second century of Rome, undoubtedly belongs not to the native legend, which of course did not specify dates, but to later chronologizing research; and it deserves no credit. Isolated incursions and immigrations may have taken place at a very early period; but the great overflowing of northern Italy by the Celts cannot be placed before the age of the decay of the Etruscan power, that is, not before the second half of the third century of the city.

In like manner, after the judicious investigations of Wickham and Cramer, we cannot doubt that the line of march of Bellovesus, like that of Hannibal, lay not over the Cottian Alps (Mont Genevre) and through the territory of the Taurini, but over the Graian Alps (the Little St. Bernard) and through the territory of the Salassi. The name of the mountain is given by Livy doubtless not on the authority of the legend, but on his own conjecture.

Whether the representation that the Italian Boii came through the more easterly pass of the Poenine Alps rested on the ground of a genuine legendary reminiscence, or only on the ground of an assumed connection with the Boii dwelling to the north of the Danube, is a question that must remain undecided.

9. This is according to the current computation 390 B. C.; but, in fact, the capture of Rome occurred in Ol. 98, 1 = 388 B. C., and has been thrown out of its proper place merely by the confusion of the Roman calendar.

10. I. XIV. Development of Alphabets in Italy

CHAPTER V

Subjugation of the Latins and Campanians by Rome

The Hegemony of Rome over Latium Shaken and Re-established

The great achievement of the regal period was the establishment of the sovereignty of Rome over Latium under the form of hegemony. It is in the nature of the case evident that the change in the constitution of Rome could not but powerfully affect both the relations of the Roman state towards Latium and the internal organization of the Latin communities themselves; and that it did so, is obvious from tradition. The fluctuations which the revolution in Rome occasioned in the Romano-Latin confederacy are attested by the legend, unusually vivid and various in its hues, of the victory at the lake Regillus, which the dictator or consul Aulus Postumius (255? 258?) is said to have gained over the Latins with the help of the Dioscuri, and still more definitely by the renewal of the perpetual league between Rome and Latium by Spurius Cassius in his second consulate (261). These narratives, however, give us no information as to the main matter, the legal relation between the new Roman republic and the Latin confederacy; and what from other sources we learn regarding that relation comes to us without date, and can only be inserted here with an approximation to probability.

Original Equality of Rights between Rome and Latium

The nature of a hegemony implies that it becomes gradually converted into sovereignty by the mere inward force of circumstances; and the Roman hegemony over Latium formed no exception to the rule. It was based upon the essential equality of rights between the Roman state on the one side and the Latin confederacy on the other;(1) but at least in matters of war and in the treatment of the acquisitions thereby made this relation between the single state on the one hand and the league of states on the other virtually involved a hegemony. According to the original constitution of the league not only was the right of making wars and treaties with foreign states—in other words, the full right of political self-determination—-reserved in all probability both to Rome and to the individual towns of the Latin league; and when a joint war took place, Rome and Latium probably furnished the like contingent, each, as a rule, an "army" of 8400 men;(2) but the chief command was held by the Roman general, who then nominated the officers of the staff, and so the leaders-of-division (-tribuni militum-), according to his own choice. In case of victory the moveable part of the spoil, as well as the conquered territory, was shared between Rome and the confederacy; when the establishment of fortresses in the conquered territory was resolved on, their garrisons and population were composed partly of Roman, partly of confederate colonists; and not only so, but the newly-founded community was received as a sovereign federal state into the Latin confederacy and furnished with a seat and vote in the Latin diet.

Encroachments on That Equality of Rights—
As to Wars and Treaties—
As to the Officering of the Army—
As to Acquisitions in War

These stipulations must probably even in the regal period, certainly in the republican epoch, have undergone alteration more and more to the disadvantage of the confederacy and to the further development of the hegemony of Rome. The earliest that fell into abeyance was beyond doubt the right of the confederacy to make wars and treaties with foreigners;(3) the decision of war and treaty passed once for all to Rome. The staff officers for the Latin troops must doubtless in earlier times have been likewise Latins; afterwards for that purpose Roman citizens were taken, if not exclusively, at any rate predominantly.(4) On the other hand, afterwards as formerly, no stronger contingent could be demanded from the Latin confederacy as a whole than was furnished by the Roman community; and the Roman commander-in-chief was likewise bound not to break up the Latin contingents, but to keep the contingent sent by each community as a separate division of the army under the leader whom that community had appointed.(5) The right of the Latin confederacy to an equal share in the moveable spoil and in the conquered land continued to subsist in form; in reality, however, the substantial fruits of war beyond doubt went, even at an early period, to the leading state. Even in the founding of the federal fortresses or the so-called Latin colonies as a rule presumably most, and not unfrequently all, of the colonists were Romans; and although by the transference they were converted from Roman burgesses into members of an allied community, the newly planted township in all probability frequently retained a preponderant—and for the confederacy dangerous—attachment to the real mother-city.

Private Rights

The rights, on the contrary, which were secured by the federal treaties to the individual burgess of one of the allied communities in every city belonging to the league, underwent no restriction. These included, in particular, full equality of rights as to the acquisition of landed property and moveable estate, as to traffic and exchange, marriage and testament, and an unlimited liberty of migration; so that not only was a man who had burgess-rights in a town of the league legally entitled to settle in any other, but whereever he settled, he as a right-sharer (-municeps-) participated in all private and political rights and duties with the exception of eligibility to office, and was even—although in a limited fashion —entitled to vote at least in the -comitia tributa-.(6)

Of some such nature, in all probability, was the relation between the Roman community and the Latin confederacy in the first period of the republic. We cannot, however ascertain what elements are to be referred to earlier stipulations, and what to the revision of the alliance in 261.

With somewhat greater certainty the remodelling of the arrangements of the several communities belonging to the Latin confederacy, after the pattern of the consular constitution in Rome, may be characterized as an innovation and introduced in this connection. For, although the different communities may very well have arrived at the abolition of royalty in itself independently of each other,(7) the identity in the appellation of the new annual kings in the Roman and other commonwealths of Latium, and the comprehensive application of the peculiar principle of collegiateness,(8) evidently point to some external connection. At some time or other after the expulsion of the Tarquins from Rome the arrangements of the Latin communities must have been throughout revised in accordance with the scheme of the consular constitution. This adjustment of the Latin constitutions in conformity with that of the leading city may possibly belong only to a later period; but internal probability rather favours the supposition that the Roman nobility, after having effected the abolition of royalty for life at home, suggested a similar change of constitution to the communities of the Latin confederacy, and at length introduced aristocratic government everywhere in Latium— notwithstanding the serious resistance, imperilling the stability of the Romano-Latin league itself, which seems to have been offered on the one hand by the expelled Tarquins, and on the other by the royal clans and by partisans well affected to monarchy in the other communities of Latium. The mighty development of the power of Etruria that occurred at this very time, the constant assaults of the Veientes, and the expedition of Porsena, may have materially contributed to secure the adherence of the Latin nation to the once-established form of union, or, in other words, to the continued recognition of the supremacy of Rome, and disposed them for its sake to acquiesce in a change of constitution for which, beyond doubt, the way had been in many respects prepared even in the bosom of the Latin communities, nay perhaps to submit even to an enlargement of the rights of hegemony.

Extension of Rome and Latium to the East and South

The permanently united nation was able not only to maintain, but also to extend on all sides its power. We have already(9) mentioned that the Etruscans remained only for a short time in possession of supremacy over Latium, and that the relations there soon returned to the position in which they stood during the regal period; but it was not till more than a century after the expulsion of the kings from Rome that any real extension of the Roman boundaries took place in this direction.

With the Sabines who occupied the middle mountain range from the borders of the Umbrians down to the region between the Tiber and the Anio, and who, at the epoch when the history of Rome begins, penetrated fighting and conquering as far as Latium itself, the Romans notwithstanding their immediate neighbourhood subsequently came comparatively little into contact. The feeble sympathy of the Sabines with the desperate resistance offered by the neighbouring peoples in the east and south, is evident even from the accounts of the annals; and—what is of more importance—we find here no fortresses to keep the land in subjection, such as were so numerously established especially in the Volscian plain. Perhaps this lack of opposition was connected with the fact that the Sabine hordes probably about this very time poured themselves over Lower Italy. Allured by the pleasantness of the settlements on the Tifernus and Volturnus, they appear to have interfered but little in the conflicts of which the region to the south of the Tiber was the arena.

At the Expense of the Aequi and Volsci—
League with the Hernici

Far more vehement and lasting was the resistance of the Aequi, who, having their settlements to the eastward of Rome as far as the valleys of the Turano and Salto and on the northern verge of the Fucine lake, bordered with the Sabines and Marsi,(10) and of the Volsci, who to the south of the Rutuli settled around Ardea, and of the Latins extending southward as far as Cora, possessed the coast almost as far as the river Liris along with the adjacent islands and in the interior the whole region drained by the Liris. We do not intend to narrate the feuds annually renewed with these two peoples—feuds which are related in the Roman chronicles in such a way that the most insignificant foray is scarcely distinguishable from a momentous war, and historical connection is totally disregarded; it is sufficient to indicate the permanent results. We plainly perceive that it was the especial aim of the Romans and Latins to separate the Aequi from the Volsci, and to become masters of the communications between them; in the region between the southern slope of the Alban range, the Volscian mountains and the Pomptine marshes, moreover, the Latins and the Volscians appear to have come first into contact and to have even had their settlements intermingled.(11) In this region the Latins took the first steps beyond the bounds of their own land, and federal fortresses on foreign soil—Latin colonies, as they were called—were first established, namely: in the plain Velitrae (as is alleged, about 260) beneath the Alban range itself, and Suessa in the Pomptine low lands, in the mountains Norba (as is alleged, in 262) and Signia (alleged to have been strengthened in 259), both of which lie at the points of connection between the Aequian and Volscian territories. The object was attained still more fully by the accession of the Hernici to the league of the Romans and Latins (268), an accession which isolated the Volscians completely, and provided the league with a bulwark against the Sabellian tribes dwelling on the south and east; it is easy therefore to perceive why this little people obtained the concession of full equality with the two others in counsel and in distribution of the spoil. The feebler Aequi were thenceforth but little formidable; it was sufficient to undertake from time to time a plundering expedition against them. The Rutuli also, who bordered with Latium on the south in the plain along the coast, early succumbed; their town Ardea was converted into a Latin colony as early as 312.(12) The Volscians opposed a more serious resistance. The first notable success, after those mentioned above, achieved over them by the Romans was, remarkably enough, the foundation of Circeii in 361, which, as long as Antium and Tarracina continued free, can only have held communication with Latium by sea. Attempts were often made to occupy Antium, and one was temporarily successful in 287; but in 295 the town recovered its freedom, and it was not till after the Gallic conflagration that, in consequence of a violent war of thirteen years (365-377), the Romans gained a decided superiority in the Antiate and Pomptine territory. Satricum, not far from Antium, was occupied with a Latin colony in 369, and not long afterwards probably Antium itself as well as Tarracina.(13) The Pomptine territory was secured by the founding of the fortress Setia (372, strengthened in 375), and was distributed into farm-allotments and burgess-districts in the year 371 and following years. After this date the Volscians still perhaps rose in revolt, but they waged no further wars against Rome.

Crises within the Romano-Latin League

But the more decided the successes that the league of Romans, Latins, and Hernici achieved against the Etruscans, Aequi, Volsci, and Rutuli, the more that league became liable to disunion. The reason lay partly in the increase of the hegemonic power of Rome, of which we have already spoken as necessarily springing out of the existing circumstances, but which nevertheless was felt as a heavy burden in Latium; partly in particular acts of odious injustice perpetrated by the leading community. Of this nature was especially the infamous sentence of arbitration between the Aricini and the Rutuli in Ardea in 308, in which the Romans, called in to be arbiters regarding a border territory in dispute between the two communities, took it to themselves; and when this decision occasioned in Ardea internal dissensions in which the people wished to join the Volsci, while the nobility adhered to Rome, these dissensions were still more disgracefully employed as a pretext for the— already mentioned —sending of Roman colonists into the wealthy city, amongst whom the lands of the adherents of the party opposed to Rome were distributed (312). The main cause however of the internal breaking up of the league was the very subjugation of the common foe; forbearance ceased on one side, devotedness ceased on the other, from the time when they thought that they had no longer need of each other. The open breach between the Latins and Hernici on the one hand and the Romans on the other was more immediately occasioned partly by the capture of Rome by the Celts and the momentary weakness which it produced, partly by the definitive occupation and distribution of the Pomptine territory. The former allies soon stood opposed in the field. Already Latin volunteers in great numbers had taken part in the last despairing struggle of the Antiates: now the most famous of the Latin cities, Lanuvium (371), Praeneste (372-374, 400), Tusculum (373), Tibur (394, 400), and even several of the fortresses established in the Volscian land by the Romano-Latin league, such as Velitrae and Circeii, had to be subdued by force of arms, and the Tiburtines were not afraid even to make common cause against Rome with the once more advancing hordes of the Gauls. No concerted revolt however took place, and Rome mastered the individual towns without much trouble.

Tusculum was even compelled (in 373) to give up its political independence, and to enter into the burgess-union of Rome as a subject community (-civitas sine suffragio-) so that the town retained its walls and an—although limited—self-administration, including magistrates and a burgess-assembly of its own, whereas its burgesses as Romans lacked the right of electing or being elected —the first instance of a whole burgess-body being incorporated as a dependent community with the Roman commonwealth.

Renewal of the Treaties of Alliance

The struggle with the Hernici was more severe (392-396); the first consular commander-in-chief belonging to the plebs, Lucius Genucius, fell in it; but here too the Romans were victorious. The crisis terminated with the renewal of the treaties between Rome and the Latin and Hernican confederacies in 396. The precise contents of these treaties are not known, but it is evident that both confederacies submitted once more, and probably on harder terms, to the Roman hegemony. The institution which took place in the same year of two new tribes in the Pomptine territory shows clearly the mighty advances made by the Roman power.

Closing of the Latin Confederation

In manifest connection with this crisis in the relations between Rome and Latium stands the closing of the Latin confederation,(14) which took place about the year 370, although we cannot precisely determine whether it was the effect or, as is more probable, the cause of the revolt of Latium against Rome which we have just described. As the law had hitherto stood, every sovereign city founded by Rome and Latium took its place among the communes entitled to participate in the federal festival and federal diet, whereas every community incorporated with another city and thereby politically annihilated was erased from the ranks of the members of the league. At the same time, however, according to Latin use and wont the number once fixed of thirty confederate communities was so adhered to, that of the participating cities never more and never less than thirty were entitled to vote, and a number of the communities that were of later admission, or were disqualified for their slight importance or for the crimes they had committed, were without the right of voting. In this way the confederacy was constituted about 370 as follows. Of old Latin townships there were—besides some which have now fallen into oblivion, or whose sites are unknown—still autonomous and entitled to vote, Nomentum, between the Tiber and the Anio; Tibur, Gabii, Scaptia, Labici,(15) Pedum, and Praeneste, between the Anio and the Alban range; Corbio, Tusculum, Bovillae, Aricia, Corioli, and Lanuvium on the Alban range; Cora in the Volscian mountains, and lastly, Laurentum in the plain along the coast. To these fell to be added the colonies instituted by Rome and the Latin league; Ardea in the former territory of the Rutuli, and Satricum, Velitrae, Norba, Signia, Setia and Circeii in that of the Volsci. Besides, seventeen other townships, whose names are not known with certainty, had the privilege of participating in the Latin festival without the right of voting. On this footing—of forty-seven townships entitled to participate and thirty entitled to vote— the Latin confederacy continued henceforward unalterably fixed. The Latin communities founded subsequently, such as Sutrium, Nepete,(16) Antium, Tarracina,(17) and Gales, were not admitted into the confederacy, nor were the Latin communities subsequently divested of their autonomy, such as Tusculum and Lanuvium, erased from the list.

Fixing of the Limits of Latium

With this closing of the confederacy was connected the geographical settlement of the limits of Latium. So long as the Latin confederacy continued open, the bounds of Latium had advanced with the establishment of new federal cities: but as the later Latin colonies had no share in the Alban festival, they were not regarded geographically as part of Latium. For this reason doubtless Ardea and Circeii were reckoned as belonging to Latium, but not Sutrium or Tarracina.

Isolation of the Later Latin Cities as Respected Private Rights

But not only were the places on which Latin privileges were bestowed after 370 kept aloof from the federal association; they were isolated also from one another as respected private rights. While each of them was allowed to have reciprocity of commercial dealings and probably also of marriage (-commercium et conubium-) with Rome, no such reciprocity was permitted with the other Latin communities. The burgess of Satrium, for example, might possess in full property a piece of ground in Rome, but not in Praeneste; and might have legitimate children with a Roman, but not with a Tiburtine, wife.(18)

Prevention of Special Leagues

If hitherto considerable freedom of movement had been allowed within the confederacy, and for example the six old Latin communities, Aricia, Tusculum, Tibur, Lanuvium, Cora, and Laurentum, and the two new Latin, Ardea and Suessa Pometia, had been permitted to found in common a shrine for the Aricine Diana; it is doubtless not the mere result of accident that we find no further instance in later times of similar separate confederations fraught with danger to the hegemony of Rome.

Revision of the Municipal Constitutions. Police Judges

We may likewise assign to this epoch the further remodelling which the Latin municipal constitutions underwent, and their complete assimilation to the constitution of Rome. If in after times two aediles, intrusted with the police-supervision of markets and highways and the administration of justice in connection therewith, make their appearance side by side with the two praetors as necessary elements of the Latin magistracy, the institution of these urban police functionaries, which evidently took place at the same time and at the instigation of the leading power in all the federal communities, certainly cannot have preceded the establishment of the curule aedileship in Rome, which occurred in 387; probably it took place about that very time. Beyond doubt this arrangement was only one of a series of measures curtailing the liberties and modifying the organization of the federal communities in the interest of aristocratic policy.

Domination of the Romans; Exasperation of the Latins—
Collision between the Romans and the Samnites

After the fall of Veii and the conquest of the Pomptine territory, Rome evidently felt herself powerful enough to tighten the reins of her hegemony and to reduce the whole of the Latin cities to a position so dependent that they became in fact completely subject. At this period (406) the Carthaginians, in a commercial treaty concluded with Rome, bound themselves to inflict no injury on the Latins who were subject to Rome, -viz-. the maritime towns of Ardea, Antium, Circeii, and Tarracina; if, however, any one of the Latin towns should fall away from the Roman alliance, the Phoenicians were to be allowed to attack it, but in the event of conquering it they were bound not to raze it, but to hand it over to the Romans. This plainly shows by what chains the Roman community bound to itself the towns protected by it and how much a town, which dared to withdraw from the native protectorate, sacrificed or risked by such a course.

It is true that even now the Latin confederacy at least—if not also the Hernican—-retained its formal title to a third of the gains of war, and doubtless some other remnants of the former equality of rights; but what was palpably lost was important enough to explain the exasperation which at this period prevailed among the Latins against Rome. Not only did numerous Latin volunteers fight under foreign standards against the community at their head, wherever they found armies in the field against Rome; but in 405 even the Latin federal assembly resolved to refuse to the Romans its contingent. To all appearance a renewed rising of the whole Latin confederacy might be anticipated at no distant date; and at that very moment a collision was imminent with another Italian nation, which was able to encounter on equal terms the united strength of the Latin stock. After the overthrow of the northern Volscians no considerable people in the first instance opposed the Romans in the south; their legions unchecked approached the Liris. As early as 397 they had contended; successfully with the Privernates; and in 409 occupied Sora on the upper Liris. Thus the Roman armies had reached the Samnite frontier; and the friendly alliance, which the two bravest and most powerful of the Italian nations concluded with each other in 400, was the sure token of an approaching struggle for the supremacy of Italy—a struggle which threatened to become interwoven with the crisis within the Latin nation.

Conquests of the Samnites in the South of Italy

The Samnite nation, which, at the time of the expulsion of the Tarquins from Rome, had doubtless already been for a considerable period in possession of the hill-country which rises between the Apulian and Campanian plains and commands them both, had hitherto found its further advance impeded on the one side by the Daunians —-the power and prosperity of Arpi fall within this period—on the other by the Greeks and Etruscans. But the fall of the Etruscan power towards the end of the third, and the decline of the Greek colonies in the course of the fourth century, made room for them towards the west and south; and now one Samnite host after another marched down to, and even moved across, the south Italian seas. They first made their appearance in the plain adjoining the bay, with which the name of the Campanians has been associated from the beginning of the fourth century; the Etruscans there were suppressed, and the Greeks were confined within narrower bounds; Capua was wrested from the former (330), Cumae from the latter (334). About the same time, perhaps even earlier, the Lucanians appeared in Magna Graecia: at the beginning of the fourth century they were involved in conflict with the people of Terina and Thurii; and a considerable time before 364 they had established themselves in the Greek Laus. About this period their levy amounted to 30,000 infantry and 4000 cavalry. Towards the end of the fourth century mention first occurs of the separate confederacy of the Bruttii,(19) who had detached themselves from the Lucanians—-not, like the other Sabellian stocks, as a colony, but through a quarrel —and had become mixed up with many foreign elements. The Greeks of Lower Italy tried to resist the pressure of the barbarians; the league of the Achaean cities was reconstructed in 361; and it was determined that, if any of the allied towns should be assailed by the Lucanians, all should furnish contingents, and that the leaders of contingents which failed to appear should suffer the punishment of death. But even the union of Magna Graecia no longer availed; for the ruler of Syracuse, Dionysius the Elder, made common cause with the Italians against his countrymen. While Dionysius wrested from the fleets of Magna Graecia the mastery of the Italian seas, one Greek city after another was occupied or annihilated by the Italians. In an incredibly short time the circle of flourishing cities was destroyed or laid desolate. Only a few Greek settlements, such as Neapolis, succeeded with difficulty, and more by means of treaties than by force of arms, in preserving at least their existence and their nationality. Tarentum alone remained thoroughly independent and powerful, maintaining its ground in consequence of its more remote position and its preparation for war—the result of its constant conflicts with the Messapians. Even that city, however, had constantly to fight for its existence with the Lucanians, and was compelled to seek for alliances and mercenaries in the mother-country of Greece.

About the period when Veii and the Pomptine plain came into the hands of Rome, the Samnite hordes were already in possession of all Lower Italy, with the exception of a few unconnected Greek colonies, and of the Apulo-Messapian coast. The Greek Periplus, composed about 418, sets down the Samnites proper with their "five tongues" as reaching from the one sea to the other; and specifies the Campanians as adjoining them on the Tyrrhene sea to the north, and the Lucanians to the south, amongst whom in this instance, as often, the Bruttii are included, and who already had the whole coast apportioned among them from Paestum on the Tyrrhene, to Thurii on the Ionic sea. In fact to one who compares the achievements of the two great nations of Italy, the Latins and the Samnites, before they came into contact, the career of conquest on the part of the latter appears far wider and more splendid than that of the former. But the character of their conquests was essentially different. From the fixed urban centre which Latium possessed in Rome the dominion of the Latin stock spread slowly on all sides, and lay within limits comparatively narrow; but it planted its foot firmly at every step, partly by founding fortified towns of the Roman type with the rights of dependent allies, partly by Romanizing the territory which it conquered. It was otherwise with Samnium. There was in its case no single leading community and therefore no policy of conquest. While the conquest of the Veientine and Pomptine territories was for Rome a real enlargement of power, Samnium was weakened rather than strengthened by the rise of the Campanian cities and of the Lucanian and Bruttian confederacies; for every swarm, which had sought and found new settlements, thenceforward pursued a path of its own.

Relations between the Samnites and the Greeks

The Samnite tribes filled a disproportionately large space, while yet they showed no disposition to make it thoroughly their own. The larger Greek cities, Tarentum, Thurii, Croton, Metapontum, Heraclea, Rhegium, and Neapolis, although weakened and often dependent, continued to exist; and the Hellenes were tolerated even in the open country and in the smaller towns, so that Cumae for instance, Posidonia, Laus, and Hipponium, still remained—as the Periplus already mentioned and coins show—Greek cities even under Samnite rule. Mixed populations thus arose; the bi-lingual Bruttii, in particular, included Hellenic as well as Samnite elements and even perhaps remains of the ancient autochthones; in Lucania and Campania also similar mixtures must to a lesser extent have taken place.

Campanian Hellenism

The Samnite nation, moreover, could not resist the dangerous charm of Hellenic culture; least of all in Campania, where Neapolis early entered into friendly intercourse with the immigrants, and where the sky itself humanized the barbarians. Nola, Nuceria, and Teanum, although having a purely Samnite population, adopted Greek manners and a Greek civic constitution; in fact the indigenous cantonal form of constitution could not possibly subsist under these altered circumstances. The Samnite cities of Campania began to coin money, in part with Greek inscriptions; Capua became by its commerce and agriculture the second city in Italy in point of size—the first in point of wealth and luxury. The deep demoralization, in which, according to the accounts of the ancients, that city surpassed all others in Italy, is especially reflected in the mercenary recruiting and in the gladiatorial sports, both of which pre-eminently flourished in Capua. Nowhere did recruiting officers find so numerous a concourse as in this metropolis of demoralized civilization; while Capua knew not how to save itself from the attacks of the aggressive Samnites, the warlike Campanian youth flocked forth in crowds under self-elected -condottteri-, especially to Sicily. How deeply these soldiers of fortune influenced by their enterprises the destinies of Italy, we shall have afterwards to show; they form as characteristic a feature of Campanian life as the gladiatorial sports which likewise, if they did not originate, were at any rate carried to perfection in Capua. There sets of gladiators made their appearance even during banquets; and their number was proportioned to the rank of the guests invited. This degeneracy of the most important Samnite city—a degeneracy which beyond doubt was closely connected with the Etruscan habits that lingered there—must have been fatal for the nation at large; although the Campanian nobility knew how to combine chivalrous valour and high mental culture with the deepest moral corruption, it could never become to its nation what the Roman nobility was to the Latin. Hellenic influence had a similar, though less powerful, effect on the Lucanians and Bruttians as on the Campanians. The objects discovered in the tombs throughout all these regions show how Greek art was cherished there in barbaric luxuriance; the rich ornaments of gold and amber and the magnificent painted pottery, which are now disinterred from the abodes of the dead, enable us to conjecture how extensive had been their departure from the ancient manners of their fathers. Other indications are preserved in their writing. The old national writing which they had brought with them from the north was abandoned by the Lucanians and Bruttians, and exchanged for Greek; while in Campania the national alphabet, and perhaps also the language, developed itself under the influence of the Greek model into greater clearness and delicacy. We meet even with isolated traces of the influence of Greek philosophy.

The Samnite Confederacy

The Samnite land, properly so called, alone remained unaffected by these innovations, which, beautiful and natural as they may to some extent have been, powerfully contributed to relax still more the bond of national unity which even from the first was loose. Through the influence of Hellenic habits a deep schism took place in the Samnite stock. The civilized "Philhellenes" of Campania were accustomed to tremble like the Hellenes themselves before the ruder tribes of the mountains, who were continually penetrating into Campania and disturbing the degenerate earlier settlers. Rome was a compact state, having the strength of all Latium at its disposal; its subjects might murmur, but they obeyed. The Samnite stock was dispersed and divided; and, while the confederacy in Samnium proper had preserved unimpaired the manners and valour of their ancestors, they were on that very account completely at variance with the other Samnite tribes and towns.

Submission of Capua to Rome—
Rome and Samnium Come to Terms—
Revolt of the Latins and Campanians against Rome—
Victory of the Romans—
Dissolution of the Latin League—
Colonization of the Land of the Volsci

In fact, it was this variance between the Samnites of the plain and the Samnites of the mountains that led the Romans over the Liris. The Sidicini in Teanum, and the Campanians in Capua, sought aid from the Romans (411) against their own countrymen, who in swarms ever renewed ravaged their territory and threatened to establish themselves there. When the desired alliance was refused, the Campanian envoys made offer of the submission of their country to the supremacy of Rome: and the Romans were unable to resist the bait. Roman envoys were sent to the Samnites to inform them of the new acquisition, and to summon them to respect the territory of the friendly power. The further course of events can no longer be ascertained in detail;(20) we discover only that—whether after a campaign, or without the intervention of a war—Rome and Samnium came to an agreement, by which Capua was left at the disposal of the Romans, Teanum in the hands of the Samnites, and the upper Liris in those of the Volscians.

The consent of the Samnites to treat is explained by the energetic exertions made about this very period by the Tarentines to get quit of their Sabellian neighbours. But the Romans also had good reason for coming to terms as quickly as possible with the Samnites; for the impending transition of the region bordering on the south of Latium into the possession of the Romans converted the ferment that had long existed among the Latins into open insurrection. All the original Latin towns, even the Tusculans who had been received into the burgess-union of Rome, took up arms against Rome, with the single exception of the Laurentes, whereas of the colonies founded beyond the bounds of Latium only the old Volscian towns Velitrae, Antium, and Tarracina adhered to the revolt. We can readily understand how the Capuans, notwithstanding their very recent and voluntarily offered submission to the Romans, should readily embrace the first opportunity of again ridding themselves of the Roman rule and, in spite of the opposition of the optimate party that adhered to the treaty with Rome, should make common cause with the Latin confederacy, whereas the still independent Volscian towns, such as Fundi and Formiae, and the Hernici abstained like the Campanian aristocracy from taking part in this revolt. The position of the Romans was critical; the legions which had crossed the Liris and occupied Campania were cut off by the revolt of the Latins and Volsci from their home, and a victory alone could save them. The decisive battle was fought near Trifanum (between Minturnae, Suessa, and Sinuessa) in 414; the consul Titus Manlius Imperiosus Torquatus achieved a complete victory over the united Latins and Campanians. In the two following years the individual towns, so far as they still offered resistance, were reduced by capitulation or assault, and the whole country was brought into subjection. The effect of the victory was the dissolution of the Latin league. It was transformed from an independent political federation into a mere association for the purpose of a religious festival; the ancient stipulated rights of the confederacy as to a maximum for the levy of troops and a share of the gains of war perished as such along with it, and assumed, where they were recognized in future, the character of acts of grace. Instead of the one treaty between Rome on the one hand and the Latin confederacy on the other, there came at best perpetual alliances between Rome and the several confederate towns. To this footing of treaty there were admitted of the old-Latin places, besides Laurentum, also Tibur and Praeneste, which however were compelled to cede portions of their territory to Rome. Like terms were obtained by the communities of Latin rights founded outside of Latium, so far as they had not taken part in the war. The principle of isolating the communities from each other, which had already been established in regard to the places founded after 370,(21) was thus extended to the whole Latin nation. In other respects the several places retained their former privileges and their autonomy. The other old-Latin communities as well as the colonies that had revolted lost—all of them—independence and entered in one form or another into the Roman burgess-union. The two important coast towns Antium (416) and Tarracina (425) were, after the model of Ostia, occupied with Roman full-burgesses and restricted to a communal independence confined within narrow limits, while the previous burgesses were deprived in great part of their landed property in favour of the Roman colonists and, so far as they retained it, likewise adopted into the full burgess-union. Lanuvium, Aricia, Momentum, Pedum became Roman burgess-communities after the model of Tusculum.(22) The walls of Velitrae were demolished, its senate was ejected -en masse- and deported to the interior of Roman Etruria, and the town was probably constituted a dependent community with Caerite rights.(23) Of the land acquired a portion—the estates, for instance, of the senators of Velitrae—was distributed to Roman burgesses: with these special assignations was connected the erection of two new tribes in 422. The deep sense which prevailed in Rome of the enormous importance of the result achieved is attested by the honorary column, which was erected in the Roman Forum to the victorious dictator of 416, Gaius Maenius, and by the decoration of the orators' platform in the same place with the beaks taken from the galleys of Antium that were found unserviceable.

Complete Submission of the Volscian and Campanian Provinces

In like manner the dominion of Rome was established and confirmed in the south Volscian and Campanian territories. Fundi, Formiae, Capua, Cumae, and a number of smaller towns became dependent Roman communities with self-administration. To secure the pre-eminently important city of Capua, the breach between the nobility and commons was artfully widened, the communal constitution was revised in the Roman interest, and the administration of the town was controlled by Roman officials annually sent to Campania. The same treatment was measured out some years after to the Volscian Privernum, whose citizens, supported by Vitruvius Vaccus a bold partisan belonging to Fundi, had the honour of fighting the last battle for the freedom of this region; the struggle ended with the storming of the town (425) and the execution of Vaccus in a Roman prison. In order to rear a population devoted to Rome in these regions, they distributed, out of the lands won in war particularly in the Privernate and Falernian territories, so numerous allotments to Roman burgesses, that a few years later (436) they were able to institute there also two new tribes. The establishment of two fortresses as colonies with Latin rights finally secured the newly won land. These were Cales (420) in the middle of the Campanian plain, whence the movements of Teanum and Capua could be observed, and Fregellae (426), which commanded the passage of the Liris. Both colonies were unusually strong, and rapidly became flourishing, notwithstanding the obstacles which the Sidicines interposed to the founding of Cales and the Samnites to that of Fregellae. A Roman garrison was also despatched to Sora, a step of which the Samnites, to whom this district had been left by the treaty, complained with reason, but in vain. Rome pursued her purpose with undeviating steadfastness, and displayed her energetic and far-reaching policy—more even than on the battlefield—in the securing of the territory which she gained by enveloping it, politically and militarily, in a net whose meshes could not be broken.

Inaction of the Samnites

As a matter of course, the Samnites could not behold the threatening progress of the Romans with satisfaction, and they probably put obstacles in its way; nevertheless they neglected to intercept the new career of conquest, while there was still perhaps time to do so, with that energy which the circumstances required. They appear indeed in accordance with their treaty with Rome to have occupied and strongly garrisoned Teanum; for while in earlier times that city sought help against Samnium from Capua and Rome, in the later struggles it appears as the bulwark of the Samnite power on the west. They spread, conquering and destroying, on the upper Liris, but they neglected to establish themselves permanently in that quarter. They destroyed the Volscian town Fregellae—by which they simply facilitated the institution of the Roman colony there which we have just mentioned —and they so terrified two other Volscian towns, Fabrateria (Ceccano) and Luca (site unknown), that these, following the example of Capua, surrendered themselves to the Romans (424). The Samnite confederacy allowed the Roman conquest of Campania to be completed before they in earnest opposed it; and the reason for their doing so is to be sought partly in the contemporary hostilities between the Samnite nation and the Italian Hellenes, but principally in the remiss and distracted policy which the confederacy pursued.

Notes for Book II Chapter V

1. I. VII. Relation of Rome to Latium

2. The original equality of the two armies is evident from Liv. i. 52; viii. 8, 14, and Dionys. viii, 15; but most clearly from Polyb. vi. 26.

3. Dionysius (viii. 15) expressly states, that in the later federal treaties between Rome and Latium the Latin communities were interdicted from calling out their contingents of their own motion and sending them into the field alone.

4. These Latin staff-officers were the twelve -praefecti sociorum-, who subsequently, when the old phalanx had been resolved into the later legions and -alae-, had the charge of the two -alae- of the federal contingents, six to each -ala-, just as the twelve war-tribunes of the Roman army had charge of the two legions, six to each legion. Polybius (vi. 26, 5) states that the consul nominated the former, as he originally nominated the latter. Now, as according to the ancient maxim of law, that every person under obligation of service might become an officer (p. 106), it was legally allowable for the general to appoint a Latin as leader of a Roman, as well as conversely a Roman as leader of a Latin, legion, this led to the practical result that the -tribuni militum- were wholly, and the -praefecti sociorum-at least ordinarily, Romans.

5. These were the -decuriones turmarum- and -praefecti cohortium-(Polyb. vi. 21, 5; Liv. xxv. 14; Sallust. Jug. 69, *et al*.) Of course, as the Roman consuls were in law and ordinarily also in fact commanders-in-chief, the presidents of the community in the dependent towns also were perhaps throughout, or at least very frequently, placed at the head of the community-contingents (Liv. xxiii. 19; Orelli, Inscr. 7022). Indeed, the usual name given to the Latin magistrates (-praetores-) indicates that they were officers.

6. Such a —metoikos— was not like an actual burgess assigned to a specific voting district once for all, but before each particular vote the district in which the —metoeci— were upon that occasion to vote was fixed by lot. In reality this probably amounted to the concession to the Latins of one vote in the Roman -comitia tributa-. As a place in some tribe was a preliminary condition of the ordinary centuriate suffrage, if the —metoeci— shared in the voting in the assembly of the centuries-which we do not know-a similar allotment must have been fixed for the latter. In the curies they must have taken part like the plebeians.

7. II. I. Abolition of the Life-Presidency of the Community

8. Ordinarily, as is well known, the Latin communities were presided over by two praetors. Besides these there occur in several communities single magistrates, who in that case bear the title of dictator; as in Alba (Orelli-Henzen, Inscr. 2293), Tusculum (p. 445, note 2), Lanuvium (Cicero, pro Mil. 10, 27; 17, 45; Asconius, in

Mil. p. 32, Orell.; Orelli, n. 2786, 5157, 6086); Compitum (Orelli, 3324); Nomentum (Orelli, 208, 6138, 7032; comp. Henzen, Bullett. 1858, p. 169); and Aricia (Orelli, n. 1455). To these falls to be added the similar dictator in the -civitas sine suffragio- of Caere (Orelli, n. 3787, 5772; also Garrucci Diss. arch., i. p. 31, although erroneously placed after Sutrium); and further the officials of the like name at Fidenae (Orelli, 112). All these magistracies or priesthoods that originated in magistracies (the dictator of Caere is to be explained in accordance with Liv. ix. 43: -Anagninis—-magistratibus praeter quam sacrorum curatione interdictum-), were annual (Orelli, 208). The statement of Macer likewise and of the annalists who borrowed from him, that Alba was at the time of its fall no longer under kings, but under annual directors (Dionys. v. 74; Plutarch, Romul. 27; Liv. i. 23), is presumably a mere inference from the institution, with which he was acquainted, of the sacerdotal Alban dictatorship which was beyond doubt annual like that of Nomentum; a view in which, moreover, the democratic partisanship of its author may have come into play. It may be a question whether the inference is valid, and whether, even if Alba at the time of its dissolution was under rulers holding office for life, the abolition of monarchy in Rome might not subsequently lead to the conversion of the Alban dictatorship into an annual office.

All these Latin magistracies substantially coincide in reality, as well as specially in name, with the arrangement established in Rome by the revolution in a way which is not adequately explained by the mere similarity of the political circumstances underlying them.

9. II. IV. Etruscans Driven Back from Latium

10. The country of the Aequi embraces not merely the valley of the Anio above Tibur and the territory of the later Latin colonies Carsioli (on the upper part of the Turano) and Alba (on the Fucine lake), but also the district of the later municipium of the Aequiculi, who are nothing but that remnant of the Aequi to which, after the subjugation by the Romans, and after the assignation of the largest portion of the territory to Roman or Latin colonists, municipal independence was left.

11. To all appearance Velitrae, although situated in the plain, was originally Volscian, and so a Latin colony; Cora, on the other hand, on the Volscian mountains, was originally Latin.

12. Not long afterwards must have taken place the founding of the -Nemus Dianae- in the forest of Aricia, which, according to Cato's account (p. 12, Jordan), a Tusculan dictator accomplished for the urban communities of old Latium, Tusculum, Aricia, Lanuvium, Laurentum, Cora, and Tibur, and of the two Latin colonies (which therefore stand last) Suessa Pometia and Ardea (-populus Ardeatis Rutulus-). The absence of Praeneste and of the smaller communities of the old Latium shows, as was implied in the nature of the case, that not all the communities of the Latin league at that time took part in the consecration. That it falls before 372 is proved by the emergence of Pometia (ii. V. Closing Of The Latin Confederation), and the list quite

accords with what can otherwise be ascertained as to the state of the league shortly after the accession of Ardea.

More credit may be given to the traditional statements regarding the years of the foundations than to most of the oldest traditions, seeing that the numbering of the year -ab urbe condita-, common to the Italian cities, has to all appearance preserved, by direct tradition, the year in which the colonies were founded.

13. The two do not appear as Latin colonies in the so-called Cassian list about 372, but they so appear in the Carthaginian treaty of 406; the towns had thus become Latin colonies in the interval.

14. In the list given by Dionysius (v. 61) of the thirty Latin federal cities—the only list which we possess—there are named the Ardeates, Aricini, Bovillani, Bubentani (site unknown), Corni (rather Corani), Carventani (site unknown), Circeienses, Coriolani, Corbintes, Cabani (perhaps the Cabenses on the Alban Mount, Bull, dell' Inst. 1861, p. 205), Fortinei (unknown), Gabini, Laurentes, Lanuvini, Lavinates, Labicani, Nomentani, Norbani, Praenestini, Pedani, Querquetulani (site unknown), Satricani, Scaptini, Setini, Tiburtini, Tusculani, Tellenii (site unknown), Tolerini (site unknown), and Veliterni. The occasional notices of communities entitled to participate, such as of Ardea (Liv. xxxii. x), Laurentum (Liv. xxxvii. 3), Lanuvium (Liv. xli. 16), Bovillae, Gabii, Labici (Cicero, pro Plane. 9, 23) agree with this list. Dionysius gives it on occasion of the declaration of war by Latium against Rome in 256, and it was natural therefore to regard—as Niebuhr did—this list as derived from the well-known renewal of the league in 261, But, as in this list drawn up according to the Latin alphabet the letter -g appears in a position which it certainly had not at the time of the Twelve Tables and scarcely came to occupy before the fifth century (see my Unteritalische Dial. p. 33), it must be taken from a much more recent source; and it is by far the simplest hypothesis to recognize it as a list of those places which were afterwards regarded as the ordinary members of the Latin confederacy, and which Dionysius in accordance with his systematizing custom specifies as its original component elements. As was to be expected, the list presents not a single non-Latin community; it simply enumerates places originally Latin or occupied by Latin colonies—no one will lay stress on Corbio and Corioli as exceptions. Now if we compare with this list that of the Latin colonies, there had been founded down to 372 Suessa Pometia, Velitrae, Norba, Signia, Ardea, Circeii (361), Satricum (369), Sutrium (371), Nepete (371), Setia (372). Of the last three founded at nearly the same time the two Etruscan ones may very well date somewhat later than Setia, since in fact the foundation of every town claimed a certain amount of time, and our list cannot be free from minor inaccuracies. If we assume this, then the list contains all the colonies sent out up to the year 372, including the two soon afterwards deleted from the list, Satricum destroyed in 377 and Velitrae divested of Latin rights in 416; there are wanting only Suessa Pometia, beyond doubt as having been destroyed before 372, and Signia, probably because in the text of Dionysius, who mentions only twenty-nine names, —SIGNINON— has dropped out after —SEITINON—. In entire harmony with this view there are absent from this list all the Latin colonies founded after 372 as well as all places, which like Ostia, Antemnae, Alba, were

incorporated with the Roman community before the year 370, whereas those incorporated subsequently, such as Tusculum, Lanuvium, Velitrae, are retained in it.

As regards the list given by Pliny of thirty-two townships extinct in his time which had formerly participated in the Alban festival, after deduction of seven that also occur in Dionysius (for the Cusuetani of Pliny appear to be the Carventani of Dionysius), there remain twenty-five townships, most of them quite unknown, doubtless made up partly of those seventeen non-voting communities—most of which perhaps were just the oldest subsequently disqualified members of the Alban festal league—partly of a number of other decayed or ejected members of the league, to which latter class above all the ancient presiding township of Alba, also named by Pliny, belonged.

15. Livy certainly states (iv. 47) that Labici became a colony in 336. But—apart from the fact that Diodorus (xiii. 6) says nothing of it—Labici cannot have been a burgess-colony, for the town did not lie on the coast and besides it appears subsequently as still in possession of autonomy; nor can it have been a Latin one, for there is not, nor can there be from the nature of these foundations, a single other example of a Latin colony established in the original Latium. Here as elsewhere it is most probable—especially as two -jugera- are named as the portion of land allotted—that a public assignation to the burgesses has been confounded with a colonial assignation (I. XIII. System of Joint Cultivation).

16. II. IV. South Etruria Roman

17. II. V. League with the Hernici

18. This restriction of the ancient full reciprocity of Latin rights first occurs in the renewal of the treaty in 416 (Liv. viii. 14); but as the system of isolation, of which it was an essential part, first began in reference to the Latin colonies settled after 370, and was only generalized in 416, it is proper to mention this alteration here.

19. The name itself is very ancient; in fact it is the most ancient indigenous name for the inhabitants of the present Calabria (Antiochus, Fr. 5. Mull.). The well-known derivation is doubtless an invention.

20. Perhaps no section of the Roman annals has been more disfigured than the narrative of the first Samnite-Latin war, as it stands or stood in Livy, Dionysius, and Appian. It runs somewhat to the following effect. After both consuls had marched into Campania in 411, first the consul Marcus Valerius Corvus gained a severe and bloody victory over the Samnites at Mount Gaurus; then his colleague Aulus Cornelius Cossus gained another, after he had been rescued from annihilation in a narrow pass by the self-devotion of a division led by the military tribune Publius Decius. The third and decisive battle was fought by both consuls at the entrance of the Caudine Pass near Suessula; the Samnites were completely vanquished—forty thousand of their shields were picked up on the field of battle—and they were compelled to make a peace, in which the Romans retained Capua, which had given

itself over to their possession, while they left Teanum to the Samnites (413). Congratulations came from all sides, even from Carthage. The Latins, who had refused their contingent and seemed to be arming against Rome, turned their arms not against Rome but against the Paeligni, while the Romans were occupied first with a military conspiracy of the garrison left behind in Campania (412), then with the capture of Privernum (413) and the war against the Antiates. But now a sudden and singular change occurred in the position of parties. The Latins, who had demanded in vain Roman citizenship and a share in the consulate, rose against Rome in conjunction with the Sidicines, who had vainly offered to submit to the Romans and knew not how to save themselves from the Samnites, and with the Campanians, who were already tired of the Roman rule. Only the Laurentes in Latium and the - equites- of Campania adhered to the Romans, who on their part found support among the Paeligni and Samnites. The Latin army fell upon Samnium; the Romano-Samnite army, after it had marched to the Fucine lake and from thence, avoiding Latium, into Campania, fought the decisive battle against the combined Latins and Campanians at Vesuvius; the consul Titus Manlius Imperiosus, after he had himself restored the wavering discipline of the army by the execution of his own son who had slain a foe in opposition to orders from headquarters, and after his colleague Publius Decius Mus had appeased the gods by sacrificing his life, at length gained the victory by calling up the last reserves. But the war was only terminated by a second battle, in which the consul Manlius engaged the Latins and Campanians near Trifanum; Latium and Capua submitted, and were mulcted in a portion of their territory.

The judicious and candid reader will not fail to observe that this report swarms with all sorts of impossibilities. Such are the statement of the Antiates waging war after the surrender of 377 (Liv. vi. 33); the independent campaign of the Latins against the Paeligni, in distinct contradiction to the stipulations of the treaties between Rome and Latium; the unprecedented march of the Roman army through the Marsian and Samnite territory to Capua, while all Latium was in arms against Rome; to say nothing of the equally confused and sentimental account of the military insurrection of 412, and the story of its forced leader, the lame Titus Quinctius, the Roman Gotz von Berlichingen. Still more suspicious perhaps, are the repetitions. Such is the story of the military tribune Publius Decius modelled on the courageous deed of Marcus Calpurnius Flamma, or whatever he was called, in the first Punic war; such is the recurrence of the conquest of Privernum by Gaius Plautius in the year 425, which second conquest alone is registered in the triumphal Fasti; such is the self-immolation of Publius Decius, repeated, as is well known, in the case of his son in 459. Throughout this section the whole representation betrays a different period and a different hand from the other more credible accounts of the annals. The narrative is full of detailed pictures of battles; of inwoven anecdotes, such as that of the praetor of Setia, who breaks his neck on the steps of the senate-house because he had been audacious enough to solicit the consulship, and the various anecdotes concocted out of the surname of Titus Manlius; and of prolix and in part suspicious archaeological digressions. In this class we include the history of the legion—of which the notice, most probably apocryphal, in Liv. i. 52, regarding the maniples of Romans and Latins intermingled formed by the second Tarquin, is evidently a second fragment, the erroneous view given of the treaty between Capua and Rome (see my Rom. Munzwesen, p. 334, n. 122); the formularies of self-devotion, the Campanian -denarius-, the Laurentine alliance, and the -bina jugera- in the assignation (p. 450, note). Under such circumstances it appears a fact of great weight that Diodorus, who follows other and often older accounts, knows absolutely nothing of any of these events except the last battle at Trifanum; a battle in fact that ill accords with the rest of the narrative, which, in accordance with the rules of poetical justice, ought to have concluded with the death of Decius.

21. II. V. Isolation of the Later Latin Cities as Respected Private Rights

22. II. V. Crises within the Romano-Latin League

23. II. IV. South Etruria Roman

CHAPTER VI

Struggle of the Italians against Rome

Wars between the Sabellians and Tarentines—
Archidamus—
Alexander the Molossian—

While the Romans were fighting on the Liris and Volturnus, other conflicts agitated the south-east of the peninsula. The wealthy merchant-republic of Tarentum, daily exposed to more serious peril from the Lucanian and Messapian bands and justly distrusting its own sword, gained by good words and better coin the help of - condottieri-from the mother-country. The Spartan king, Archidamus, who with a strong band had come to the assistance of his fellow-Dorians, succumbed to the Lucanians on the same day on which Philip conquered at Chaeronea (416); a retribution, in the belief of the pious Greeks, for the share which nineteen years previously he and his people had taken in pillaging the sanctuary of Delphi. His place was taken by an abler commander, Alexander the Molossian, brother of Olympias the mother of Alexander the Great. In addition to the troops which he had brought along with him he united under his banner the contingents of the Greek cities, especially those of the Tarentines and Metapontines; the Poediculi (around Rubi, now Ruvo), who like the Greeks found themselves in danger from the Sabellian nation; and lastly, even the Lucanian exiles themselves, whose considerable numbers point to the existence of violent internal troubles in that confederacy. Thus he soon found himself superior to the enemy. Consentia (Cosenza), which seems to have been the federal headquarters of the Sabellians settled in Magna Graecia, fell into his hands. In vain the Samnites came to the help of the Lucanians; Alexander defeated their combined forces near Paestum. He subdued the Daunians around Sipontum, and the Messapians in the south-eastern peninsula; he already commanded from sea to sea, and was on the point of arranging with the Romans a joint attack on the Samnites in their native abodes. But successes so unexpected went beyond the desires of the Tarentine merchants, and filled them with alarm. War broke out between them and their captain, who had come amongst them a hired mercenary and now appeared desirous to found a Hellenic empire in the west like his nephew in the east. Alexander had at first the advantage; he wrested Heraclea from the Tarentines, restored Thurii, and seems to have called upon the other Italian Greeks to unite under his protection against the Tarentines, while he at the same time tried to bring about a peace between them and the Sabellian tribes. But his grand projects found only feeble support among the degenerate and desponding Greeks, and the forced change of sides alienated from him his former Lucanian adherents: he fell at Pandosia by the hand of a Lucanian emigrant (422).(1) On his death matters substantially reverted to their old position. The Greek cities found themselves once more isolated and once more left to protect themselves as best they might by treaty or payment of tribute, or even by extraneous aid; Croton for instance repulsed the Bruttii about 430 with the help of the Syracusans. The Samnite tribes acquire renewed ascendency, and were able, without troubling

La Confederació Europea de Sindicats convoca una jornada de lluita, solidaritat i mobilització a tot Europa per dir NO a les polítiques de retallades i austeritat marcades per la Comissió Europea, el BCE i l'FMI de manera gens democràtica, i reclamar un canvi de polítiques a Catalunya, Espanya i Europa. Aquesta és una vaga general laboral, però també social i de consum amb el suport de la Plataforma Prou Retallades, formada per més de 200 entitats socials.

14 RAONS PER FER VAGA GENERAL EL #14N

1. Atur desbocat: 900.000 persones sense feina a Catalunya i 100.000 llars sense cap ingrés.

2. Nivell de pobresa alarmant: el 30% de la població catalana està en risc de pobresa o exclusió social.

3. Augment de la pobresa entre els que tenen feina. Es retallen salaris i condicions laborals i augmenta la precarietat de treballadores i treballadors públics i privats.

4. La reforma laboral del PP trenca les regles de joc en les relacions laborals: acomiadaments fàcils i barats, convenis bloquejats i prolongacions de jornades.

5. El jovent no té futur a Catalunya. El 53% de joves estan sense feina i més de 10.000 han emigrat a l'estranger.

6. Menys recursos per a investigació: a les persones investigadores se les obliga a emigrar i es prescindeix de la generació millor preparada.

7. Més retallades en educació: 6.000 llocs de treball menys i 20.000 alumnes més, augment de taxes a la universitat i a l'FP, menys beques menjador i menys pressupost per a escoles bressol.

8. Sanitat més cara i en pitjors condicions: l'euro per recepta a Catalunya, el re-copagament sanitari i l'augment del 45% de les llistes d'espera.

9. Criminalització de les persones que reben prestacions o subsidis: retallada i enduriment de l'accés a la prestació d'atur i la renda mínima d'inserció.

10. El rescat només agreujarà aquesta situació a la qual ens ha portat la política d'austeritat: més atur, retallada de pensions, retallada de prestacions d'atur, més pobresa, més interessos per pagar als especuladors.

11. Més desigualtats fiscals: s'apuja l'IVA i els preus dels serveis bàsics i es castiga el treball autònom, mentre s'amnistien els defraudadors i no es fan pagar impostos als especuladors financers.

12. Milers de persones que perden l'habitatge i els estalvis mentre es donen diners al sistema financer sense que paguin els responsables.

13. S'ofega la cultura amb més retallades i es mercantilitza la creativitat.

14. Es reprimeix la protesta i es posen en perill les llibertats democràtiques.

també t'afecta
14N VAGA GENERAL

CCOO UGT USOC

PLATAFORMA PROU RETALLADES

QUE NO ENS PRENGUIN EL FUTUR

HI HA
MÉS ATUR   MÉS RETALLADES
MÉS POBRESA
MENYS PROTECCIÓ SOCIAL

CULPABLES
TENIM SOLUCIONS
14N VAGA GENERAL
també t'afecta

No Callem

CCOO UGT USOC
PLATAFORMA PROU RETALLADES

MANIFESTACIÓ 14N
LLEIDA
17.30 HORES
Ricard Viñes

themselves about the Greeks, once more to direct their eyes towards Campania and Latium.

But there during the brief interval a prodigious change had occurred. The Latin confederacy was broken and scattered, the last resistance of the Volsci was overcome, the province of Campania, the richest and finest in the peninsula, was in the undisputed and well-secured possession of the Romans, and the second city of Italy was a dependency of Rome. While the Greeks and Samnites were contending with each other, Rome had almost without a contest raised herself to a position of power which no single people in the peninsula possessed the means of shaking, and which threatened to render all of them subject to her yoke. A joint exertion on the part of the peoples who were not severally a match for Rome might perhaps still burst the chains, ere they became fastened completely. But the clearness of perception, the courage, the self-sacrifice required for such a coalition of numerous peoples and cities that had hitherto been for the most part foes or at any rate strangers to each other, were not to be found at all, or were found only when it was already too late.

Coalition of the Italians against Rome

After the fall of the Etruscan power and the weakening of the Greek republics, the Samnite confederacy was beyond doubt, next to Rome, the most considerable power in Italy, and at the same time that which was most closely and immediately endangered by Roman encroachments. To its lot therefore fell the foremost place and the heaviest burden in the struggle for freedom and nationality which the Italians had to wage against Rome. It might reckon upon the assistance of the small Sabellian tribes, the Vestini, Frentani, Marrucini, and other smaller cantons, who dwelt in rustic seclusion amidst their mountains, but were not deaf to the appeal of a kindred stock calling them to take up arms in defence of their common possessions. The assistance of the Campanian Greeks and those of Magna Graecia (especially the Tarentines), and of the powerful Lucanians and Bruttians would have been of greater importance; but the negligence and supineness of the demagogues ruling in Tarentum and the entanglement of that city in the affairs of Sicily, the internal distractions of the Lucanian confederacy, and above all the deep hostility that had subsisted for centuries between the Greeks of Lower Italy and their Lucanian oppressors, scarcely permitted the hope that Tarentum and Lucania would make common cause with the Samnites. From the Sabines and the Marsi, who were the nearest neighbours of the Romans and had long lived in peaceful relations with Rome, little more could be expected than lukewarm sympathy or neutrality. The Apulians, the ancient and bitter antagonists of the Sabellians, were the natural allies of the Romans. On the other hand it might be expected that the more remote Etruscans would join the league if a first success were gained; and even a revolt in Latium and the land of the Volsci and Hernici was not impossible. But the Samnites—the Aetolians of Italy, in whom national vigour still lived unimpaired—had mainly to rely on their own energies for such perseverance in the unequal struggle as would give the other peoples time for a generous sense of shame, for calm deliberation, and for the mustering of their forces; a single success might then kindle the flames of war and insurrection all around Rome. History cannot but do the noble people the justice of acknowledging that they understood and performed their duty.

Outbreak of War between Samnium and Rome—
Pacification of Campania

Differences had already for several years existed between Rome and Samnium in consequence of the continual aggressions in which the Romans indulged on the Liris, and of which the founding of Fregellae in 426 was the latest and most important. But it was the Greeks of Campania that gave occasion to the outbreak of the contest. After Cumae and Capua had become Roman, nothing so naturally suggested itself to the Romans as the subjugation of the Greek city Neapolis, which ruled also over the Greek islands in the bay—the only town not yet reduced to subjection within the field of the Roman power. The Tarentines and Samnites, informed of the scheme of the Romans to obtain possession of the town, resolved to anticipate them; and while the Tarentines were too remiss perhaps rather than too distant for the execution of this plan, the Samnites actually threw into it a strong garrison. The Romans immediately declared war nominally against the Neapolitans, really against the Samnites (427), and began the siege of Neapolis. After it had lasted a while, the Campanian Greeks became weary of the disturbance of their commerce and of the foreign garrison; and the Romans, whose whole efforts were directed to keep states of the second and third rank by means of separate treaties aloof from the coalition which was about to be formed, hastened, as soon as the Greeks consented to negotiate, to offer them the most favourable terms—full equality of rights and exemption from land service, equal alliance and perpetual peace. Upon these conditions, after the Neapolitans had rid themselves of the garrison by stratagem, a treaty was concluded (428).

The Sabellian towns to the south of the Volturnus, Nola, Nuceria, Herculaneum, and Pompeii, took part with Samnium in the beginning of the war; but their greatly exposed situation and the machinations of the Romans—who endeavoured to bring over to their side the optimate party in these towns by all the levers of artifice and self-interest, and found a powerful support to their endeavours in the precedent of Capua—induced these towns to declare themselves either in favour of Rome or neutral not long after the fall of Neapolis.

Alliance between the Romans and Lucanians

A still more important success befell the Romans in Lucania. There also the people with true instinct was in favour of joining the Samnites; but, as an alliance with the Samnites involved peace with Tarentum and a large portion of the governing lords of Lucania were not disposed to suspend their profitable pillaging expeditions, the Romans succeeded in concluding an alliance with Lucania—an alliance which was invaluable, because it provided employment for the Tarentines and thus left the whole power of Rome available against Samnium.

108

War in Samnium—
The Caudine Pass and the Caudine Peace

Thus Samnium stood on all sides unsupported; excepting that some of the eastern mountain districts sent their contingents. In the year 428 the war began within the Samnite land itself: some towns on the Campanian frontier, Rufrae (between Venafrum and Teanum) and Allifae, were occupied by the Romans. In the following years the Roman armies penetrated Samnium, fighting and pillaging, as far as the territory of the Vestini, and even as far as Apulia, where they were received with open arms; everywhere they had very decidedly the advantage. The courage of the Samnites was broken; they sent back the Roman prisoners, and along with them the dead body of the leader of the war party, Brutulus Papius, who had anticipated the Roman executioners, when the Samnite national assembly determined to ask the enemy for peace and to procure for themselves more tolerable terms by the surrender of their bravest general. But when the humble, almost suppliant, request was not listened to by the Roman people (432), the Samnites, under their new general Gavius Pontius, prepared for the utmost and most desperate resistance. The Roman army, which under the two consuls of the following year (433) Spurius Postumius and Titus Veturius was encamped near Calatia (between Caserta and Maddaloni), received accounts, confirmed by the affirmation of numerous captives, that the Samnites had closely invested Luceria, and that that important town, on which depended the possession of Apulia, was in great danger. They broke up in haste. If they wished to arrive in good time, no other route could be taken than through the midst of the enemy's territory—where afterwards, in continuation of the Appian Way, the Roman road was constructed from Capua by way of Beneventum to Apulia. This route led, between the present villages of Arpaja and Montesarchio (Caudium), through a watery meadow, which was wholly enclosed by high and steep wooded hills and was only accessible through deep defiles at the entrance and outlet. Here the Samnites had posted themselves in ambush. The Romans, who had entered the valley unopposed, found its outlet obstructed by abattis and strongly occupied; on marching back they saw that the entrance was similarly closed, while at the same time the crests of the surrounding mountains were crowned by Samnite cohorts. They perceived, when it was too late, that they had suffered themselves to be misled by a stratagem, and that the Samnites awaited them, not at Luceria, but in the fatal pass of Caudium. They fought, but without hope of success and without earnest aim; the Roman army was totally unable to manoeuvre and was completely vanquished without a struggle. The Roman generals offered to capitulate. It is only a foolish rhetoric that represents the Samnite general as shut up to the simple alternatives of disbanding or of slaughtering the Roman army; he could not have done better than accept the offered capitulation and make prisoners of the hostile army—the whole force which for the moment the Roman community could bring into action—with both its commanders-in-chief. In that case the way to Campania and Latium would have stood open; and in the then existing state of feeling, when the Volsci and Hernici and the larger portion of the Latins would have received him with open arms, the political existence of Rome would have been in serious danger. But instead of taking this course and concluding a military convention, Gavius Pontius thought that he could at once terminate the whole quarrel by an equitable peace; whether it was that he shared that foolish longing of the confederates for peace, to which Brutulus

Papius had fallen a victim in the previous year, or whether it was that he was unable to prevent the party which was tired of the war from spoiling his unexampled victory. The terms laid down were moderate enough; Rome was to raze the fortresses which she had constructed in defiance of the treaty—Cales and Fregellae—and to renew her equal alliance with Samnium. After the Roman generals had agreed to these terms and had given six hundred hostages chosen from the cavalry for their faithful execution—besides pledging their own word and that of all their staff-officers on oath to the same effect —the Roman army was dismissed uninjured, but disgraced; for the Samnite army, drunk with victory, could not resist the desire to subject their hated enemies to the disgraceful formality of laying down their arms and passing under the yoke.

But the Roman senate, regardless of the oath of their officers and of the fate of the hostages, cancelled the agreement, and contented themselves with surrendering to the enemy those who had concluded it as personally responsible for its fulfilment. Impartial history can attach little importance to the question whether in so doing the casuistry of Roman advocates and priests kept the letter of the law, or whether the decree of the Roman senate violated it; under a human and political point of view no blame in this matter rests upon the Romans. It was a question of comparative indifference whether, according to the formal state law of the Romans, the general in command was or was not entitled to conclude peace without reserving its ratification by the burgesses. According to the spirit and practice of the constitution it was quite an established principle that in Rome every state-agreement, not purely military, pertained to the province of the civil authorities, and a general who concluded peace without the instructions of the senate and the burgesses exceeded his powers. It was a greater error on the part of the Samnite general to give the Roman generals the choice between saving their army and exceeding their powers, than it was on the part of the latter that they had not the magnanimity absolutely to repel such a suggestion; and it was right and necessary that the Roman senate should reject such an agreement. A great nation does not surrender what it possesses except under the pressure of extreme necessity: all treaties making concessions are acknowledgments of such a necessity, not moral obligations. If every people justly reckons it a point of honour to tear to pieces by force of arms treaties that are disgraceful, how could honour enjoin a patient adherence to a convention like the Caudine to which an unfortunate general was morally compelled, while the sting of the recent disgrace was keenly felt and the vigour of the nation subsisted unimpaired?

Victory of the Romans

Thus the convention of Caudium did not produce the rest which the enthusiasts for peace in Samnium had foolishly expected from it, but only led to war after war with exasperation aggravated on either side by the opportunity forfeited, by the breach of a solemn engagement, by military honour disgraced, and by comrades that had been abandoned. The Roman officers given up were not received by the Samnites, partly because they were too magnanimous to wreak their vengeance on those unfortunates, partly because they would thereby have admitted the Roman plea that the agreement bound only those who swore to it, not the Roman state. Magnanimously they spared even the hostages whose lives had been forfeited by the rules of war, and preferred to resort at once to arms.

Luceria was occupied by them and Fregellae surprised and taken by assault (434) before the Romans had reorganized their broken army; the passing of the Satricans(2) over to the Samnites shows what they might have accomplished, had they not allowed their advantage to slip through their hands. But Rome was only momentarily paralyzed, not weakened; full of shame and indignation the Romans raised all the men and means they could, and placed the highly experienced Lucius Papirius Cursor, equally distinguished as a soldier and as a general, at the head of the newly formed army. The army divided; the one-half marched by Sabina and the Adriatic coast to appear before Luceria, the other proceeded to the same destination through Samnium itself, successfully engaging and driving before it the Samnite army. They formed a junction again under the walls of Luceria, the siege of which was prosecuted with the greater zeal, because the Roman equites lay in captivity there; the Apulians, particularly the Arpani, lent the Romans important assistance in the siege, especially by procuring supplies. After the Samnites had given battle for the relief of the town and been defeated, Luceria surrendered to the Romans (435). Papirius enjoyed the double satisfaction of liberating his comrades who had been given up for lost, and of requiting the yoke of Caudium on the Samnite garrison of Luceria. In the next years (435-437) the war was carried on(3) not so much in Samnium itself as in the adjoining districts. In the first place the Romans chastised the allies of the Samnites in the Apulian and Frentanian territories, and concluded new conventions with the Teanenses of Apulia and the Canusini. At the same time Satricum was again reduced to subjection and severely punished for its revolt. Then the war turned to Campania, where the Romans conquered the frontier town towards Samnium, Saticula (perhaps S. Agata de' Goti) (438). But now the fortune of war seemed disposed once more to turn against them. The Samnites gained over the Nucerians (438), and soon afterwards the Nolans, to their side; on the upper Liris the Sorani of themselves expelled the Roman garrison (439); the Ausonians were preparing to rise, and threatened the important Cales; even in Capua the party opposed to Rome was vigorously stirring. A Samnite army advanced into Campania and encamped before the city, in the hope that its vicinity might place the national party in the ascendant (440). But Sora was immediately attacked by the Romans and recaptured after the defeat of a Samnite relieving force (440). The movements among the Ausonians were suppressed with cruel rigour ere the insurrection fairly broke out, and at the same time a special dictator was nominated to institute and decide political processes against the leaders of the Samnite party in Capua, so that the most illustrious of them died a voluntary death to escape from the Roman executioner (440). The Samnite army before Capua was defeated and compelled to retreat from Campania; the Romans, following close at the heels of the enemy, crossed the Matese and encamped in the winter of 440 before Bovianum, the capital of Samnium. Nola was abandoned by its allies; and the Romans had the sagacity to detach the town for ever from the Samnite party by a very favourable convention, similar to that concluded with Neapolis (441). Fregellae, which after the catastrophe of Caudium had fallen into the hands of the party adverse to Rome and had been their chief stronghold in the district on the Liris, finally fell in the eighth year after its occupation by the Samnites (441); two hundred of the citizens, the chief members of the national party, were conveyed to Rome, and there openly beheaded in the Forum as an example and a warning to the patriots who were everywhere bestirring themselves.

New Fortresses in Apulia and Campania

Apulia and Campania were thus in the hands of the Romans. In order finally to secure and permanently to command the conquered territory, several new fortresses were founded in it during the years 440-442: Luceria in Apulia, to which on account of its isolated and exposed situation half a legion was sent as a permanent garrison; Pontiae (the Ponza islands) for the securing of the Campanian waters; Saticula on the Campano-Samnite frontier, as a bulwark against Samnium; and lastly Interamna (near Monte Cassino) and Suessa Aurunca (Sessa) on the road from Rome to Capua. Garrisons moreover were sent to Caiatia (Cajazzo), Sora, and other stations of military importance. The great military road from Rome to Capua, which with the necessary embankment for it across the Pomptine marshes the censor Appius Claudius caused to be constructed in 442, completed the securing of Campania. The designs of the Romans were more and more fully developed; their object was the subjugation of Italy, which was enveloped more closely from year to year in a network of Roman fortresses and roads. The Samnites were already on both sides surrounded by the Roman meshes; already the line from Rome to Luceria severed north and south Italy from each other, as the fortresses of Norba and Signia had formerly severed the Volsci and Aequi; and Rome now rested on the Arpani, as it formerly rested on the Hernici. The Italians could not but see that the freedom of all of them was gone if Samnium succumbed, and that it was high time at length to hasten with all their might to the help of the brave mountain people which had now for fifteen years singly sustained the unequal struggle with the Romans.

Intervention of the Tarentines

The most natural allies of the Samnites would have been the Tarentines; but it was part of that fatality that hung over Samnium and over Italy in general, that at this moment so fraught with the destinies of the future the decision lay in the hands of these Athenians of Italy. Since the constitution of Tarentum, which was originally after the old Doric fashion strictly aristocratic, had become changed to a complete democracy, a life of singular activity had sprung up in that city, which was inhabited chiefly by mariners, fishermen, and artisans. The sentiments and conduct of the population, more wealthy than noble, discarded all earnestness amidst the giddy bustle and witty brilliance of their daily life, and oscillated between the grandest boldness of enterprise and elevation of spirit on the one hand, and a shameful frivolity and childish whim on the other. It may not be out of place, in connection with a crisis wherein the existence or destruction of nations of noble gifts and ancient renown was at stake, to mention that Plato, who came to Tarentum some sixty years before this time, according to his own statement saw the whole city drunk at the Dionysia, and that the burlesque farce, or "merry tragedy" as it was called, was created in Tarentum about the very time of the great Samnite war. This licentious life and buffoon poetry of the Tarentine fashionables and literati had a fitting counterpart in the inconstant, arrogant, and short-sighted policy of the Tarentine demagogues, who regularly meddled in matters with which they had nothing to do, and kept aloof where their immediate interests called for action. After the Caudine catastrophe, when the Romans and Samnites stood opposed in Apulia, they had sent envoys thither to enjoin both parties to lay down their arms (434). This diplomatic intervention in the decisive struggle of the Italians could not rationally have any other meaning than that of an announcement that Tarentum had at length resolved to abandon the neutrality which it had hitherto maintained. It had in fact sufficient reason to do so. It was no doubt a difficult and dangerous thing for Tarentum to be entangled in such a war; for the democratic development of the state had directed its energies entirely to the fleet, and while that fleet, resting upon the strong commercial marine of Tarentum, held the first rank among the maritime powers of Magna Graecia, the land force, on which they were in the present case dependent, consisted mainly of hired soldiers and was sadly disorganized. Under these circumstances it was no light undertaking for the Tarentine republic to take part in the conflict between Rome and Samnium, even apart from the—at least troublesome—feud in which Roman policy had contrived to involve them with the Lucanians. But these obstacles might be surmounted by an energetic will; and both the contending parties construed the summons of the Tarentine envoys that they should desist from the strife as meant in earnest. The Samnites, as the weaker, showed themselves ready to comply with it; the Romans replied by hoisting the signal for battle. Reason and honour dictated to the Tarentines the propriety of now following up the haughty injunction of their envoys by a declaration of war against Rome; but in Tarentum neither reason nor honour characterized the government, and they had simply been trifling in a very childish fashion with very serious matters. No declaration of war against Rome took place; in its stead they preferred to support the oligarchical party in the Sicilian towns against Agathocles of Syracuse who had at a former period been in the Tarentine service and had been dismissed in disgrace, and following the example of Sparta, they sent a fleet to the island—a fleet which would have rendered better service in the Campanian seas (440).

Accession of the Etruscans to the Coalition—
Victory at the Vadimonian Lake

The peoples of northern and central Italy, who seem to have been roused especially by the establishment of the fortress of Luceria, acted with more energy. The Etruscans first drew the sword (443), the armistice of 403 having already expired some years before. The Roman frontier-fortress of Sutrium had to sustain a two years' siege, and in the vehement conflicts which took place under its walls the Romans as a rule were worsted, till the consul of the year 444 Quintus Fabius Rullianus, a leader who had gained experience in the Samnite wars, not only restored the ascendency of the Roman arms in Roman Etruria, but boldly penetrated into the land of the Etruscans proper, which had hitherto from diversity of language and scanty means of communication remained almost unknown to the Romans. His march through the Ciminian Forest which no Roman army had yet traversed, and his pillaging of a rich region that had long been spared the horrors of war, raised all Etruria in arms. The Roman government, which had seriously disapproved the rash expedition and had when too late forbidden the daring leader from crossing the frontier, collected in the greatest haste new legions, in order to meet the expected onslaught of the whole Etruscan power. But a seasonable and decisive victory of Rullianus, the battle at the Vadimonian lake which long lived in the memory of the people, converted an imprudent enterprise into a celebrated feat of heroism and broke the resistance of the Etruscans. Unlike the Samnites who had now for eighteen years maintained the unequal struggle, three of the most powerful Etruscan towns—- Perusia, Cortona, and Arretium—consented after the first defeat to a separate peace for three hundred months (444), and after the Romans had once more beaten the other Etruscans near Perusia in the following year, the Tarquinienses also agreed to a peace of four hundred months (446); whereupon the other cities desisted from the contest, and a temporary cessation of arms took place throughout Etruria.

Last Campaigns in Samnium

While these events were passing, the war had not been suspended in Samnium. The campaign of 443 was confined like the preceding to the besieging and storming of several strongholds of the Samnites; but in the next year the war took a more vigorous turn. The dangerous position of Rullianus in Etruria, and the reports which spread as to the annihilation of the Roman army in the north, encouraged the Samnites to new exertions; the Roman consul Gaius Marcius Rutilus was vanquished by them and severely wounded in person. But the sudden change in the aspect of matters in Etruria destroyed their newly kindled hopes. Lucius Papirius Cursor again appeared at the head of the Roman troops sent against the Samnites, and again remained the victor in a great and decisive battle (445), in which the confederates had put forth their last energies. The flower of their army—the wearers of the striped tunics and golden shields, and the wearers of the white tunics and silver shields—were there extirpated, and their splendid equipments thenceforth on festal occasions decorated the rows of shops along the Roman Forum. Their distress was ever increasing; the struggle was becoming ever more hopeless. In the following year (446) the Etruscans laid down their arms; and in the same year the last town of Campania which still adhered to the Samnites, Nuceria, simultaneously assailed on the part of the Romans by water and by land, surrendered under favourable conditions. The Samnites found new allies in the Umbrians of northern, and in the Marsi and Paeligni of central, Italy, and numerous volunteers even from the Hernici joined their ranks; but movements which might have decidedly turned the scale against Rome, had the Etruscans still remained under arms, now simply augmented the results of the Roman victory without seriously adding to its difficulties. The Umbrians, who gave signs of marching on Rome, were intercepted by Rullianus with the army of Samnium on the upper Tiber—a step which the enfeebled Samnites were unable to prevent; and this sufficed to disperse the Umbrian levies. The war once more returned to central Italy. The Paeligni were conquered, as were also the Marsi; and, though the other Sabellian tribes remained nominally foes of Rome, in this quarter Samnium gradually came to stand practically alone. But unexpected assistance came to them from the district of the Tiber. The confederacy of the Hernici, called by the Romans to account for their countrymen found among the Samnite captives, now declared war against Rome (in 448)—more doubtless from despair than from calculation. Some of the more considerable Hernican communities from the first kept aloof from hostilities; but Anagnia, by far the most eminent of the Hernican cities, carried out this declaration of war. In a military point of view the position of the Romans was undoubtedly rendered for the moment highly critical by this unexpected rising in the rear of the army occupied with the siege of the strongholds of Samnium. Once more the fortune of war favoured the Samnites; Sora and Caiatia fell into their hands. But the Anagnines succumbed with unexpected rapidity before troops despatched from Rome, and these troops also gave seasonable relief to the army stationed in Samnium: all in fact was lost. The Samnites sued for peace, but in vain; they could not yet come to terms. The final decision was reserved for the campaign of 449. Two Roman consular armies penetrated—the one, under Tiberius Minucius and after his fall under Marcus Fulvius, from Campania through the mountain passes, the other, under Lucius Postumius, from the Adriatic upwards by the Biferno—into Samnium, there to unite in front of Bovianum the capital; a decisive victory was achieved, the Samnite general Statius Gellius was taken prisoner, and Bovianum was carried by storm.

Peace with Samnium

The fall of the chief stronghold of the land terminated the twenty-two years' war. The Samnites withdrew their garrisons from Sora and Arpinum, and sent envoys to Rome to sue for peace; the Sabellian tribes, the Marsi, Marrucini, Paeligni, Frentani, Vestini, and Picentes followed their example. The terms granted by Rome were tolerable; cessions of territory were required from some of them, from the Paeligni for instance, but they do not seem to have been of much importance. The equal alliance was renewed between the Sabellian tribes and the Romans (450).

And with Tarentum

Presumably about the same time, and in consequence doubtless of the Samnite peace, peace was also made between Rome and Tarentum. The two cities had not indeed directly opposed each other in the field. The Tarentines had been inactive spectators of the long contest between Rome and Samnium from its beginning to its close, and had only kept up hostilities in league with the Sallentines against the Lucanians who were allies of Rome. In the last years of the Samnite war no doubt they had shown some signs of more energetic action. The position of embarrassment to which the ceaseless attacks of the Lucanians reduced them on the one hand, and on the other hand the feeling ever obtruding itself on them more urgently that the complete subjugation of Samnium would endanger their own independence, induced them, notwithstanding their unpleasant experiences with Alexander, once more to entrust themselves to a -condottiere-. There came at their call the Spartan prince Cleonymus, accompanied by five thousand mercenaries; with whom he united a band equally numerous raised in Italy, as well as the contingents of the Messapians and of the smaller Greek towns, and above all the Tarentine civic army of twenty-two thousand men. At the head of this considerable force he compelled the Lucanians to make peace with Tarentum and to install a government of Samnite tendencies; in return for which Metapontum was abandoned to them. The Samnites were still in arms when this occurred; there was nothing to prevent the Spartan from coming to their aid and casting the weight of his numerous army and his military skill into the scale in favour of freedom for the cities and peoples of Italy. But Tarentum did not act as Rome would in similar circumstances have acted; and prince Cleonymus himself was far from being an Alexander or a Pyrrhus. He was in no hurry to undertake a war in which he might expect more blows than booty, but preferred to make common cause with the Lucanians against Metapontum, and made himself comfortable in that city, while he talked of an expedition against Agathocles of Syracuse and of liberating the Sicilian Greeks. Thereupon the Samnites made peace; and when after its conclusion Rome began to concern herself more seriously about the south-east of the peninsula—in token of which in the year 447 a Roman force levied contributions, or rather reconnoitred by order of the government, in the territory of the Sallentines—the Spartan -condottiere- embarked with his mercenaries and surprised the island of Corcyra, which was admirably situated as a basis for piratical expeditions against Greece and Italy. Thus abandoned by their general, and at the same time deprived of their allies in central Italy, the Tarentines and their Italian allies, the Lucanians and Sallentines, had now no course left but to solicit an accommodation with Rome, which appears to have been granted on tolerable terms. Soon afterwards (451) even an incursion of Cleonymus, who had landed in the Sallentine territory and laid siege to Uria, was repulsed by the inhabitants with Roman aid.

Consolidation of the Roman Rule in Central Italy

The victory of Rome was complete; and she turned it to full account. It was not from magnanimity in the conquerors—for the Romans knew nothing of the sort—but from shrewd and far-seeing calculation that terms so moderate were granted to the Samnites, the Tarentines, and the more distant peoples generally. The first and main object was not so much to compel southern Italy as quickly as possible to recognize formally the Roman supremacy, as to supplement and complete the subjugation of central Italy, for which the way had been prepared by the military roads and fortresses already established in Campania and Apulia during the last war, and by that means to separate the northern and southern Italians into two masses cut off in a military point of view from direct contact with each other. To this object accordingly the next undertakings of the Romans were with consistent energy directed. Above all they used, or made, the opportunity for getting rid of the confederacies of the Aequi and the Hernici which had once been rivals of the Roman single power in the region of the Tiber and were not yet quite set aside. In the same year, in which the peace with Samnium took place (450), the consul Publius Sempronius Sophus waged war on the Aequi; forty townships surrendered in fifty days; the whole territory with the exception of the narrow and rugged mountain valley, which still in the present day bears the old name of the people (Cicolano), passed into the possession of the Romans, and here on the northern border of the Fucine lake was founded the fortress Alba with a garrison of 6000 men, thenceforth forming a bulwark against the valiant Marsi and a curb for central Italy; as was also two years afterwards on the upper Turano, nearer to Rome, Carsioli —both as allied communities with Latin rights.

The fact that in the case of the Hernici at least Anagnia had taken part in the last stage of the Samnite war, furnished the desired reason for dissolving the old relation of alliance. The fate of the Anagnines was, as might be expected, far harder than that which had under similar circumstances been meted out to the Latin communities in the previous generation. They not merely had, like these, to acquiesce in the Roman citizenship without suffrage, but they also like the Caerites lost self-administration; out of a portion of their territory on the upper Trerus (Sacco), moreover, a new tribe was instituted, and another was formed at the same time on the lower Anio (455). The only regret was that the three Hernican communities next in importance to Anagnia, Aletrium, Verulae, and Ferentinum, had not also revolted; for, as they courteously declined the suggestion that they should voluntarily enter into the bond of Roman citizenship and there existed no pretext for compelling them to do so, the Romans were obliged not only to respect their autonomy, but also to allow to them even the right of assembly and of intermarriage, and in this way still to leave a shadow of the old Hernican confederacy. No such considerations fettered their action in that portion of the Volscian country which had hitherto been held by the Samnites. There Arpinum and Frusino became subject, the latter town was deprived of a third of its domain, and on the upper Liris in addition to Fregellae the Volscian town of Sora, which had previously been garrisoned, was now permanently converted into a Roman fortress and occupied by a legion of 4000 men. In this way the old Volscian territory was completely subdued, and became rapidly Romanized. The region which separated Samnium from Etruria was penetrated by two military roads, both of which were secured by new fortresses. The northern road, which afterwards became the Flaminian, covered the line of the Tiber; it led through Ocriculum, which was in alliance with Rome, to Narnia, the name which the Romans gave to the old Umbrian fortress Nequinum when they settled a military colony there (455). The southern, afterwards the Valerian, ran along the Fucine lake by way of the just mentioned fortresses of Carsioli and Alba. The small tribes within whose bounds these colonies were instituted, the Umbrians who obstinately defended Nequinum, the Aequians who once more assailed Alba, and the Marsians who attacked Carsioli, could not arrest the course of Rome: the two strong curb-fortresses were inserted almost without hindrance between Samnium and Etruria. We have already mentioned the great roads and fortresses instituted for permanently securing Apulia and above all Campania: by their means Samnium was further surrounded on the east and west with the net of Roman strongholds. It is a significant token of the comparative weakness of Etruria that it was not deemed necessary to secure the passes through the Ciminian Forest in a similar mode—by a highway and corresponding fortresses. The former frontier fortress of Sutrium continued to be in this quarter the terminus of the Roman military line, and the Romans contented themselves with having the road leading thence to Arretium kept in a serviceable state for military purposes by the communities through whose territories it passed.(4)

Renewed Outbreak of the Samnite-Etruscan War—
Junction of the Troops of the Coalition in Etruria

The high-spirited Samnite nation perceived that such a peace was more ruinous than the most destructive war; and, what was more, it acted accordingly. The Celts in northern Italy were just beginning to bestir themselves again after a long suspension of warfare; moreover several Etruscan communities there were still in arms against the Romans, and brief armistices alternated in that quarter with vehement but indecisive conflicts. All central Italy was still in ferment and partly in open insurrection; the fortresses were still only in course of construction; the way between Etruria and Samnium was not yet completely closed. Perhaps it was not yet too late to save freedom; but, if so, there must be no delay; the difficulty of attack increased, the power of the assailants diminished with every year by which the peace was prolonged. Five years had scarce elapsed since the contest ended, and all the wounds must still have been bleeding which the twenty-two years' war had inflicted on the peasantry of Samnium, when in the year 456 the Samnite confederacy renewed the struggle. The last war had been decided in favour of Rome mainly through the alliance of Lucania with the Romans and the consequent standing aloof of Tarentum. The Samnites, profiting by that lesson, now threw themselves in the first instance with all their might on the Lucanians, and succeeded in bringing their party in that quarter to the helm of affairs, and in concluding an alliance between Samnium and Lucania. Of course the Romans immediately declared war; the Samnites had expected no other issue. It is a significant indication of the state of feeling, that the Samnite government informed the Roman envoys that it was not able to guarantee their inviolability, if they should set foot on Samnite ground.

The war thus began anew (456), and while a second army was fighting in Etruria, the main Roman army traversed Samnium and compelled the Lucanians to make peace and send hostages to Rome. The following year both consuls were able to proceed to Samnium; Rullianus conquered at Tifernum, his faithful comrade in arms, Publius Decius Mus, at Maleventum, and for five months two Roman armies encamped in the land of the enemy. They were enabled to do so, because the Tuscan states had on their own behalf entered into negotiations for peace with Rome. The Samnites, who from the beginning could not but see that their only chance of victory lay in the combination of all Italy against Rome, exerted themselves to the utmost to prevent the threatened separate peace between Etruria and Rome; and when at last their general, Gellius Egnatius, offered to bring aid to the Etruscans in their own country, the Etruscan federal council in reality agreed to hold out and once more to appeal to the decision of arms. Samnium made the most energetic efforts to place three armies simultaneously in the field, the first destined for the defence of its own territory, the second for an invasion of Campania, the third and most numerous for Etruria; and in the year 458 the last, led by Egnatius himself, actually reached Etruria in safety through the Marsian and Umbrian territories, with whose inhabitants there was an understanding. Meanwhile the Romans were capturing some strong places in Samnium and breaking the influence of the Samnite party in Lucania; they were not in a position to prevent the departure of the army led by Egnatius. When information reached Rome that the Samnites had succeeded in frustrating all the enormous efforts made to sever the southern from the northern Italians, that the arrival of the Samnite bands in Etruria had become the signal for an almost universal rising against Rome, and that the Etruscan communities were labouring with the utmost zeal to get their own forces ready for war and to take into their pay Gallic bands, every nerve was strained also in Rome; the freedmen and the married were formed into cohorts—it was felt on all hands that the decisive crisis was near. The year 458 however passed

118

away, apparently, in armings and marchings. For the following year (459) the Romans placed their two best generals, Publius Decius Mus and the aged Quintus Fabius Rullianus, at the head of their army in Etruria, which was reinforced with all the troops that could be spared from Campania, and amounted to at least 60,000 men, of whom more than a third were full burgesses of Rome. Besides this, two reserves were formed, the first at Falerii, the second under the walls of the capital. The rendezvous of the Italians was Umbria, towards which the roads from the Gallic, Etruscan, and Sabellian territories converged; towards Umbria the consuls also moved off their main force, partly along the left, partly along the right bank of the Tiber, while at the same time the first reserve made a movement towards Etruria, in order if possible to recall the Etruscan troops from the main scene of action for the defence of their homes. The first engagement did not prove fortunate for the Romans; their advanced guard was defeated by the combined Gauls and Samnites in the district of Chiusi. But that diversion accomplished its object. Less magnanimous than the Samnites, who had marched through the ruins of their towns that they might not be absent from the chosen field of battle, a great part of the Etruscan contingents withdrew from the federal army on the news of the advance of the Roman reserve into Etruria, and its ranks were greatly thinned when the decisive battle came to be fought on the eastern declivity of the Apennines near Sentinum.

Battle of Sentinum—
Peace with Etruria

Nevertheless it was a hotly contested day. On the right wing of the Romans, where Rullianus with his two legions fought against the Samnite army, the conflict remained long undecided. On the left, which Publius Decius commanded, the Roman cavalry was thrown into confusion by the Gallic war chariots, and the legions also already began to give way. Then the consul called to him Marcus Livius the priest, and bade him devote to the infernal gods both the head of the Roman general and the army of the enemy; and plunging into the thickest throng of the Gauls he sought death and found it. This heroic deed of despair on the part of one so eminent as a man and so beloved as a general was not in vain. The fugitive soldiers rallied; the bravest threw themselves after their leader into the hostile ranks, to avenge him or to die with him; and just at the right moment the consular Lucius Scipio, despatched by Rullianus, appeared with the Roman reserve on the imperilled left wing. The excellent Campanian cavalry, which fell on the flank and rear of the Gauls, turned the scale; the Gauls fled, and at length the Samnites also gave way, their general Egnatius falling at the gate of the camp. Nine thousand Romans strewed the field of battle; but dearly as the victory was purchased, it was worthy of such a sacrifice. The army of the coalition was dissolved, and with it the coalition itself; Umbria remained in the power of the Romans, the Gauls dispersed, the remnant of the Samnites still in compact order retreated homeward through the Abruzzi. Campania, which the Samnites had overrun during the Etruscan war, was after its close re-occupied with little difficulty by the Romans. Etruria sued for peace in the following year (460); Volsinii, Perusia, Arretium, and in general all the towns that had joined the league against Rome, promised a cessation of hostilities for four hundred months.

But the Samnites were of a different mind; they prepared for their hopeless resistance with the courage of free men, which cannot compel success but may put it to shame. When the two consular armies advanced into Samnium, in the year 460, they encountered everywhere the most desperate resistance; in fact Marcus Atilius was discomfited near Luceria, and the Samnites were able to penetrate into Campania and to lay waste the territory of the Roman colony Interamna on the Liris. In the ensuing year Lucius Papirius Cursor, the son of the hero of the first Samnite war, and Spurius Carvilius, gave battle on a great scale near Aquilonia to the Samnite army, the flower of which —the 16,000 in white tunics—had sworn a sacred oath to prefer death to flight. Inexorable destiny, however, heeds neither the oaths nor the supplications of despair; the Roman conquered and stormed the strongholds where the Samnites had sought refuge for themselves and their property. Even after this great defeat the confederates still for years resisted the ever-increasing superiority of the enemy with unparalleled perseverance in their fastnesses and mountains, and still achieved various isolated advantages. The experienced arm of the old Rullianus was once more called into the field against them (462), and Gavius Pontius, a son perhaps of the victor of Caudium, even gained for his nation a last victory, which the Romans meanly enough avenged by causing him when subsequently taken to be executed in prison (463). But there was no further symptom of movement in Italy; for the war, which Falerii began in 461, scarcely deserves such a name. The Samnites doubtless turned with longing eyes towards Tarentum, which alone was still in a position to grant them aid; but it held aloof. The same causes as before occasioned its inaction—internal misgovernment, and the passing over of the Lucanians once more to the Roman party in the year 456; to which fell to be added a not unfounded dread of Agathocles of Syracuse, who just at that time had reached the height of his power and began to turn his views towards Italy. About 455 the latter established himself in Corcyra whence Cleonymus had been expelled by Demetrius Poliorcetes, and now threatened the Tarentines from the Adriatic as well as from the Ionian sea. The cession of the island to king Pyrrhus of Epirus in 459 certainly removed to a great extent the apprehensions which they had cherished; but the affairs of Corcyra continued to occupy the Tarentines—in the year 464, for instance, they helped to protect Pyrrhus in possession of the island against Demetrius—and in like manner Agathocles did not cease to give the Tarentines uneasiness by his Italian policy. When he died (465) and with him the power of the Syracusans in Italy went to wreck, it was too late; Samnium, weary of the thirty-seven years' struggle, had concluded peace in the previous year (464) with the Roman consul Manius Curius Dentatus, and had in form renewed its league with Rome. On this occasion, as in the peace of 450, no disgraceful or destructive conditions were imposed on the brave people by the Romans; no cessions even of territory seem to have taken place. The political sagacity of Rome preferred to follow the path which it had hitherto pursued, and to attach in the first place the Campanian and Adriatic coast more and more securely to Rome before proceeding to the direct conquest of the interior. Campania, indeed, had been long in subjection; but the far-seeing policy of Rome found it needful, in order to secure the Campanian coast, to establish two coast-fortresses there, Minturnae and Sinuessa (459), the new burgesses of which were admitted according to the settled rule in the case of maritime colonies to the full citizenship of

Rome. With still greater energy the extension of the Roman rule was prosecuted in central Italy. As the subjugation of the Aequi and Hernici was the immediate sequel of the first Samnite war, so that of the Sabines followed on the end of the second. The same general, who ultimately subdued the Samnites, Manius Curius broke down in the same year (464) the brief and feeble resistance of the Sabines and forced them to unconditional surrender. A great portion of the subjugated territory was immediately taken into possession of the victors and distributed to Roman burgesses, and Roman subject-rights (-civitas sine suffragio-) were imposed on the communities that were left—Cures, Reate, Amiternum, Nursia. Allied towns with equal rights were not established here; on the contrary the country came under the immediate rule of Rome, which thus extended as far as the Apennines and the Umbrian mountains. Nor was it even now restricted to the territory on Rome's side of the mountains; the last war had shown but too clearly that the Roman rule over central Italy was only secured, if it reached from sea to sea. The establishment of the Romans beyond the Apennines begins with the laying out of the strong fortress of Atria (Atri) in the year 465, on the northern slope of the Abruzzi towards the Picenian plain, not immediately on the coast and hence with Latin rights, but still near to the sea, and the keystone of the mighty wedge separating northern and southern Italy. Of a similar nature and of still greater importance was the founding of Venusia (463), whither the unprecedented number of 20,000 colonists was conducted. That city, founded at the boundary of Samnium, Apulia, and Lucania, on the great road between Tarentum and Samnium, in an uncommonly strong position, was destined as a curb to keep in check the surrounding tribes, and above all to interrupt the communications between the two most powerful enemies of Rome in southern Italy. Beyond doubt at the same time the southern highway, which Appius Claudius had carried as far as Capua, was prolonged thence to Venusia. Thus, at the close of the Samnite wars, the Roman domain closely compact—that is, consisting almost exclusively of communities with Roman or Latin rights—extended on the north to the Ciminian Forest, on the east to the Abruzzi and to the Adriatic, on the south as far as Capua, while the two advanced posts, Luceria and Venusia, established towards the east and south on the lines of communication of their opponents, isolated them on every side. Rome was no longer merely the first, but was already the ruling power in the peninsula, when towards the end of the fifth century of the city those nations, which had been raised to supremacy in their respective lands by the favour of the gods and by their own capacity, began to come into contact in council and on the battle-field; and, as at Olympia the preliminary victors girt themselves for a second and more serious struggle, so on the larger arena of the nations, Carthage, Macedonia, and Rome now prepared for the final and decisive contest.

Notes for Book II Chapter VI

1. It may not be superfluous to mention that our knowledge Archidamus and Alexander is derived from Greek annals, and that the synchronism between these and the Roman is in reference to the present epoch only approximately established. We must beware, therefore, of pursuing too far into detail the unmistakable general connection between the events in the west and those in the east of Italy.

2. These were not the inhabitants of Satricum near Antium (*ii.* V. League with The Hernici), but those of another Volscian town constituted at that time as a Roman burgess-community without right of voting, near Arpinum.

3. That a formal armistice for two years subsisted between the Romans and Samnites in 436-437 is more than improbable.

4. The operations in the campaign of 537, and still more plainly the formation of the highway from Arretium to Bononia in 567, show that the road from Rome to Arretium had already been rendered serviceable before that time. But it cannot at that period have been a Roman military road, because, judging from its later appellation of the "Cassian way," it cannot have been constructed as a -via consularis-earlier than 583; for no Cassian appears in the lists of Roman consuls and censors between Spurius Cassius, consul in 252, 261, and 268—who of course is out of the question—and Gaius Cassius Longinus, consul in 583.

CHAPTER VII

Struggle between Pyrrhus and Rome, and Union of Italy

Relations between the East and West

After Rome had acquired the undisputed mastery of the world, the Greeks were wont to annoy their Roman masters by the assertion that Rome was indebted for her greatness to the fever of which Alexander of Macedonia died at Babylon on the 11th of June, 431. As it was not too agreeable for them to reflect on the actual past, they were fond of allowing their thoughts to dwell on what might have happened, had the great king turned his arms—as was said to have been his intention at the time of his death—towards the west and contested the Carthaginian supremacy by sea with his fleet, and the Roman supremacy by land with his phalanxes. It is not impossible that Alexander may have cherished such thoughts; nor is it necessary to resort for an explanation of their origin to the mere difficulty which an autocrat, who is fond of war and is well provided with soldiers and ships, experiences in setting limits to his warlike career. It was an enterprise worthy of a Greek great king to protect the Siceliots against Carthage and the Tarentines against Rome, and to put an end to piracy on either sea; and the Italian embassies from the Bruttians, Lucanians, and Etruscans,(1) that along with numerous others made their appearance at Babylon, afforded him sufficient opportunities of becoming acquainted with the circumstances of the peninsula and of entering into relations with it. Carthage with its many connections in the east could not but attract the attention of the mighty monarch, and it was probably one of his designs to convert the nominal sovereignty of the Persian king over the Tyrian colony into a real one: it was not for nothing that a Phoenician spy was found in the retinue of Alexander. Whether, however, these ideas were dreams or actual projects, the king died without having interfered in the affairs of the west, and his ideas were buried with him. For but a few brief years a Greek ruler had held in his hand the whole intellectual vigour of the Hellenic race combined with the whole material resources of the east. On his death the work to which his life had been devoted—the establishment of Hellenism in the east—was by no means undone; but his empire had barely been united when it was again dismembered, and, amidst the constant quarrels of the different states that were formed out of its ruins, the object of world-wide interest which they were destined to promote—the diffusion of Greek culture in the east—though not abandoned, was prosecuted on a feeble and stunted scale. Under such circumstances, neither the Greek nor the Asiatico-Egyptian states could think of acquiring a footing in the west or of turning their efforts against the Romans or the Carthaginians. The eastern and western state-systems subsisted side by side for a time without crossing, politically, each other's path; and Rome in particular remained substantially aloof from the complications in the days of Alexander's successors. The only relations established were of a mercantile kind; as in the instance of the free state of Rhodes, the leading representative of the policy of commercial neutrality in Greece and in consequence the universal medium of intercourse in an age of perpetual wars, which about 448 concluded a treaty with Rome —a commercial convention of course, such as was natural between a mercantile people and the masters of the Caerite and Campanian coasts. Even in the supply of mercenaries from Hellas, the universal recruiting field of those times, to Italy, and to Tarentum in particular, political relations—such as subsisted, for instance, between Tarentum and Sparta its mother-city—exercised but a very subordinate influence. In general the raising of mercenaries was simply a matter of traffic, and Sparta, although it regularly supplied the Tarentines with captains for their Italian wars, was by that course as little involved in hostilities with the Italians, as in the North American war of independence the German states were involved in hostilities with the Union, to whose opponents they sold the services of their subjects.

The Historical Position of Pyrrhus

Pyrrhus, king of Epirus, was himself simply a military adventurer. He was none the less a soldier of fortune that he traced back his pedigree to Aeacus and Achilles, and that, had he been more peacefully disposed, he might have lived and died as "king" of a small mountain tribe under the supremacy of Macedonia or perhaps in isolated independence. He has been compared to Alexander of Macedonia; and certainly the idea of founding a Hellenic empire of the west—which would have had as its core Epirus, Magna Graecia, and Sicily, would have commanded both the Italian seas, and would have reduced Rome and Carthage to the rank of barbarian peoples bordering on the Hellenistic state-system, like the Celts and the Indians—was analogous in greatness and boldness to the idea which led the Macedonian king over the Hellespont. But it was not the mere difference of issue that formed the distinction between the expedition to the east and that to the west. Alexander with his Macedonian army, in which the staff especially was excellent, could fully make head against the great-king; but the king of Epirus, which stood by the side of Macedonia somewhat as Hesse by the side of Prussia, could only raise an army worthy of the name by means of mercenaries and of alliances based on accidental political combinations. Alexander made his appearance in the Persian empire as a conqueror; Pyrrhus appeared in Italy as the general of a coalition of secondary states. Alexander left his hereditary dominions completely secured by the unconditional subjection of Greece, and by the strong army that remained behind under Antipater; Pyrrhus had no security for the integrity of his native dominions but the word of a doubtful neighbour. In the case of both conquerors, if their plans should be crowned with success, their native country would necessarily cease to be the centre of their new empire; but it was far more practicable to transfer the seat of the Macedonian military monarchy to Babylon than to found a soldier-dynasty in Tarentum or Syracuse. The democracy of the Greek republics—perpetual agony though it was—could not be at all coerced into the stiff forms of a military state; Philip had good reason for not incorporating the Greek republics with his empire. In the east no national resistance was to be expected; ruling and subject races had long lived there side by side, and a change of despot was a matter of indifference or even of satisfaction to the mass of the population. In the west the Romans, the Samnites, the Carthaginians, might be vanquished; but no conqueror could have transformed the Italians into Egyptian fellahs, or rendered the Roman farmers tributaries of Hellenic barons. Whatever we take into view—whether their own power, their allies, or the resources of their antagonists—in all points the plan of the Macedonian appears as a feasible, that of the Epirot an impracticable, enterprise; the former as the completion of a great historical task, the latter as a remarkable blunder; the former as the foundation of a new system of states and of a new phase of civilization, the latter as a mere episode in history. The work of Alexander outlived him, although its creator met an untimely death; Pyrrhus saw with his own eyes the wreck of all his plans, ere death called him away. Both were by nature daring and great, but Pyrrhus was only the foremost general, Alexander was eminently the most gifted statesman, of his time; and, if it is insight into what is and what is not possible that distinguishes the hero from the adventurer, Pyrrhus must be numbered among the latter class, and may as little be placed on a parallel with his greater kinsman as the Constable of Bourbon may be put in comparison with Louis the Eleventh.

And yet a wondrous charm attaches to the name of the Epirot—a peculiar sympathy, evoked certainly in some degree by his chivalrous and amiable character, but still more by the circumstance that he was the first Greek that met the Romans in battle. With him began those direct relations between Rome and Hellas, on which the whole subsequent development of ancient, and an essential part of modern, civilization are based. The struggle between phalanxes and cohorts, between a mercenary army and a militia, between military monarchy and senatorial government, between individual talent and national vigour —this struggle between Rome and Hellenism was first fought out in the battles between Pyrrhus and the Roman generals; and though the defeated party often afterwards appealed anew to the arbitration of arms, every succeeding day of battle simply confirmed the decision. But while the Greeks were beaten in the battlefield as well as in the senate-hall, their superiority was none the less decided on every other field of rivalry than that of politics; and these very struggles already betokened that the victory of Rome over the Hellenes would be different from her victories over Gauls and Phoenicians, and that the charm of Aphrodite only begins to work when the lance is broken and the helmet and shield are laid aside.

Character and Earlier History of Pyrrhus

King Pyrrhus was the son of Aeacides, ruler of the Molossians (about Janina), who, spared as a kinsman and faithful vassal by Alexander, had been after his death drawn into the whirlpool of Macedonian family-politics, and lost in it first his kingdom and then his life (441). His son, then six years of age, was saved by Glaucias the ruler of the Illyrian Taulantii, and in the course of the conflicts for the possession of Macedonia he was, when still a boy, restored by Demetrius Poliorcetes to his hereditary principality (447)—but only to lose it again after a few years through the influence of the opposite party (about 452), and to begin his military career as an exiled prince in the train of the Macedonian generals. Soon his personality asserted itself. He shared in the last campaigns of Antigonus; and the old marshal of Alexander took delight in the born soldier, who in the judgment of the grey-headed general only wanted years to be already the first warrior of the age. The unfortunate battle at Ipsus brought him as a hostage to Alexandria, to the court of the founder of the Lagid dynasty, where by his daring and downright character, and his soldierly spirit thoroughly despising everything that was not military, he attracted the attention of the politic king Ptolemy no less than he attracted the notice of the royal ladies by his manly beauty, which was not impaired by his wild look and stately tread. Just at this time the enterprising Demetrius was once more establishing himself in a new kingdom, which on this occasion was Macedonia; of course with the intention of using it as a lever to revive the monarchy of Alexander. To keep down his ambitious designs, it was important to give him employment at home; and Ptolemy, who knew how to make admirable use of such fiery spirits as the Epirot youth in the prosecution of his subtle policy, not only met the wishes of his consort queen Berenice, but also promoted his own ends, by giving his stepdaughter the princess Antigone in marriage to the young prince, and lending his aid and powerful influence to support the return of his beloved "son" to his native land (458). Restored to his paternal kingdom, he soon carried all before him. The brave Epirots, the Albanians of antiquity, clung with hereditary loyalty and fresh enthusiasm to the high-spirited youth—the "eagle," as they called him. In the confusion that arose regarding the succession to the Macedonian throne after the death of Cassander (457), the Epirot extended his dominions: step by step he gained the regions on the Ambracian gulf with the important town of Ambracia, the island of Corcyra,(2) and even a part of the Macedonian territory, and with forces far inferior he made head against king Demetrius to the admiration of the Macedonians themselves. Indeed, when Demetrius was by his own folly hurled from the Macedonian throne, it was voluntarily proffered by them to his chivalrous opponent, a kinsman of the Alexandrid house (467). No one was in reality worthier than Pyrrhus to wear the royal diadem of Philip and of Alexander. In an age of deep depravity, in which princely rank and baseness began to be synonymous, the personally unspotted and morally pure character of Pyrrhus shone conspicuous. For the free farmers of the hereditary Macedonian soil, who, although diminished and impoverished, were far from sharing in that decay of morals and of valour which the government of the Diadochi produced in Greece and Asia, Pyrrhus appeared exactly formed to be the fitting king, —Pyrrhus, who, like Alexander, in his household and in the circle of his friends preserved a heart open to all human sympathies, and constantly avoided the bearing of an Oriental sultan which was so odious to the Macedonians; and who, like Alexander, was acknowledged to be the first tactician of his time. But the singularly overstrained national feeling of the Macedonians, which preferred the most paltry Macedonian sovereign to the ablest foreigner, and the irrational insubordination of the Macedonian troops towards every non-Macedonian leader, to which Eumenes the Cardian, the greatest general of the school of Alexander, had fallen a victim, put a speedy termination to the rule of the prince of Epirus. Pyrrhus, who could not exercise sovereignty over Macedonia with the consent of the Macedonians, and who was too powerless and perhaps too high spirited to force himself on the nation against its will, after reigning seven months left the country to its native misgovernment, and went home to his faithful Epirots (467). But the man who had worn the crown of Alexander, the brother-in-law of Demetrius, the son-in-law of Ptolemy Lagides and of Agathocles of Syracuse, the highly-trained tactician who wrote memoirs and scientific dissertations on the military art, could not possibly end his days in inspecting at a set time yearly the accounts of the royal cattle steward, in receiving from his brave Epirots their customary gifts of oxen and sheep, in thereupon, at the altar of Zeus, procuring the renewal of their oath of allegiance and repeating his own engagement to respect the laws, and—for the better confirmation of the whole—in carousing with them all night long. If there was no place for him on the throne of Macedonia, there was no abiding in the land of his nativity at all; he was fitted for the first place, and he could not be content with the second. His views therefore turned abroad. The kings, who were quarrelling for the possession of Macedonia, although agreeing in nothing else, were ready and glad to concur in aiding the voluntary departure of their dangerous rival; and that his faithful war-comrades would follow him where-ever he led, he knew full well. Just at that time the circumstances of Italy were such, that the project which had been meditated forty years before by Pyrrhus's kinsman, his father's cousin, Alexander of Epirus, and quite recently by his father-in-law Agathocles, once more seemed feasible; and so Pyrrhus resolved to abandon his Macedonian schemes and to found for himself and for the Hellenic nation a new empire in the west.

Rising of the Italians against Rome—
The Lucanians—
The Etruscans and Celts—
The Samnites—
The Senones Annihilated

The interval of repose, which the peace with Samnium in 464 had procured for Italy, was of brief duration; the impulse which led to the formation of a new league against Roman ascendency came on this occasion from the Lucanians. This people, by taking part with Rome during the Samnite wars, paralyzed the action of the Tarentines and essentially contributed to the decisive issue; and in consideration of their services, the Romans gave up to them the Greek cities in their territory. Accordingly after the conclusion of peace they had, in concert with the Bruttians, set themselves to subdue these cities in succession. The Thurines, repeatedly assailed by Stenius Statilius the general of the Lucanians and reduced to extremities, applied for assistance against the Lucanians to the Roman senate—just as formerly the Campanians had asked the aid of Rome against the Samnites—and beyond doubt with a like sacrifice of their liberty and independence. In consequence of the founding of the fortress Venusia, Rome could dispense with the alliance of the Lucanians; so the Romans granted the prayer of the Thurines, and enjoined their friends and allies to desist from their designs on a city which had surrendered itself to Rome. The Lucanians and Bruttians, thus cheated by their more powerful allies of their share in the common spoil, entered into negotiations with the opposition-party among the Samnites and Tarentines to bring about a new Italian coalition; and when the Romans sent an embassy to warn them, they detained the envoys in captivity and began the war against Rome with a new attack on Thurii (about 469), while at the same time they invited not only the Samnites and Tarentines, but the northern Italians also—the Etruscans, Umbrians, and Gauls—to join them in the struggle for freedom. The Etruscan league actually revolted, and hired numerous bands of Gauls; the Roman army, which the praetor Lucius Caecilius was leading to the help of the Arretines who had remained faithful, was annihilated under the walls of Arretium by the Senonian mercenaries of the Etruscans: the general himself fell with 13,000 of his men (470). The Senones were reckoned allies of Rome; the Romans accordingly sent envoys to them to complain of their furnishing warriors to serve against Rome, and to require the surrender of their captives without ransom. But by the command of their chieftain Britomaris, who had to take vengeance on the Romans for the death of his father, the Senones slew the Roman envoys and openly took the Etruscan side. All the north of Italy, Etruscans, Umbrians, Gauls, were thus in arms against Rome; great results might be achieved, if its southern provinces also should seize the moment and declare, so far as they had not already done so, against Rome. In fact the Samnites, ever ready to make a stand on behalf of liberty, appear to have declared war against the Romans; but weakened and hemmed in on all sides as they were, they could be of little service to the league; and Tarentum manifested its wonted delay. While her antagonists were negotiating alliances, settling treaties as to subsidies, and collecting mercenaries, Rome was acting. The Senones were first made to feel how dangerous it was to gain a victory over the Romans. The consul Publius Cornelius Dolabella advanced with a strong army into their territory; all that were not put to the sword were driven forth from the land, and this tribe was erased from the list of the Italian nations (471). In the case of a people subsisting chiefly on its flocks and herds such an expulsion en masse was quite practicable; and the Senones thus expelled from Italy probably helped to make up the Gallic hosts which soon after inundated the countries of the Danube, Macedonia, Greece, and Asia Minor.

The Boii

The next neighbours and kinsmen of the Senones, the Boii, terrified and exasperated by a catastrophe which had been accomplished with so fearful a rapidity, united instantaneously with the Etruscans, who still continued the war, and whose Senonian mercenaries now fought against the Romans no longer as hirelings, but as desperate avengers of their native land. A powerful Etrusco-Gallic army marched against Rome to retaliate the annihilation of the Senonian tribe on the enemy's capital, and to extirpate Rome from the face of the earth more completely than had been formerly done by the chieftain of these same Senones. But the combined army was decidedly defeated by the Romans at its passage of the Tiber in the neighbourhood of the Vadimonian lake (471). After they had once more in the following year risked a general engagement near Populonia with no better success, the Boii deserted their confederates and concluded a peace on their own account with the Romans (472). Thus the Gauls, the most formidable member of the league, were conquered in detail before the league was fully formed, and by that means the hands of Rome were left free to act against Lower Italy, where during the years 469-471 the contest had not been carried on with any vigour. Hitherto the weak Roman army had with difficulty maintained itself in Thurii against the Lucanians and Bruttians; but now (472) the consul Gaius Fabricius Luscinus appeared with a strong army in front of the town, relieved it, defeated the Lucanians in a great engagement, and took their general Statilius prisoner. The smaller non-Doric Greek towns, recognizing the Romans as their deliverers, everywhere voluntarily joined them. Roman garrisons were left behind in the most important places, in Locri, Croton, Thurii, and especially in Rhegium, on which latter town the Carthaginians seem also to have had designs. Everywhere Rome had most decidedly the advantage. The annihilation of the Senones had given to the Romans a considerable tract of the Adriatic coast. With a view, doubtless, to the smouldering feud with Tarentum and the already threatened invasion of the Epirots, they hastened to make themselves sure of this coast as well as of the Adriatic sea. A burgess colony was sent out (about 471) to the seaport of Sena (Sinigaglia), the former capital of the Senonian territory; and at the same time a Roman fleet sailed from the Tyrrhene sea into the eastern waters, manifestly for the purpose of being stationed in the Adriatic and of protecting the Roman possessions there.

The Tarentines since the treaty of 450 had lived at peace with Rome. They had been spectators of the long struggle of the Samnites, and of the rapid extirpation of the Senones; they had acquiesced without remonstrance in the establishment of Venusia, Atria, and Sena, and in the occupation of Thurii and of Rhegium. But when the Roman fleet, on its voyage from the Tyrrhene to the Adriatic sea, now arrived in the Tarentine waters and cast anchor in the harbour of the friendly city, the long, cherished resentment at length overflowed. Old treaties, which prohibited the war-vessels of Rome from sailing to the east of the Lacinian promontory, were appealed to by popular orators in the assembly of the citizens. A furious mob fell upon the Roman ships of war, which, assailed suddenly in a piratical fashion, succumbed after a sharp struggle; five ships were taken and their crews executed or sold into slavery; the Roman admiral himself had fallen in the engagement. Only the supreme folly and supreme unscrupulousness of mob-rule can account for those disgraceful proceedings. The treaties referred to belonged to a period long past and forgotten; it is clear that they no longer had any meaning, at least subsequently to the founding of Atria and Sena, and that the Romans entered the bay on the faith of the existing alliance; indeed, it was very much their interest—as the further course of things showed—to afford the Tarentines no sort of pretext for declaring war. In declaring war against Rome—if such was their wish—the statesmen of Tarentum were only doing what they should have done long before; and if they preferred to rest their declaration of war upon the formal pretext of a breach of treaty rather than upon the real ground, no further objection could be taken to that course, seeing that diplomacy has always reckoned it beneath its dignity to speak the plain truth in plain language. But to make an armed attack upon the fleet without warning, instead of summoning the admiral to retrace his course, was a foolish no less than a barbarous act—one of those horrible barbarities of civilization, when moral principle suddenly forsakes the helm and the merest coarseness emerges in its room, as if to warn us against the childish belief that civilization is able to extirpate brutality from human nature.

And, as if what they had done had not been enough, the Tarentines after this heroic feat attacked Thurii, the Roman garrison of which capitulated in consequence of the surprise (in the winter of 472-473); and inflicted: severe chastisement on the Thurines—the same, whom Tarentine policy had abandoned to the Lucanians and thereby forcibly constrained into surrender to Rome—for their desertion from the Hellenic party to the barbarians.

Attempts at Peace

The barbarians, however, acted with a moderation which, considering their power and the provocation they had received, excites astonishment. It was the interest of Rome to maintain as long as possible the Tarentine neutrality, and the leading men in the senate accordingly rejected the proposal, which a minority had with natural resentment submitted, to declare war at once against the Tarentines. In fact, the continuance of peace on the part of Rome was proffered on the most moderate terms consistent with her honour—the release of the captives, the restoration of Thurii, the

130

surrender of the originators of the attack on the fleet. A Roman embassy proceeded with these proposals to Tarentum (473), while at the same time, to add weight to their words, a Roman army under the consul Lucius Aemilius advanced into Samnium. The Tarentines could, without forfeiting aught of their independence, accept these terms; and considering the little inclination for war in so wealthy a commercial city, the Romans had reason to presume that an accommodation was still possible. But the attempt to preserve peace failed, whether through the opposition of those Tarentines who recognized the necessity of meeting the aggressions of Rome, the sooner the better, by a resort to arms, or merely through the unruliness of the city rabble, which with characteristic Greek naughtiness subjected the person of the envoy to an unworthy insult. The consul now advanced into the Tarentine territory; but instead of immediately commencing hostilities, he offered once more the same terms of peace; and, when this proved in vain, he began to lay waste the fields and country houses, and he defeated the civic militia. The principal persons captured, however, were released without ransom; and the hope was not abandoned that the pressure of war would give to the aristocratic party ascendency in the city and so bring about peace. The reason of this reserve was, that the Romans were unwilling to drive the city into the arms of the Epirot king. His designs on Italy were no longer a secret. A Tarentine embassy had already gone to Pyrrhus and returned without having accomplished its object. The king had demanded more than it had powers to grant. It was necessary that they should come to a decision. That the civic militia knew only how to run away from the Romans, had been made sufficiently clear. There remained only the choice between a peace with Rome, which the Romans still were ready to agree to on equitable terms, and a treaty with Pyrrhus on any condition that the king might think proper; or, in other words, the choice between submission to the supremacy of Rome, and subjection to the —tyrannis— of a Greek soldier.

Pyrrhus Summoned to Italy

The parties in the city were almost equally balanced. At length the ascendency remained with the national party—a result, that was due partly to the justifiable predilection which led them, if they must yield to a master at all, to prefer a Greek to a barbarian, but partly also to the dread of the demagogues that Rome, notwithstanding the moderation now forced upon it by circumstances, would not neglect on a fitting opportunity to exact vengeance for the outrages perpetrated by the Tarentine rabble. The city, accordingly, came to terms with Pyrrhus. He obtained the supreme command of the troops of the Tarentines and of the other Italians in arms against Rome, along with the right of keeping a garrison in Tarentum. The expenses of the war were, of course, to be borne by the city. Pyrrhus, on the other hand, promised to remain no longer in Italy than was necessary; probably with the tacit reservation that his own judgment should fix the time during which he would be needed there. Nevertheless, the prey had almost slipped out of his hands. While the Tarentine envoys—the chiefs, no doubt, of the war party—were absent in Epirus, the state of feeling in the city, now hard pressed by the Romans, underwent a change. The chief command was already entrusted to Agis, a man favourable to Rome, when the return of the envoys with the concluded treaty, accompanied by Cineas the confidential minister of Pyrrhus, again brought the war party to the helm.

Landing of Pyrrhus

A firmer hand now grasped the reins, and put an end to the pitiful vacillation. In the autumn of 473 Milo, the general of Pyrrhus, landed with 3000 Epirots and occupied the citadel of the town. He was followed in the beginning of the year 474 by the king himself, who landed after a stormy passage in which many lives were lost. He transported to Tarentum a respectable but miscellaneous army, consisting partly of the household troops, Molossians, Thesprotians, Chaonians, and Ambraciots; partly of the Macedonian infantry and the Thessalian cavalry, which Ptolemy king of Macedonia had conformably to stipulation handed over to him; partly of Aetolian, Acarnanian, and Athamanian mercenaries. Altogether it numbered 20,000 phalangitae, 2000 archers, 500 slingers, 3000 cavalry, and 20 elephants, and thus was not much smaller than the army with which fifty years before Alexander had crossed the Hellespont

Pyrrhus and the Coalition

The affairs of the coalition were in no very favourable state when the king arrived. The Roman consul indeed, as soon as he saw the soldiers of Milo taking the field against him instead of the Tarentine militia, had abandoned the attack on Tarentum and retreated to Apulia; but, with the exception of the territory of Tarentum, the Romans virtually ruled all Italy. The coalition had no army in the field anywhere in Lower Italy; and in Upper Italy the Etruscans, who alone were still in arms, had in the last campaign (473) met with nothing but defeat. The allies had, before the king embarked, committed to him the chief command of all their troops, and declared that they were able to place in the field an army of 350,000 infantry and 20,000 cavalry. The reality formed a sad contrast to these great promises. The army, whose chief command had been committed to Pyrrhus, had still to be created; and for the time being the main resources available for forming it were those of Tarentum alone. The king gave orders for the enlisting of an army of Italian mercenaries with Tarentine money, and called out the able-bodied citizens to serve in the war. But the Tarentines had not so understood the agreement. They had thought to purchase victory, like any other commodity, with money; it was a sort of breach of contract, that the king should compel them to fight for it themselves. The more glad the citizens had been at first after Milo's arrival to be quit of the burdensome service of mounting guard, the more unwillingly they now rallied to the standards of the king: it was necessary to threaten the negligent with the penalty of death. This result now justified the peace party in the eyes of all, and communications were entered into, or at any rate appeared to have been entered into, even with Rome. Pyrrhus, prepared for such opposition, immediately treated Tarentum as a conquered city; soldiers were quartered in the houses, the assemblies of the people and the numerous clubs (—-sussitia—) were suspended, the theatre was shut, the promenades were closed, and the gates were occupied with Epirot guards. A number of the leading men were sent over the sea as hostages; others escaped the like fate by flight to Rome. These strict measures were necessary, for it was absolutely impossible in any sense to rely upon the Tarentines. It was only now that the king, in possession of that important city as a basis, could begin operations in the field.

Preparations in Rome—
Commencement of the Conflict in Lower Italy

The Romans too were well aware of the conflict which awaited them. In order first of all to secure the fidelity of their allies or, in other words, of their subjects, the towns that could not be depended on were garrisoned, and the leaders of the party of independence, where it seemed needful, were arrested or executed: such was the case with a number of the members of the senate of Praeneste. For the war itself great exertions were made; a war contribution was levied; the full contingent was called forth from all their subjects and allies; even the proletarians who were properly exempt from obligation of service were called to arms. A Roman army remained as a reserve in the capital. A second advanced under the consul Tiberius Coruncanius into Etruria, and dispersed the forces of Volci and Volsinii. The main force was of course destined for Lower Italy; its departure was hastened as much as possible, in order to reach Pyrrhus while still in the territory of Tarentum, and to prevent him and his forces from forming a junction with the Samnites and other south Italian levies that were in arms against Rome. The Roman garrisons, that were placed in the Greek towns of Lower Italy, were intended temporarily to check the king's progress. But the mutiny of the troops stationed in Rhegium—one of the legions levied from the Campanian subjects of Rome under a Campanian captain Decius—deprived the Romans of that important town. It was not, however, transferred to the hands of Pyrrhus. While on the one hand the national hatred of the Campanians against the Romans undoubtedly contributed to produce this military insurrection, it was impossible on the other hand that Pyrrhus, who had crossed the sea to shield and protect the Hellenes, could receive as his allies troops who had put to death their Rhegine hosts in their own houses. Thus they remained isolated, in close league with their kinsmen and comrades in crime, the Mamertines, that is, the Campanian mercenaries of Agathocles, who had by similar means gained possession of Messana on the opposite side of the straits; and they pillaged and laid waste for their own behoof the adjacent Greek towns, such as Croton, where they put to death the Roman garrison, and Caulonia, which they destroyed. On the other hand the Romans succeeded, by means of a weak corps which advanced along the Lucanian frontier and of the garrison of Venusia, in preventing the Lucanians and Samnites from uniting with Pyrrhus; while the main force—four legions as it would appear, and so, with a corresponding number of allied troops, at least 50,000 strong—-marched against Pyrrhus, under the consul Publius Laevinus.

Battle near Heraclea

With a view to cover the Tarentine colony of Heraclea, the king had taken up a position with his own and the Tarentine troops between that city and Pandosia (3) (474). The Romans, covered by their cavalry, forced the passage of the Siris, and opened the battle with a vehement and successful cavalry charge; the king, who led his cavalry in person, was thrown from his horse, and the Greek horsemen, panic-struck by the disappearance of their leader, abandoned the field to the squadrons of the enemy. Pyrrhus, however, put himself at the head of his infantry, and began a fresh and more decisive engagement. Seven times the legions and the phalanx met in shock of battle, and still the conflict was undecided. Then Megacles, one of the best officers of the king, fell, and, because on this hotly-contested day he had worn the king's armour, the army for the second time believed that the king had fallen; the ranks wavered; Laevinus already felt sure of the victory and threw the whole of his cavalry on the flank of the Greeks. But Pyrrhus, marching with uncovered head through the ranks of the infantry, revived the sinking courage of his troops. The elephants which had hitherto been kept in reserve were brought up to meet the cavalry; the horses took fright at them; the soldiers, not knowing how to encounter the huge beasts, turned and fled; the masses of disordered horsemen and the pursuing elephants at length broke the compact ranks of the Roman infantry, and the elephants in concert with the excellent Thessalian cavalry wrought great slaughter among the fugitives. Had not a brave Roman soldier, Gaius Minucius, the first hastate of the fourth legion, wounded one of the elephants and thereby thrown the pursuing troops into confusion, the Roman army would have been extirpated; as it was, the remainder of the Roman troops succeeded in retreating across the Siris. Their loss was great; 7000 Romans were found by the victors dead or wounded on the field of battle, 2000 were brought in prisoners; the Romans themselves stated their loss, including probably the wounded carried off the field, at 15,000 men. But Pyrrhus's army had suffered not much less: nearly 4000 of his best soldiers strewed the field of battle, and several of his ablest captains had fallen. Considering that his loss fell chiefly on the veteran soldiers who were far more difficult to be replaced than the Roman militia, and that he owed his victory only to the surprise produced by the attack of the elephants which could not be often repeated, the king, skilful judge of tactics as he was, may well at an after period have described this victory as resembling a defeat; although he was not so foolish as to communicate that piece of self-criticism to the public—as the Roman poets afterwards invented the story—in the inscription of the votive offering presented by him at Tarentum. Politically it mattered little in the first instance at what sacrifices the victory was bought; the gain of the first battle against the Romans was of inestimable value for Pyrrhus. His talents as a general had been brilliantly displayed on this new field of battle, and if anything could breathe unity and energy into the languishing league of the Italians, the victory of Heraclea could not fail to do so. But even the immediate results of the victory were considerable and lasting. Lucania was lost to the Romans: Laevinus collected the troops stationed there and marched to Apulia, The Bruttians, Lucanians, and Samnites joined Pyrrhus unmolested. With the exception of Rhegium, which pined under the oppression of the Campanian mutineers, the whole of the Greek cities joined the king, and Locri even voluntarily delivered up to him the Roman garrison; in his case they were persuaded, and with reason, that they would not be abandoned to the Italians. The Sabellians and Greeks thus passed over to Pyrrhus; but the victory produced no further effect. The Latins showed no inclination to get quit of the Roman rule, burdensome as it might be, by the help of a foreign dynast. Venusia, although now wholly surrounded by enemies, adhered with unshaken steadfastness to Rome. Pyrrhus proposed to the prisoners taken on the Siris, whose brave demeanour the chivalrous king requited by the most honourable treatment, that they should enter his army in accordance with the Greek fashion; but he learned that he was fighting not with mercenaries, but with a nation. Not one, either Roman or Latin, took service with him.

Attempts at Peace

Pyrrhus offered peace to the Romans. He was too sagacious a soldier not to recognize the precariousness of his footing, and too skilled a statesman not to profit opportunely by the moment which placed him in the most favourable position for the conclusion of peace. He now hoped that under the first impression made by the great battle on the Romans he should be able to secure the freedom of the Greek towns in Italy, and to call into existence between them and Rome a series of states of the second and third order as dependent allies of the new Greek power; for such was the tenor of his demands: the release of all Greek towns—and therefore of the Campanian and Lucanian towns in particular—from allegiance to Rome, and restitution of the territory taken from the Samnites, Daunians, Lucanians, and Bruttians, or in other words especially the surrender of Luceria and Venusia. If a further struggle with Rome could hardly be avoided, it was not desirable at any rate to begin it till the western Hellenes should be united under one ruler, till Sicily should be acquired and perhaps Africa be conquered.

Provided with such instructions, the Thessalian Cineas, the confidential minister of Pyrrhus, went to Rome. That dexterous negotiator, whom his contemporaries compared to Demosthenes so far as a rhetorician might be compared to a statesman and the minister of a sovereign to a popular leader, had orders to display by every means the respect which the victor of Heraclea really felt for his vanquished opponents, to make known the wish of the king to come to Rome in person, to influence men's minds in the king's favour by panegyrics which sound so well in the mouth of an enemy, by earnest flatteries, and, as opportunity offered, also by well-timed gifts—in short to try upon the Romans all the arts of cabinet policy, as they had been tested at the courts of Alexandria and Antioch. The senate hesitated; to many it seemed a prudent course to draw back a step and to wait till their dangerous antagonist should have further entangled himself or should be no more. But the grey-haired and blind consular Appius Claudius (censor 442, consul 447, 458), who had long withdrawn from state affairs but had himself conducted at this decisive moment to the senate, breathed the unbroken energy of his own vehement nature with words of fire into the souls of the younger generation. They gave to the message of the king the proud reply, which was first heard on this occasion and became thenceforth a maxim of the state, that Rome never negotiated so long as there were foreign troops on Italian ground; and to make good their words they dismissed the ambassador at once from the city. The object of the mission had failed, and the dexterous diplomatist, instead of producing an effect by his oratorical art, had on the contrary been himself impressed by such manly earnestness after so severe a defeat—he declared at home that every burgess in that city had seemed to him a king; in truth, the courtier had gained a sight of a free people.

Pyrrhus Marches against Rome

Pyrrhus, who during these negotiations had advanced into Campania, immediately on the news of their being broken off marched against Rome, to co-operate with the Etruscans, to shake the allies of Rome, and to threaten the city itself. But the

Romans as little allowed themselves to be terrified as cajoled. At the summons of the herald "to enrol in the room of the fallen," the young men immediately after the battle of Heraclea had pressed forward in crowds to enlist; with the two newly-formed legions and the corps withdrawn from Lucania, Laevinus, stronger than before, followed the march of the king. He protected Capua against him, and frustrated his endeavours to enter into communications with Neapolis. So firm was the attitude of the Romans that, excepting the Greeks of Lower Italy, no allied state of any note dared to break off from the Roman alliance. Then Pyrrhus turned against Rome itself. Through a rich country, whose flourishing condition he beheld with astonishment, he marched against Fregellae which he surprised, forced the passage of the Liris, and reached Anagnia, which is not more than forty miles from Rome. No army crossed his path; but everywhere the towns of Latium closed their gates against him, and with measured step Laevinus followed him from Campania, while the consul Tiberius Coruncanius, who had just concluded a seasonable peace with the Etruscans, brought up a second Roman army from the north, and in Rome itself the reserve was preparing for battle under the dictator Gnaeus Domitius Calvinus. In these circumstances Pyrrhus could accomplish nothing; no course was left to him but to retire. For a time he still remained inactive in Campania in presence of the united armies of the two consuls; but no opportunity occurred of striking an effective blow. When winter came on, the king evacuated the enemy's territory, and distributed his troops among the friendly towns, taking up his own winter quarters in Tarentum. Thereupon the Romans also desisted from their operations. The army occupied standing quarters near Firmum in Picenum, where by command of the senate the legions defeated on the Siris spent the winter by way of punishment under tents.

Second Year of the War

Thus ended the campaign of 474. The separate peace which at the decisive moment Etruria had concluded with Rome, and the king's unexpected retreat which entirely disappointed the high-strung hopes of the Italian confederates, counterbalanced in great measure the impression of the victory of Heraclea. The Italians complained of the burdens of the war, particularly of the bad discipline of the mercenaries quartered among them, and the king, weary of the petty quarrelling and of the impolitic as well as unmilitary conduct of his allies, began to have a presentiment that the problem which had fallen to him might be, despite all tactical successes, politically insoluble. The arrival of a Roman embassy of three consulars, including Gaius Fabricius the conqueror of Thurii, again revived in him for a moment the hopes of peace; but it soon appeared that they had only power to treat for the ransom or exchange of prisoners. Pyrrhus rejected their demand, but at the festival of the Saturnalia he released all the prisoners on their word of honour. Their keeping of that word, and the repulse by the Roman ambassador of an attempt at bribery, were celebrated by posterity in a manner most unbecoming and betokening rather the dishonourable character of the later, than the honourable feeling of that earlier, epoch.

Battle of Ausculum

In the spring of 475 Pyrrhus resumed the offensive, and advanced into Apulia, whither the Roman army marched to meet him. In the hope of shaking the Roman symmachy in these regions by a decisive victory, the king offered battle a second time, and the Romans did not refuse it. The two armies encountered each other near Ausculum (Ascoli di Puglia). Under the banners of Pyrrhus there fought, besides his Epirot and Macedonian troops, the Italian mercenaries, the burgess-force—the white shields as they were called—of Tarentum, and the allied Lucanians, Bruttians, and Samnites—altogether 70,000 infantry, of whom 16,000 were Greeks and Epirots, more than 8000 cavalry, and nineteen elephants. The Romans were supported on that day by the Latins, Campanians, Volscians, Sabines, Umbrians, Marrucinians, Paelignians, Frentanians, and Arpanians. They too numbered above 70,000 infantry, of whom 20,000 were Roman citizens, and 8000 cavalry. Both parties had made alterations in their military system. Pyrrhus, perceiving with the sharp eye of a soldier the advantages of the Roman manipular organization, had on the wings substituted for the long front of his phalanxes an arrangement by companies with intervals between them in imitation of the cohorts, and— perhaps for political no less than for military reasons—had placed the Tarentine and Samnite cohorts between the subdivisions of his own men. In the centre alone the Epirot phalanx stood in close order. For the purpose of keeping off the elephants the Romans produced a species of war-chariot, from which projected iron poles furnished with chafing-dishes, and on which were fastened moveable masts adjusted with a view to being lowered, and ending in an iron spike—in some degree the model of the boarding-bridges which were to play so great a part in the first Punic war.

According to the Greek account of the battle, which seems less one-sided than the Roman account also extant, the Greeks had the disadvantage on the first day, as they did not succeed in deploying their line along the steep and marshy banks of the river where they were compelled to accept battle, or in bringing their cavalry and elephants into action. On the second day, however, Pyrrhus anticipated the Romans in occupying the intersected ground, and thus gained without loss the plain where he could without disturbance draw up his phalanx. Vainly did the Romans with desperate courage fall sword in hand on the -sarissae-; the phalanx preserved an unshaken front under every assault, but in its turn was unable to make any impression on the Roman legions. It was not till the numerous escort of the elephants had, with arrows and stones hurled from slings, dislodged the combatants stationed in the Roman war-chariots and had cut the traces of the horses, and the elephants pressed upon the Roman line, that it began to waver. The giving way of the guard attached to the Roman chariots formed the signal for universal flight, which, however, did not involve the sacrifice of many lives, as the adjoining camp received the fugitives. The Roman account of the battle alone mentions the circumstance, that during the principal engagement an Arpanian corps detached from the Roman main force had attacked and set on fire the weakly-guarded Epirot camp; but, even if this were correct, the Romans are not at all justified in their assertion that the battle remained undecided. Both accounts, on the contrary, agree in stating that the Roman army retreated across the river, and that Pyrrhus remained in possession of the field of battle. The number of the fallen was, according to the Greek account, 6000 on the side of the Romans, 3505 on that of the Greeks.(4) Amongst the wounded was the king himself, whose arm had been pierced with a javelin, while he was fighting, as was his wont, in the thickest of the fray. Pyrrhus had achieved a victory, but his were unfruitful laurels; the victory was creditable to the king as a general and as a soldier, but it did not promote his political designs. What Pyrrhus needed was a brilliant success which should break up the Roman army and give an opportunity and impulse to the wavering allies to change sides; but the Roman army and the Roman confederacy still remained unbroken, and the Greek army, which was nothing without its leader, was fettered for a considerable time in consequence of his wound. He was obliged to renounce the campaign and to go into winter quarters; which the king took up in Tarentum, the Romans on this occasion in Apulia. It was becoming daily more evident that in a military point of view the resources of the king were inferior to those of the Romans, just as, politically, the loose and refractory coalition could not stand a comparison with the firmly-established Roman symmachy. The sudden and vehement style of the Greek warfare and the genius of the general might perhaps achieve another such victory as those of Heraclea and Ausculum, but every new victory was wearing out his resources for further enterprise, and it was clear that the Romans already felt themselves the stronger, and awaited with a courageous patience final victory. Such a war as this was not the delicate game of art that was practised and understood by the Greek princes. All strategical combinations were shattered against the full and mighty energy of the national levy. Pyrrhus felt how matters stood: weary of his victories and despising his allies, he only persevered because military honour required him not to leave Italy till he should have secured his clients from barbarian assault. With his impatient temperament it might be presumed that he would embrace the first pretext to get rid of the burdensome duty; and an opportunity of withdrawing from Italy was soon presented to him by the affairs of Sicily.

Relations of Sicily, Syracuse, and Carthage—
Pyrrhus Invited to Syracuse

After the death of Agathocles (465) the Greeks of Sicily were without any leading power. While in the several Hellenic cities incapable demagogues and incapable tyrants were replacing each other, the Carthaginians, the old rulers of the western point, were extending their dominion unmolested. After Agrigentum had surrendered to them, they believed that the time had come for taking final steps towards the end which they had kept in view for centuries, and for reducing the whole island under their authority; they set themselves to attack Syracuse. That city, which formerly by its armies and fleets had disputed the possession of the island with Carthage, had through internal dissension and the weakness of its government fallen so low that it was obliged to seek for safety in the protection of its walls and in foreign aid; and none could afford that aid but king Pyrrhus. Pyrrhus was the husband of Agathocles's daughter, and his son Alexander, then sixteen years of age, was Agathocles's grandson. Both were in every respect natural heirs of the ambitious schemes of the ruler of Syracuse; and if her freedom was at an end, Syracuse might find compensation in becoming the capital of a Hellenic empire of the West. So the Syracusans, like the Tarentines, and under similar conditions, voluntarily offered their sovereignty to king Pyrrhus (about 475); and by a singular conjuncture of affairs everything seemed to concur towards the success of the magnificent plans of the Epirot king, based as they primarily were on the possession of Tarentum and Syracuse.

League between Rome and Carthage—
Third Year of the War

The immediate effect, indeed, of this union of the Italian and Sicilian Greeks under one control was a closer concert also on the part of their antagonists. Carthage and Rome now converted their old commercial treaties into an offensive and defensive league against Pyrrhus (475), the tenor of which was that, if Pyrrhus invaded Roman or Carthaginian territory, the party which was not attacked should furnish that which was assailed with a contingent on its own territory and should itself defray the expense of the auxiliary troops; that in such an event Carthage should be bound to furnish transports and to assist the Romans also with a war fleet, but the crews of that fleet should not be obliged to fight for the Romans by land; that lastly, both states should pledge themselves not to conclude a separate peace with Pyrrhus. The object of the Romans in entering into the treaty was to render possible an attack on Tarentum and to cut off Pyrrhus from his own country, neither of which ends could be attained without the co-operation of the Punic fleet; the object of the Carthaginians was to detain the king in Italy, so that they might be able without molestation to carry into effect their designs on Syracuse.(5) It was accordingly the interest of both powers in the first instance to secure the sea between Italy and Sicily. A powerful Carthaginian fleet of 120 sail under the admiral Mago proceeded from Ostia, whither Mago seems to have gone to conclude the treaty, to the Sicilian straits. The Mamertines, who anticipated righteous punishment for their outrage upon the Greek population of Messana in the event of Pyrrhus becoming ruler of Sicily and Italy, attached themselves closely to the Romans and Carthaginians, and secured for them the Sicilian side of the straits. The allies would willingly have brought Rhegium also on the opposite coast under their power; but Rome could not possibly pardon the Campanian garrison, and an attempt of the combined Romans and Carthaginians to gain the city by force of arms miscarried. The Carthaginian fleet sailed thence for Syracuse and blockaded the city by sea, while at the same time a strong Phoenician army began the siege by land (476). It was high time that Pyrrhus should appear at Syracuse: but, in fact, matters in Italy were by no means in such a condition that he and his troops could be dispensed with there. The two consuls of 476, Gaius Fabricius Luscinus, and Quintus Aemilius Papus, both experienced generals, had begun the new campaign with vigour, and although the Romans had hitherto sustained nothing but defeat in this war, it was not they but the victors that were weary of it and longed for peace. Pyrrhus made another attempt to obtain accommodation on tolerable terms. The consul Fabricius had handed over to the king a wretch, who had proposed to poison him on condition of being well paid for it. Not only did the king in token of gratitude release all his Roman prisoners without ransom, but he felt himself so moved by the generosity of his brave opponents that he offered, by way of personal recompense, a singularly fair and favourable peace. Cineas appears to have gone once more to Rome, and Carthage seems to have been seriously apprehensive that Rome might come to terms. But the senate remained firm, and repeated its former answer. Unless the king was willing to allow Syracuse to fall into the hands of the Carthaginians and to have his grand scheme thereby disconcerted, no other course remained than to abandon his Italian allies and to confine himself for the time being to the occupation of the most important seaports, particularly Tarentum and Locri. In vain the Lucanians and Samnites conjured him not to desert them; in vain the Tarentines summoned him either to comply with his duty as their general or to give them back their city. The king met their complaints and reproaches with the consolatory assurance that better times were coming, or with abrupt dismissal. Milo remained behind in Tarentum; Alexander, the king's son, in Locri; and Pyrrhus, with his main force, embarked in the spring of 476 at Tarentum for Syracuse.

Embarkation of Pyrrhus for Sicily—
The War in Italy Flags

By the departure of Pyrrhus the hands of the Romans were set free in Italy; none ventured to oppose them in the open field, and their antagonists everywhere confined themselves to their fastnesses or their forests. The struggle however was not terminated so rapidly as might have been expected; partly in consequence of its nature as a warfare of mountain skirmishes and sieges, partly also, doubtless, from the exhaustion of the Romans, whose fearful losses are indicated by a decrease of 17,000 in the burgess-roll from 473 to 479. In 476 the consul Gaius Fabricius succeeded in inducing the considerable Tarentine settlement of Heraclea to enter into a separate peace, which was granted to it on the most favourable terms. In the campaign of 477 a desultory warfare was carried on in Samnium, where an attack thoughtlessly made on some entrenched heights cost the Romans many lives, and thereafter in southern Italy, where the Lucanians and Bruttians were defeated. On the other hand Milo, issuing from Tarentum, anticipated the Romans in their attempt to surprise Croton: whereupon the Epirot garrison made even a successful sortie against the besieging army. At length, however, the consul succeeded by a stratagem in inducing it to march forth, and in possessing himself of the undefended town (477). An incident of more moment was the slaughter of the Epirot garrison by the Locrians, who had formerly surrendered the Roman garrison to the king, and now atoned for one act of treachery by another. By that step the whole south coast came into the hands of the Romans, with the exception of Rhegium and Tarentum. These successes, however, advanced the main object but little. Lower Italy itself had long been defenceless; but Pyrrhus was not subdued so long as Tarentum remained in his hands and thus rendered it possible for him to renew the war at his pleasure, and the Romans could not think of undertaking the siege of that city. Even apart from the fact that in siege-warfare, which had been revolutionized by Philip of Macedonia and Demetrius Poliorcetes, the Romans were at a very decided disadvantage when matched against an experienced and resolute Greek commandant, a strong fleet was needed for such an enterprise, and, although the Carthaginian treaty promised to the Romans support by sea, the affairs of Carthage herself in Sicily were by no means in such a condition as to enable her to grant that support.

Pyrrhus Master of Sicily

The landing of Pyrrhus on the island, which, in spite of the Carthaginian fleet, had taken place without interruption, had changed at once the aspect of matters there. He had immediately relieved Syracuse, had in a short time united under his sway all the free Greek cities, and at the head of the Sicilian confederation had wrested from the Carthaginians nearly their whole possessions. It was with difficulty that the Carthaginians could, by the help of their fleet which at that time ruled the Mediterranean without a rival, maintain themselves in Lilybaeum; it was with difficulty, and amidst constant assaults, that the Mamertines held their ground in Messana. Under such circumstances, agreeably to the treaty of 475, it would have been the duty of Rome to lend her aid to the Carthaginians in Sicily, far rather than that of Carthage to help the Romans with her fleet to conquer Tarentum; but on the side of neither ally was there much inclination to secure or to extend the power of the other. Carthage had only offered help to the Romans when the real danger was past; they in their turn had done nothing to prevent the departure of the king from Italy and the fall of the Carthaginian power in Sicily. Indeed, in open violation of the treaties Carthage had even proposed to the king a separate peace, offering, in return for the undisturbed possession of Lilybaeum, to give up all claim to her other Sicilian possessions and even to place at the disposal of the king money and ships of war, of course with a view to his crossing to Italy and renewing the war against Rome. It was evident, however, that with the possession of Lilybaeum and the departure of the king the position of the Carthaginians in the island would be nearly the same as it had been before the landing of Pyrrhus; the Greek cities if left to themselves were powerless, and the lost territory would be easily regained. So Pyrrhus rejected the doubly perfidious proposal, and proceeded to build for himself a war fleet. Mere ignorance and shortsightedness in after times censured this step; but it was really as necessary as it was, with the resources of the island, easy of accomplishment. Apart from the consideration that the master of Ambracia, Tarentum, and Syracuse could not dispense with a naval force, he needed a fleet to conquer Lilybaeum, to protect Tarentum, and to attack Carthage at home as Agathocles, Regulus, and Scipio did before or afterwards so successfully. Pyrrhus never was so near to the attainment of his aim as in the summer of 478, when he saw Carthage humbled before him, commanded Sicily, and retained a firm footing in Italy by the possession of Tarentum, and when the newly-created fleet, which was to connect, to secure, and to augment these successes, lay ready for sea in the harbour of Syracuse.

The Sicilian Government of Pyrrhus

The real weakness of the position of Pyrrhus lay in his faulty internal policy. He governed Sicily as he had seen Ptolemy rule in Egypt: he showed no respect to the local constitutions; he placed his confidants as magistrates over the cities whenever, and for as long as, he pleased; he made his courtiers judges instead of the native jurymen; he pronounced arbitrary sentences of confiscation, banishment, or death, even against those who had been most active in promoting his coming thither; he placed garrisons in the towns, and ruled over Sicily not as the leader of a national league, but as a king. In so doing he probably reckoned himself according to oriental-Hellenistic ideas a good and wise ruler, and perhaps he really was so; but the Greeks bore this transplantation of the system of the Diadochi to Syracuse with all the impatience of a nation that in its long struggle for freedom had lost all habits of discipline; the Carthaginian yoke very soon appeared to the foolish people more tolerable than their new military government. The most important cities entered into communications with the Carthaginians, and even with the Mamertines; a strong Carthaginian army ventured again to appear on the island; and everywhere supported by the Greeks, it made rapid progress. In the battle which Pyrrhus fought with it fortune was, as always, with the "Eagle"; but the circumstances served to show what the state of feeling was in the island, and what might and must ensue, if the king should depart.

Departure of Pyrrhus to Italy

To this first and most essential error Pyrrhus added a second; he proceeded with his fleet, not to Lilybaeum, but to Tarentum. It was evident, looking to the very ferment in the minds of the Sicilians, that he ought first of all to have dislodged the Carthaginians wholly from the island, and thereby to have cut off the discontented from their last support, before he turned his attention to Italy; in that quarter there was nothing to be lost, for Tarentum was safe enough for him, and the other allies were of little moment now that they had been abandoned. It is conceivable that his soldierly spirit impelled him to wipe off the stain of his not very honourable departure in the year 476 by a brilliant return, and that his heart bled when he heard the complaints of the Lucanians and Samnites. But problems, such as Pyrrhus had proposed to himself, can only be solved by men of iron nature, who are able to control their feelings of compassion and even their sense of honour; and Pyrrhus was not one of these.

Fall of the Sicilian Kingdom—
Recommencement of the Italian War

The fatal embarkation took place towards the end of 478. On the voyage the new Syracusan fleet had to sustain a sharp engagement with that of Carthage, in which it lost a considerable number of vessels. The departure of the king and the accounts of this first misfortune sufficed for the fall of the Sicilian kingdom. On the arrival of the news all the cities refused to the absent king money and troops; and the brilliant state collapsed even more rapidly than it had arisen, partly because the king had himself undermined in the hearts of his subjects the loyalty and affection on which every commonwealth depends, partly because the people lacked the devotedness to renounce freedom for perhaps but a short term in order to save their nationality. Thus the enterprise of Pyrrhus was wrecked, and the plan of his life was ruined irretrievably; he was thenceforth an adventurer, who felt that he had been great and was so no longer, and who now waged war no longer as a means to an end, but in order to drown thought amidst the reckless excitement of the game and to find, if possible, in the tumult of battle a soldier's death. Arrived on the Italian coast, the king began by an attempt to get possession of Rhegium; but the Campanians repulsed the attack with the aid of the Mamertines, and in the heat of the conflict before the town the king himself was wounded in the act of striking down an officer of the enemy. On the other hand he surprised Locri, whose inhabitants suffered severely for their slaughter of the Epirot garrison, and he plundered the rich treasury of the temple of Persephone there, to replenish his empty exchequer. Thus he arrived at Tarentum, it is said with 20,000 infantry and 3000 cavalry. But these were no longer the experienced veterans of former days, and the Italians no longer hailed them as deliverers; the confidence and hope with which they had received the king five years before were gone; the allies were destitute of money and of men.

Battle near Beneventum—
Pyrrhus Leaves Italy—
Death of Pyrrhus

The king took the field in the spring of 479 with the view of aiding the hard-pressed Samnites, in whose territory the Romans had passed the previous winter; and he forced the consul Manius Curius to give battle near Beneventum on the -campus Arusinus-, before he could form a junction with his colleague advancing from Lucania. But the division of the army, which was intended to take the Romans in flank, lost its way during its night march in the woods, and failed to appear at the decisive moment; and after a hot conflict the elephants again decided the battle, but decided it this time in favour of the Romans, for, thrown into confusion by the archers who were stationed to protect the camp, they attacked their own people. The victors occupied the camp; there fell into their hands 1300 prisoners and four elephants—the first that were seen in Rome—besides an immense spoil, from the proceeds of which the aqueduct, which conveyed the water of the Anio from Tibur to Rome, was subsequently built. Without troops to keep the field and without money, Pyrrhus applied to his allies who had contributed to his equipment for Italy, the kings of Macedonia and Asia; but even in his native land he was no longer feared, and his request was refused. Despairing of success against Rome and exasperated by these refusals, Pyrrhus left a garrison in Tarentum, and went home himself in the same year (479) to Greece, where some prospect of gain might open up to the desperate player sooner than amidst the steady and measured course of Italian affairs. In fact, he not only rapidly recovered the portion of his kingdom that had been taken away, but once more grasped, and not without success, at the Macedonian throne. But his last plans also were thwarted by the calm and cautious policy of Antigonus Gonatas, and still more by his own vehemence and inability to tame his proud spirit; he still gained battles, but he no longer gained any lasting success, and met his death in a miserable street combat in Peloponnesian Argos (482).

Last Struggles in Italy—
Capture of Tarentum

In Italy the war came to an end with the battle of Beneventum; the last convulsive struggles of the national party died slowly away. So long indeed as the warrior prince, whose mighty arm had ventured to seize the reins of destiny in Italy, was still among the living, he held, even when absent, the stronghold of Tarentum against Rome. Although after the departure of the king the peace party recovered ascendency in the city, Milo, who commanded there on behalf of Pyrrhus, rejected their suggestions and allowed the citizens favourable to Rome, who had erected a separate fort for themselves in the territory of Tarentum, to conclude peace with

Rome as they pleased, without on that account opening his gates. But when after the death of Pyrrhus a Carthaginian fleet entered the harbour, and Milo saw that the citizens were on the point of delivering up the city to the Carthaginians, he preferred to hand over the citadel to the Roman consul Lucius Papirius (482), and by that means to secure a free departure for himself and his troops. For the Romans this was an immense piece of good fortune. After the experiences of Philip before Perinthus and Byzantium, of Demetrius before Rhodes, and of Pyrrhus before Lilybaeum, it may be doubted whether the strategy of that period was at all able to compel the surrender of a town well fortified, well defended, and freely accessible by sea; and how different a turn matters might have taken, had Tarentum become to the Phoenicians in Italy what Lilybaeum was to them in Sicily! What was done, however, could not be undone. The Carthaginian admiral, when he saw the citadel in the hands of the Romans, declared that he had only appeared before Tarentum conformably to the treaty to lend assistance to his allies in the siege of the town, and set sail for Africa; and the Roman embassy, which was sent to Carthage to demand explanations and make complaints regarding the attempted occupation of Tarentum, brought back nothing but a solemn confirmation on oath of that allegation as to its ally's friendly design, with which accordingly the Romans had for the time to rest content. The Tarentines obtained from Rome, presumably on the intercession of their emigrants, the restoration of autonomy; but their arms and ships had to be given up and their walls had to be pulled down.

Submission of Lower Italy

In the same year, in which Tarentum became Roman, the Samnites, Lucanians, and Bruttians finally submitted. The latter were obliged to cede the half of the lucrative, and for ship-building important, forest of Sila.

At length also the band that for ten years had sheltered themselves in Rhegium were duly chastised for the breach of their military oath, as well as for the murder of the citizens of Rhegium and of the garrison of Croton. In this instance Rome, while vindicating her own rights vindicated the general cause of the Hellenes against the barbarians. Hiero, the new ruler of Syracuse, accordingly supported the Romans before Rhegium by sending supplies and a contingent, and in combination with the Roman expedition against the garrison of Rhegium he made an attack upon their fellow-countrymen and fellow-criminals, the Mamertines of Messana. The siege of the latter town was long protracted. On the other hand Rhegium, although the mutineers resisted long and obstinately, was stormed by the Romans in 484; the survivors of the garrison were scourged and beheaded in the public market at Rome, while the old inhabitants were recalled and, as far as possible, reinstated in their possessions. Thus all Italy was, in 484, reduced to subjection. The Samnites alone, the most obstinate antagonists of Rome, still in spite of the official conclusion of peace continued the struggle as "robbers," so that in 485 both consuls had to be once more despatched against them. But even the most high-spirited national courage—-the bravery of despair—comes to an end; the sword and the gibbet at length carried quiet even into the mountains of Samnium.

Construction of New Fortresses and Roads

For the securing of these immense acquisitions a new series of colonies was instituted: Paestum and Cosa in Lucania (481); Beneventum (486), and Aesernia (about 491) to hold Samnium in check; and, as outposts against the Gauls, Ariminum (486), Firmum in Picenum (about 490), and the burgess colony of Castrum Novum. Preparations were made for the continuation of the great southern highway—which acquired in the fortress of Beneventum a new station intermediate between Capua and Venusia—as far as the seaports of Tarentum and Brundisium, and for the colonization of the latter seaport, which Roman policy had selected as the rival and successor of the Tarentine emporium. The construction of the new fortresses and roads gave rise to some further wars with the small tribes, whose territory was thereby curtailed: with the Picentes (485, 486), a number of whom were transplanted to the district of Salernum; with the Sallentines about Brundisium (487, 488); and with the Umbrian Sassinates (487, 488), who seem to have occupied the territory of Ariminum after the expulsion of the Senones. By these establishments the dominion of Rome was extended over the interior of Lower Italy, and over the whole Italian east coast from the Ionian sea to the Celtic frontier.

Maritime Relations

Before we describe the political organization under which the Italy which was thus united was governed on the part of Rome, it remains that we should glance at the maritime relations that subsisted in the fourth and fifth centuries. At this period Syracuse and Carthage were the main competitors for the dominion of the western waters. On the whole, notwithstanding the great temporary successes which Dionysius (348-389), Agathocles (437-465), and Pyrrhus (476-478) obtained at sea, Carthage had the preponderance and Syracuse sank more and more into a naval power of the second rank. The maritime importance of Etruria was wholly gone;(6) the hitherto Etruscan island of Corsica, if it did not quite pass into the possession, fell under the maritime supremacy, of the Carthaginians. Tarentum, which for a time had played a considerable part, had its power broken by the Roman occupation. The brave Massiliots maintained their ground in their own waters; but they exercised no material influence over the course of events in those of Italy. The other maritime cities hardly came as yet into serious account.

Decline of the Roman Naval Power

Rome itself was not exempt from a similar fate; its own waters were likewise commanded by foreign fleets. It was indeed from the first a maritime city, and in the period of its vigour never was so untrue to its ancient traditions as wholly to neglect its war marine or so foolish as to desire to be a mere continental power. Latium furnished the finest timber for ship-building, far surpassing the famed growths of Lower Italy; and the very docks constantly maintained in Rome are enough to show that the Romans never abandoned the idea of possessing a fleet of their own. During the perilous crises, however, which the expulsion of the kings, the internal disturbances in the Romano-Latin confederacy, and the unhappy wars with the

Etruscans and Celts brought upon Rome, the Romans could take but little interest in the state of matters in the Mediterranean; and, in consequence of the policy of Rome directing itself more and more decidedly to the subjugation of the Italian continent, the growth of its naval power was arrested. There is hardly any mention of Latin vessels of war up to the end of the fourth century, except that the votive offering from the Veientine spoil was sent to Delphi in a Roman vessel (360). The Antiates indeed continued to prosecute their commerce with armed vessels and thus, as occasion offered, to practise the trade of piracy also, and the "Tyrrhene corsair" Postumius, whom Timoleon captured about 415, may certainly have been an Antiate; but the Antiates were scarcely to be reckoned among the naval powers of that period, and, had they been so, the fact must from the attitude of Antium towards Rome have been anything but an advantage to the latter. The extent to which the Roman naval power had declined about the year 400 is shown by the plundering of the Latin coasts by a Greek, presumably a Sicilian, war fleet in 405, while at the same time Celtic hordes were traversing and devastating the Latin land.(7) In the following year (406), and beyond doubt under the immediate impression produced by these serious events, the Roman community and the Phoenicians of Carthage, acting respectively for themselves and for their dependent allies, concluded a treaty of commerce and navigation— the oldest Roman document of which the text has reached us, although only in a Greek translation.(8) In that treaty the Romans had to come under obligation not to navigate the Libyan coast to the west of the Fair Promontory (Cape Bon) excepting in cases of necessity. On the other hand they obtained the privilege of freely trading, like the natives, in Sicily, so far as it was Carthaginian; and in Africa and Sardinia they obtained at least the right to dispose of their merchandise at a price fixed with the concurrence of the Carthaginian officials and guaranteed by the Carthaginian community. The privilege of free trading seems to have been granted to the Carthaginians at least in Rome, perhaps in all Latium; only they bound themselves neither to do violence to the subject Latin communities,(9) nor, if they should set foot as enemies on Latin soil, to take up their quarters for a night on shore—in other words, not to extend their piratical inroads into the interior—nor to construct any fortresses in the Latin land.

We may probably assign to the same period the already mentioned(10) treaty between Rome and Tarentum, respecting the date of which we are only told that it was concluded a considerable time before 472. By it the Romans bound themselves—for what concessions on the part of Tarentum is not stated—not to navigate the waters to the east of the Lacinian promontory; a stipulation by which they were thus wholly excluded from the eastern basin of the Mediterranean.

Roman Fortification of the Coast

These were disasters no less than the defeat on the Allia, and the Roman senate seems to have felt them as such and to have made use of the favourable turn, which the Italian relations assumed soon after the conclusion of the humiliating treaties with Carthage and Tarentum, with all energy to improve its depressed maritime position. The most important of the coast towns were furnished with Roman colonies: Pyrgi the seaport of Caere, the colonization of which probably falls within this period; along the west coast, Antium in 415,(11) Tarracina in 425,(12) the island of Pontia in 441,(13) so that, as Ardea and Circeii had previously received colonists, all the Latin seaports of consequence in the territory of the Rutuli and Volsci had now become Latin or burgess colonies; further, in the territory of the Aurunci, Minturnae and Sinuessa in 459;(14) in that of the Lucanians, Paestum and Cosa in 481;(15) and, on the coast of the Adriatic, Sena Gallica and Castrum Novum about 471,(16) and Ariminum in 486;(17) to which falls to be added the occupation of Brundisium, which took place immediately after the close of the Pyrrhic war. In the greater part of these places—the burgess or maritime colonies(18)—the young men were exempted from serving in the legions and destined solely for the watching of the coasts. The well judged preference given at the same time to the Greeks of Lower Italy over their Sabellian neighbours, particularly to the considerable communities of Neapolis, Rhegium, Locri, Thurii, and Heraclea, and their similar exemption under the like conditions from furnishing contingents to the land army, completed the network drawn by Rome around the coasts of Italy.

But with a statesmanlike sagacity, from which the succeeding generations might have drawn a lesson, the leading men of the Roman commonwealth perceived that all these coast fortifications and coast garrisons could not but prove inadequate, unless the war marine of the state were again placed on a footing that should command respect. Some sort of nucleus for this purpose was already furnished on the subjugation of Antium (416) by the serviceable war-galleys which were carried off to the Roman docks; but the enactment at the same time, that the Antiates should abstain from all maritime traffic,(19) is a very clear and distinct indication how weak the Romans then felt themselves at sea, and how completely their maritime policy was still summed up in the occupation of places on the coast. Thereafter, when the Greek cities of southern Italy, Neapolis leading the way in 428, were admitted to the clientship of Rome, the war-vessels, which each of these cities bound itself to furnish as a war contribution under the alliance to the Romans, formed at least a renewed nucleus for a Roman fleet. In 443, moreover, two fleet-masters (-duoviri navales-) were nominated in consequence of a resolution of the burgesses specially passed to that effect, and this Roman naval force co-operated in the Samnite war at the siege of Nuceria.(20) Perhaps even the remarkable mission of a Roman fleet of twenty-five sail to found a colony in Corsica, which Theophrastus mentions in his "History of Plants" written about 446, belongs to this period. But how little was immediately accomplished with all this preparation, is shown by the renewed treaty with Carthage in 448. While the stipulations of the treaty of 406 relating to Italy and Sicily(21) remained unchanged, the Romans were now prohibited not only from the navigation of the eastern waters, but also from that of the Atlantic Ocean which was previously permitted, as well as debarred from holding commercial intercourse with the subjects of Carthage in Sardinia and Africa, and also, in all probability, from effecting a settlement in Corsica;(22) so that only Carthaginian Sicily and Carthage itself remained open to their traffic. We recognize here the jealousy of the dominant maritime power, gradually increasing with the extension of the Roman dominion along the coasts. Carthage compelled the Romans to acquiesce in her prohibitive system, to submit to be excluded from the seats of production in the west and east (connected with which exclusion is the story of a public reward bestowed on the Phoenician mariner who at the sacrifice of his own ship decoyed a Roman vessel, steering after him into the Atlantic Ocean, to perish on a sand-bank), and to restrict their navigation under the treaty to the narrow space of the western Mediterranean—and all this for the mere purpose of averting pillage from their coasts and of securing their ancient and important trading connection with Sicily. The Romans were obliged to yield to these terms; but they did not desist from their efforts to rescue their marine from its condition of impotence.

Quaestors of the Fleet—
Variance between Rome and Carthage

A comprehensive measure with that view was the institution of four quaestors of the fleet (-quaestores classici-) in 487: of whom the first was stationed at Ostia the port of Rome; the second, stationed at Cales then the capital of Roman Campania, had to superintend the ports of Campania and Magna Graecia; the third, stationed at Ariminum, superintended the ports on the other side of the Apennines; the district assigned to the fourth is not known. These new standing officials were intended to exercise not the sole, but a conjoint, guardianship of the coasts, and to form a war marine for their protection. The objects of the Roman senate—to recover their independence by sea, to cut off the maritime communications of Tarentum, to close the Adriatic against fleets coming from Epirus, and to emancipate themselves from Carthaginian supremacy—were very obvious. Their already explained relations with Carthage during the last Italian war discover traces of such views. King Pyrrhus indeed compelled the two great cities once more—it was for the last time —to conclude an offensive alliance; but the lukewarmness and faithlessness of that alliance, the attempts of the Carthaginians to establish themselves in Rhegium and Tarentum, and the immediate occupation of Brundisium by the Romans after the termination of the war, show clearly how much their respective interests already came into collision.

Rome and the Greek Naval Powers

Rome very naturally sought to find support against Carthage from the Hellenic maritime states. Her old and close relations of amity with Massilia continued uninterrupted. The votive offering sent by Rome to Delphi, after the conquest of Veii, was preserved there in the treasury of the Massiliots. After the capture of Rome by the Celts there was a collection in Massilia for the sufferers by the fire, in which the city chest took the lead; in return the Roman senate granted commercial advantages to the Massiliot merchants, and, at the celebration of the games in the Forum assigned a position of honour (-Graecostasis-) to the Massiliots by the side of the platform for the senators. To the same category belong the treaties of commerce and amity concluded by the Romans about 448 with Rhodes and not long after with Apollonia, a considerable mercantile town on the Epirot coast, and especially the closer relation, so fraught with danger for Carthage, which immediately after the end of the Pyrrhic war sprang up between Rome and Syracuse.(23)

While the Roman power by sea was thus very far from keeping pace with the immense development of their power by land, and the war marine belonging to the

Romans in particular was by no means such as from the geographical and commercial position of the city it ought to have been, yet it began gradually to emerge out of the complete nullity to which it had been reduced about the year 400; and, considering the great resources of Italy, the Phoenicians might well follow its efforts with anxious eyes.

The crisis in reference to the supremacy of the Italian waters was approaching; by land the contest was decided. For the first time Italy was united into one state under the sovereignty of the Roman community. What political prerogatives the Roman community on this occasion withdrew from all the other Italian communities and took into its own sole keeping, or in other words, what conception in state-law is to be associated with this sovereignty of Rome, we are nowhere expressly informed, and—a significant circumstance, indicating prudent calculation—there does not even exist any generally current expression for that conception.(24) The only privileges that demonstrably belonged to it were the rights of making war, of concluding treaties, and of coining money. No Italian community could declare war against any foreign state, or even negotiate with it, or coin money for circulation. On the other hand every declaration of war made by the Roman people and every state-treaty resolved upon by it were binding in law on all the other Italian communities, and the silver money of Rome was legally current throughout all Italy. It is probable that the formulated prerogatives of the leading community extended no further. But to these there were necessarily attached rights of sovereignty that practically went far beyond them.

The Full Roman Franchise

The relations, which the Italians sustained to the leading community, exhibited in detail great inequalities. In this point of view, in addition to the full burgesses of Rome, there were three different classes of subjects to be distinguished. The full franchise itself, in the first place, was extended as far as was possible, without wholly abandoning the idea of an urban commonwealth as applied to the Roman commune. The old burgess-domain had hitherto been enlarged chiefly by individual assignation in such a way that southern Etruria as far as towards Caere and Falerii,(25) the districts taken from the Hernici on the Sacco and on the Anio(26) the largest part of the Sabine country(27) and large tracts of the territory formerly Volscian, especially the Pomptine plain(28) were converted into land for Roman farmers, and new burgess-districts were instituted mostly for their inhabitants. The same course had even already been taken with the Falernian district on the Volturnus ceded by Capua.(29) All these burgesses domiciled outside of Rome were without a commonwealth and an administration of their own; on the assigned territory there arose at the most market-villages (-fora et conciliabula-). In a position not greatly different were placed the burgesses sent out to the so-called maritime colonies mentioned above, who were likewise left in possession of the full burgess-rights of Rome, and whose self-administration was of little moment. Towards the close of this period the Roman community appears to have begun to grant full burgess-rights to the adjoining communities of passive burgesses who were of like or closely kindred nationality; this was probably done first for Tusculum,(30) and so, presumably, also for the other communities of passive burgesses in Latium proper, then at the end of this period (486) was extended to the Sabine towns, which doubtless were even then essentially Latinized and had given sufficient proof of their fidelity in the last severe war. These towns retained the restricted self-administration, which under their earlier legal position belonged to them, even after their admission into the Roman burgess-union; it was they more than the maritime colonies that furnished the model for the special commonwealths subsisting within the body of Roman full burgesses and so, in the course of time, for the Roman municipal organization. Accordingly the range of the full Roman burgesses must at the end of this epoch have extended northward as far as the vicinity of Caere, eastward as far as the Apennines, and southward as far as Tarracina; although in this case indeed we cannot speak of boundary in a strict sense, partly because a number of federal towns with Latin rights, such as Tibur, Praeneste, Signia, Norba, Circeii, were found within these bounds, partly because beyond them the inhabitants of Minturnae, Sinuessa, of the Falernian territory, of the town Sena Gallica and some other townships, likewise possessed the full franchise, and families of Roman farmers were presumably to be even now found scattered throughout Italy, either isolated or united in villages.

Subject Communities

Among the subject communities the passive burgesses (-cives sine suffragio-) apart from the privilege of electing and being elected, stood on an equality of rights and duties with the full burgesses. Their legal position was regulated by the decrees of the Roman comitia and the rules issued for them by the Roman praetor, which, however, were doubtless based essentially on the previous arrangements. Justice was administered for them by the Roman praetor or his deputies (-praefecti-) annually sent to the individual communities. Those of them in a better position, such as the city of Capua,(31) retained self-administration and along with it the continued use of the native language, and had officials of their own who took charge of the levy and the census. The communities of inferior rights such as Caere(32) were deprived even of self-administration, and this was doubtless the most oppressive among the different forms of subjection. However, as was above remarked, there is already apparent at the close of this period an effort to incorporate these communities, at least so far as they were -de facto- Latinized, among the full burgesses.

Latins

Among the subject communities the most privileged and most important class was that of the Latin towns, which obtained accessions equally numerous and important in the autonomous communities founded by Rome within and even beyond Italy—- the Latin colonies, as they were called —and was always increasing in consequence of new settlements of the same nature. These new urban communities of Roman origin, but with Latin rights, became more and more the real buttresses of the Roman rule over Italy. These Latins, however, were by no means those with whom the battles of the lake Regillus and Trifanum had been fought. They were not those old members of the Alban league, who reckoned themselves originally equal to, if not better than, the community of Rome, and who felt the dominion of Rome to be an oppressive yoke, as the fearfully rigorous measures of security taken against Praeneste at the beginning of the war with Pyrrhus, and the collisions that evidently long continued to occur with the Praenestines in particular, show. This old Latium had essentially either perished or become merged in Rome, and it now numbered but few communities politically self-subsisting, and these, with the exception of Tibur and Praeneste, throughout insignificant. The Latium of the later times of the republic, on the contrary, consisted almost exclusively of communities, which from the beginning had honoured Rome as their capital and parent city; which, settled amidst regions of alien language and of alien habits, were attached to Rome by community of language, of law, and of manners; which, as the petty tyrants of the surrounding districts, were obliged doubtless to lean on Rome for their very existence, like advanced posts leaning upon the main army; and which, in fine, in consequence of the increasing material advantages of Roman citizenship, were ever deriving very considerable benefit from their equality of rights with the Romans, limited though it was. A portion of the Roman domain, for instance, was usually assigned to them for their separate use, and participation in the state leases and contracts was open to them as to the Roman burgess. Certainly in their case also the consequences of the self-subsistence granted to them did not wholly fail to appear. Venusian inscriptions of the time of the Roman republic, and Beneventane inscriptions recently brought to light,(33) show that Venusia as well as Rome had its plebs and its tribunes of the people, and that the chief magistrates of Beneventum bore the title of consul at least about the time of the Hannibalic war. Both communities are among the most recent of the Latin colonies with older rights: we perceive what pretensions were stirring in them about the middle of the fifth century. These so-called Latins, issuing from the Roman burgess-body and feeling themselves in every respect on a level with it, already began to view with displeasure their subordinate federal rights and to strive after full equalization. Accordingly the senate had exerted itself to curtail these Latin communities—however important they were for Rome—as far as possible, in their rights and privileges, and to convert their position from that of allies to that of subjects, so far as this could be done without removing the wall of partition between them and the non-Latin communities of Italy. We have already described the abolition of the league of the Latin communities itself as well as of their former complete equality of rights, and the loss of the most important political privileges belonging to them. On the complete subjugation of Italy a further step was taken, and a beginning was made towards the restriction of the personal rights—that had not hitherto been touched—of the individual Latin, especially the important right of freedom of settlement. In the case of Ariminum founded in 486 and of all the autonomous communities constituted afterwards, the advantage enjoyed by them, as compared with other subjects, was restricted to their equalization with burgesses of the Roman community so far as regarded private rights —those of traffic and barter as well as those of inheritance.(34) Presumably about the same time the full right of free migration allowed to the Latin communities hitherto established—the title of every one of their burgesses to gain by transmigration to Rome full burgess-rights there—was, for the Latin colonies of later erection, restricted to those persons who had attained to the highest office of the community in their native home; these alone were allowed to exchange their colonial burgess-rights for the Roman. This clearly shows the complete revolution in the position of Rome. So long as Rome was still but one among the many urban communities of Italy, although that one might be the first, admission even to the unrestricted Roman franchise was universally regarded as a gain for the admitting community, and the acquisition of that franchise by non-burgesses was facilitated in every way, and was in fact often imposed on them as a punishment. But after the Roman community became sole sovereign and all the others were its servants, the state of matters changed. The Roman community began jealously to guard its franchise, and accordingly put an end in the first instance to the old full liberty of migration; although the statesmen of that period were wise enough still to keep admission to the Roman franchise legally open at least to the men of eminence and of capacity in the highest class of subject communities. The Latins were thus made to feel that Rome, after having subjugated Italy mainly by their aid, had now no longer need of them as before.

Non-Latin Allied Communities

Lastly, the relations of the non-Latin allied communities were subject, as a matter of course, to very various rules, just as each particular treaty of alliance had defined them. Several of these perpetual alliances, such as that with the Hernican communities,(35) passed over to a footing of complete equalization with the Latin. Others, in which this was not the case, such as those with Neapolis(36), Nola(37), and Heraclea(38), granted rights comparatively comprehensive; while others, such as the Tarentine and Samnite treaties, may have approximated to despotism.

Dissolution of National Leagues—
Furnishing of Contingents

As a general rule, it may be taken for granted that not only the Latin and Hernican national confederations—as to which the fact is expressly stated—but all such confederations subsisting in Italy, and the Samnite and Lucanian leagues in particular, were legally dissolved or at any rate reduced to insignificance, and that in general no Italian community was allowed the right of acquiring property or of intermarriage, or even the right of joint consultation and resolution, with any other. Further, provision must have been made, under different forms, for placing the military and financial resources of all the Italian communities at the disposal of the leading community. Although the burgess militia on the one hand, and the contingents of the "Latin name" on the other, were still regarded as the main and integral constituents of the Roman army, and in that way its national character was on the whole preserved, the Roman -cives sine suffragio-were called forth to join its ranks, and not only so, but beyond doubt the non-Latin federate communities also were either bound to furnish ships of war, as was the case with the Greek cities, or were placed on the roll of contingent-furnishing Italians (-formula togatorum-), as must have been ordained at once or gradually in the case of the Apulians, Sabellians, and Etruscans. In general this contingent, like that of the Latin communities, appears to have had its numbers definitely fixed, although, in case of necessity, the leading community was not precluded from making a larger requisition. This at the same time involved an indirect taxation, as every community was bound itself to equip and to pay its own contingent. Accordingly it was not without design that the supply of the most costly requisites for war devolved chiefly on the Latin, or non-Latin federate communities; that the war marine was for the most part kept up by the Greek cities; and that in the cavalry service the allies, at least subsequently, were called upon to furnish a proportion thrice as numerous as the Roman burgesses, while in the infantry the old principle, that the contingent of the allies should not be more numerous than the burgess army, still remained in force for a long time at least as the rule.

System of Government—
Division and Classification of the Subjects

The system, on which this fabric was constructed and kept together, can no longer be ascertained in detail from the few notices that have reached us. Even the numerical proportions of the three classes of subjects relatively to each other and to the full burgesses, can no longer be determined even approximately;(39) and in like manner the geographical distribution of the several categories over Italy is but imperfectly known. The leading ideas on which the structure was based, on the other hand, are so obvious that it is scarcely necessary specially to set them forth. First of all, as we have already said, the immediate circle of the ruling community was extended—-partly by the settlement of full burgesses, partly by the conferring of passive burgess-rights—as far as was possible without completely decentralizing the Roman community, which was an urban one and was intended to remain so. When the system of incorporation was extended up to and perhaps even beyond its natural limits, the communities that were subsequently added had to submit to a position of subjection; for a pure hegemony as a permanent relation was intrinsically impossible. Thus not through any arbitrary monopolizing of sovereignty, but through the inevitable force of circumstances, by the side of the class of ruling burgesses a second class of subjects took its place. It was one of the primary expedients of Roman rule to subdivide the governed by breaking up the Italian confederacies and instituting as large a number as possible of comparatively small communities, and to graduate the pressure of that rule according to the different categories of subjects. As Cato in the government of his household took care that the slaves should not be on too good terms with one another, and designedly fomented variances and factions among them, so the Roman community acted on a great scale. The expedient was not generous, but it was effectual.

Aristocratic Remodelling of the Constitutions of the Italian Communities

It was but a wider application of the same expedient, when in each dependent community the constitution was remodelled after the Roman pattern and a government of the wealthy and respectable families was installed, which was naturally more or less keenly opposed to the multitude and was induced by its material interests and by its wish for local power to lean on Roman support. The most remarkable instance of this sort is furnished by the treatment of Capua, which appears to have been from the first treated with suspicious precaution as the only Italian city that could come into possible rivalry with Rome. The Campanian nobility received a privileged jurisdiction, separate places of assembly, and in every respect a distinctive position; indeed they even obtained not inconsiderable pensions —sixteen hundred of them at 450 -stateres- (about 30 pounds) annually—charged on the Campanian exchequer. It was these Campanian equites, whose refusal to take part in the great Latino-Campanian insurrection of 414 mainly contributed to its failure, and whose brave swords decided the day in favour of the Romans at Sentinum in 459;(40) whereas the Campanian infantry at Rhegium was the first body of troops that in the war with Pyrrhus revolted from Rome.(41) Another remarkable instance of the Roman practice of turning to account for their own interest the variances between the orders in the dependent communities by favouring the aristocracy, is furnished by the treatment which Volsinii met with in 489. There, just as in Rome, the old and new burgesses must have stood opposed to one another, and the latter must have attained by legal means equality of political rights. In consequence of this the old burgesses of Volsinii resorted to the Roman senate with a request for the restoration of their old constitution—a step which the ruling party in the city naturally viewed as high treason, and inflicted legal punishment accordingly on the petitioners. The Roman senate, however, took part with the old burgesses, and, when the city showed no disposition to submit, not only destroyed by military violence the communal constitution of Volsinii which was In recognized operation, but also, by razing the old capital of Etruria, exhibited to the Italians a fearfully palpable proof of the mastery of Rome.

Moderation of the Government

But the Roman senate had the wisdom not to overlook the fact, that the only means of giving permanence to despotism is moderation on the part of the despots. On that account there was left with, or conferred on, the dependent communities an autonomy, which included a shadow of independence, a special share in the military and political successes of Rome, and above all a free communal constitution—so far as the Italian confederacy extended, there existed no community of Helots. On that account also Rome from the very first, with a clear-sightedness and magnanimity perhaps unparalleled in history, waived the most dangerous of all the rights of government, the right of taxing her subjects. At the most tribute was perhaps imposed on the dependent Celtic cantons: so far as the Italian confederacy extended, there was no tributary community. On that account, lastly, while the duty of bearing arms was partially devolved on the subjects, the ruling burgesses were by no means exempt from it; it is probable that the latter were proportionally far more numerous than the body of the allies; and in that body, again, probably the Latins as a whole were liable to far greater demands upon them than the non-Latin allied communities. There was thus a certain reasonableness in the appropriation by which Rome ranked first, and the Latins next to her, in the distribution of the spoil acquired in war.

Intermediate Functionaries—
Valuation of the Empire

The central administration at Rome solved the difficult problem of preserving its supervision and control over the mass of the Italian communities liable to furnish contingents, partly by means of the four Italian quaestorships, partly by the extension of the Roman censorship over the whole of the dependent communities. The quaestors of the fleet,(42) along with their more immediate duty, had to raise the revenues from the newly acquired domains and to control the contingents of the new allies; they were the first Roman functionaries to whom a residence and district out of Rome were assigned by law, and they formed the necessary intermediate authority between the Roman senate and the Italian communities. Moreover, as is shown by the later municipal constitution, the chief functionaries in every Italian community,(43) whatever might be their title, had to undertake a valuation every fourth or fifth year—an institution, the suggestion of which must necessarily have emanated from Rome, and which can only have been intended to furnish the senate with a view of the resources in men and money of the whole of Italy, corresponding to the census in Rome.

Italy and the Italians

Lastly, with this military administrative union of the whole peoples dwelling to the south of the Apennines, as far as the Iapygian promontory and the straits of Rhegium, was connected the rise of a new name common to them all—that of "the men of the toga" (-togati-), which was their oldest designation in Roman state law, or that of the "Italians," which was the appellation originally in use among the Greeks and thence became universally current. The various nations inhabiting those lands were probably first led to feel and own their unity, partly through their common contrast to the Greeks, partly and mainly through their common resistance to the Celts; for, although an Italian community may now and then have made common cause with the Celts against Rome and employed the opportunity to recover independence, yet in the long run sound national feeling necessarily prevailed. As the "Gallic field" down to a late period stood contrasted in law with the Italian, so the "men of the toga" were thus named in contrast to the Celtic "men of the hose" (-braccati-); and it is probable that the repelling of the Celtic invasions played an important diplomatic part as a reason or pretext for centralizing the military resources of Italy in the hands of the Romans. Inasmuch as the Romans on the one hand took the lead in the great national struggle and on the other hand compelled the Etruscans, Latins, Sabellians, Apulians, and Hellenes (within the bounds to be immediately described) alike to fight under their standards, that unity, which hitherto had been undefined and latent rather than expressed, obtained firm consolidation and recognition in state law; and the name -Italia-, which originally and even in the Greek authors of the fifth century—in Aristotle for instance—pertained only to the modern Calabria, was transferred to the whole land of these wearers of the toga.

Earliest Boundaries of the Italian Confederacy

The earliest boundaries of this great armed confederacy led by Rome, or of the new Italy, reached on the western coast as far as the district of Leghorn south of the Arnus,(44) on the east as far as the Aesis north of Ancona. The townships colonized by Italians, lying beyond these limits, such as Sena Gallica and Ariminum beyond the Apennines, and Messana in Sicily, were reckoned geographically as situated out of Italy—even when, like Ariminum, they were members of the confederacy or even, like Sena, were Roman burgess communities. Still less could the Celtic cantons beyond the Apennines be reckoned among the -togati-, although perhaps some of them were already among the clients of Rome.

First Steps towards the Latininzing of Italy—
New Position of Rome as a Great Power

The new Italy had thus become a political unity; it was also in the course of becoming a national unity. Already the ruling Latin nationality had assimilated to itself the Sabines and Volscians and had scattered isolated Latin communities over all Italy; these germs were merely developed, when subsequently the Latin language became the mother-tongue of every one entitled to wear the Latin toga. That the Romans already clearly recognized this as their aim, is shown by the familiar extension of the Latin name to the whole body of contingent-furnishing Italian allies.(45) Whatever can still be recognized of this grand political structure testifies to the great political sagacity of its nameless architects; and the singular cohesion, which that confederation composed of so many and so diversified ingredients subsequently exhibited under the severest shocks, stamped their great work with the seal of success. From the time when the threads of this net drawn as skilfully as firmly around Italy were concentrated in the hands of the Roman community, it was a great power, and took its place in the system of the Mediterranean states in the room of Tarentum, Lucania, and other intermediate and minor states erased by the last wars from the list of political powers. Rome received, as it were, an official recognition of its new position by means of the two solemn embassies, which in 481 were sent from Alexandria to Rome and from Rome to Alexandria, and which, though primarily they regulated only commercial relations, beyond doubt prepared the way for a political alliance. As Carthage was contending with the Egyptian government regarding Cyrene and was soon to contend with that of Rome regarding Sicily, so Macedonia was contending with the former for the predominant influence in Greece, with the latter proximately for the dominion of the Adriatic coasts. The new struggles, which were preparing on all sides, could not but influence each other, and Rome, as mistress of Italy, could not fail to be drawn into the wide arena which the victories and projects of Alexander the Great had marked out as the field of conflict for his successors.

Notes for Book II Chapter VII

1. The story that the Romans also sent envoys to Alexander at Babylon on the testimony of Clitarchus (Plin. Hist. Nat. iii. 5, 57), from whom the other authorities who mention this fact (Aristus and Asclepiades, ap. Arrian, vii. 15, 5; Memnon, c. 25) doubtless derived it. Clitarchus certainly was contemporary with these events; nevertheless, his Life of Alexander was decidedly a historical romance rather than a history; and, looking to the silence of the trustworthy biographers (Arrian, l. c.; Liv. ix. 18) and the utterly romantic details of the account—which represents the Romans, for instance, as delivering to Alexander a chaplet of gold, and the latter as prophesying the future greatness of Rome—we cannot but set down this story as one of the many embellishments which Clitarchus introduced into the history.

2. II. VI. Last Struggles of Samnium

3. Near the modern Anglona; not to be confounded with the better known town of the same name in the district of Cosenza.

4. These numbers appear credible. The Roman account assigns, probably in dead and wounded, 15,000 to each side; a later one even specifies 5000 as dead on the Roman, and 20,000 on the Greek side. These accounts may be mentioned here for the purpose of exhibiting, in one of the few instances where it is possible to check the statement, the untrustworthiness—almost without exception—of the reports of numbers, which are swelled by the unscrupulous invention of the annalists with avalanche-like rapidity.

5. The later Romans, and the moderns following them, give a version of the league, as if the Romans had designedly avoided accepting the Carthaginian help in Italy. This would have been irrational, and the facts pronounce against it. The circumstance that Mago did not land at Ostia is to be explained not by any such foresight, but simply by the fact that Latium was not at all threatened by Pyrrhus and so did not need Carthaginian aid; and the Carthaginians certainly fought for Rome in front of Rhegium.

6. II. IV. Victories of Salamis and Himera, and Their Effects

7. II. IV. Fruitlessness of the Celtic Victory

8. The grounds for assigning the document given in Polybius (iii. 22) not to 245, but to 406, are set forth in my Rom. Chronologie, p. 320 f. [translated in the Appendix to this volume].

9. II. V. Domination of the Romans; Exasperation of the Latins

10. II. VII. Breach between Rome and Tarentum

11. II. V. Colonization of the Volsci

12. II. V. Colonization of the Volsci

13. II. VI. New Fortresses in Apulia and Campania

14. II. VI. Last Struggles of Samnium

15. II. VII. Construction of New Fortresses and Roads

16. II. VII. The Boii

17. II. VII. Construction of New Fortresses and Roads

18. These were Pyrgi, Ostia, Antium, Tarracina, Minturnae, Sinuessa Sena Gallica, and Castrum Novum.

19. This statement is quite as distinct (Liv. viii. 14; -interdictum mari Antiati populo est-) as it is intrinsically credible; for Antium was inhabited not merely by colonists, but also by its former citizens who had been nursed in enmity to Rome (*ii.* V. Colonizations in The Land Of The Volsci). This view is, no doubt, inconsistent with the Greek accounts, which assert that Alexander the Great (431) and Demetrius Poliorcetes (471) lodged complaints at Rome regarding Antiate pirates. The former statement is of the same stamp, and perhaps from the same source, with that regarding the Roman embassy to Babylon (*ii.* VII. Relations Between The East and West). It seems more likely that Demetrius Poliorcetes may have tried by edict to put down piracy in the Tyrrhene sea which he had never set eyes upon, and it is not at all inconceivable that the Antiates may have even as Roman citizens, in defiance of the prohibition, continued for a time their old trade in an underhand fashion: much dependence must not however, be placed even on the second story.

20. II. VI. Last Campaigns in Samnium

21. II. VII. Decline of the Roman Naval Power

22. According to Servius (in Aen. iv. 628) it was stipulated in the Romano-Carthaginian treaties, that no Roman should set foot on (or rather occupy) Carthaginian, and no Carthaginian on Roman, soil, but Corsica was to remain in a neutral position between them (-ut neque Romani ad litora Carthaginiensium accederent neque Carthaginienses ad litora Romanorum.....Corsica esset media inter Romanos et Carthaginienses-). This appears to refer to our present period, and the colonization of Corsica seems to have been prevented by this very treaty.

23. II. VII. Submission of Lower Italy

24. The clause, by which a dependent people binds itself "to uphold in a friendly manner the sovereignty of that of Rome" (-maiestatem populi Romani comiter conservare-), is certainly the technical appellation of that mildest form of subjection, but it probably did not come into use till a considerably later period (Cic. pro Balbo, 16, 35). The appellation of clientship derived from private law, aptly as in its very indefiniteness it denotes the relation (Dig. xlix. 15, 7, i), was scarcely applied to it officially in earlier times.

25. II. IV. South Etruria Roman

26. II. VI. Consolidation of the Roman Rule in Central Italy

27. II. VI. Last Struggles of Samnium

28. II. V. Complete Submission of the Volscian and Campanian Provinces

29. II. V. Complete Submission of the Volscian and Campanian Provinces

30. That Tusculum as it was the first to obtain passive burgess-rights (*ii*. V. Crises within the Romano-Latin League) was also the first to exchange these for the rights of full burgesses, is probable in itself and presumably it is in the latter and not in the former respect that the town is named by Cicero (pro Mur. 8, 19) -municipium antiquissimum-.

31. II. V. Complete Submission of the Volscian and Campanian Provinces

32. II. IV. South Etruria Roman

33. -V. Cervio A. f. cosol dedicavit- and -Iunonei Quiritri sacra. C. Falcilius L. f. consol dedicavit-.

34. According to the testimony of Cicero (pro Caec. 35) Sulla gave to the Volaterrans the former -ius- of Ariminum, that is—adds the orator—the -ius- of the "twelve colonies" which had not the Roman -civitas- but had full -commercium- with the Romans. Few things have been so much discussed as the question to what places this -ius- of the twelve towns refers; and yet the answer is not far to seek. There were in Italy and Cisalpine Gaul—laying aside some places that soon disappeared again—thirty-four Latin colonies established in all. The twelve most recent of these—Ariminum, Beneventum, Firmum, Aesernia, Brundisium, Spoletium, Cremona, Placentia, Copia, Valentia, Bononia, and Aquileia—are those here referred to; and because Ariminum was the oldest of these and the town for which this new organization was primarily established, partly perhaps also because it was the first Roman colony founded beyond Italy, the -ius- of these colonies rightly took its name from Ariminum. This at the same time demonstrates the truth of the view—which already had on other grounds very high probability—that all the

colonies established in Italy (in the wider sense of the term) after the founding of Aquileia belonged to the class of burgess-colonies.

We cannot fully determine the extent to which the curtailment of the rights of the more recent Latin towns was carried, as compared with the earlier. If intermarriage, as is not improbable but is in fact anything but definitely established (i. 132; Diodor. p. 590, 62, fr. Vat. p. 130, Dind.), formed a constituent element of the original federal equality of rights, it was, at any rate, no longer conceded to the Latin colonies of more recent origin.

35. II. V. League with the Hernici

36. II. VI. Pacification of Campania

37. II. VI. Victory of the Romans

38. II. VII. The War in Italy Flags

39. It is to be regretted that we are unable to give satisfactory information as to the proportional numbers. We may estimate the number of Roman burgesses capable of bearing arms in the later regal period as about 20,000. (I. VI. Time And Occasion of the Reform) Now from the fall of Alba to the conquest of Veii the immediate territory of Rome received no material extension; in perfect accordance with which we find that from the first institution of the twenty-one tribes about 259, (ii. II. Coriolanus) which involved no, or at any rate no considerable, extension of the Roman bounds, no new tribes were instituted till 367. However abundant allowance we make for increase by the excess of births over deaths, by immigration, and by manumissions, it is absolutely impossible to reconcile with the narrow limits of a territory of hardly 650 square miles the traditional numbers of the census, according to which the number of Roman burgesses capable of bearing arms in the second half of the third century varied between 104,000 and 150,000, and in 362, regarding which a special statement is extant, amounted to 152,573. These numbers must rather stand on a parallel with the 84,700 burgesses of the Servian census; and in general the whole earlier census-lists, carried back to the four lustres of Servius Tullius and furnished with copious numbers, must belong to the class of those apparently documentary traditions which delight in, and betray themselves by the very fact of, such numerical details.

It was only with the second half of the fourth century that the large extensions of territory, which must have suddenly and considerably augmented the burgess roll, began. It is reported on trustworthy authority and is intrinsically credible, that about 416 the Roman burgesses numbered 165,000; which very well agrees with the statement that ten years previously, when the whole militia was called out against Latium and the Gauls, the first levy amounted to ten legions, that is, to 50,000 men. Subsequently to the great extensions of territory in Etruria, Latium, and Campania, in the fifth century the effective burgesses numbered, on an average, 250,000; immediately before the first Punic war, 280,000 to 290,000. These numbers are certain enough, but they are not quite available historically for another reason, namely, that in them probably the Roman full burgesses and the "burgesses without vote" not serving, like the Campanians, in legions of their own, —such, e. g., as the Caerites, —are included together in the reckoning, while the latter must at any rate - de facto- be counted among the subjects (Rom. Forsch. ii. 396).

40. II. VI. Battle of Sentinum

41. II. VII. Commencement of the Conflict in Lower Italy

42. II. VII. Quaestors of the Fleet

43. Not merely in every Latin one; for the censorship or so-called -quinquennalitas- occurs, as is well known, also among communities whose constitution was not formed according to the Latin scheme.

44. This earliest boundary is probably indicated by the two small townships -Ad fines-, of which one lay north of Arezzo on the road to Florence, the second on the coast not far from Leghorn. Somewhat further to the south of the latter, the brook and valley of Vada are still called -Fiume della fine-, -Valle della fine- (Targioni Tozzetti, Viaggj, iv. 430).

45. In strict official language, indeed, this was not the case. The fullest designation of the Italians occurs in the agrarian law of 643, line 21; -[ceivis] Romanus sociumve nominisve Latini, quibus ex formula togatorum [milites in terra Italia imperare solent]-; in like manner at the 29th line of the same -peregrinus- is distinguished from the -Latinus-, and in the decree of the senate as to the Bacchanalia in 568 the expression is used: -ne quis ceivis Romanus neve nominis Latini neve socium quisquam-. But in common use very frequently the second or third of these three subdivisions is omitted, and along with the Romans sometimes only those Latini nominis are mentioned, sometimes only the -socii- (Weissenborn on Liv. xxii. 50, 6), while there is no difference in the meaning. The designation -homines nominis Latini ac socii Italici- (Sallust. Jug. 40), correct as it is in itself, is foreign to the official -usus loquendi, which knows -Italia-, but not -Italici-.

CHAPTER VIII

Law, Religion, Military System, Economic Condition, Nationality

Development of Law

In the development which law underwent during this period within the Roman community, probably the most important material innovation was that peculiar control which the community itself, and in a subordinate degree its office-bearers, began to exercise over the manners and habits of the individual burgesses. The germ of it is to be sought in the right of the magistrate to inflict property-fines (-multae-) for offences against order.(1) In the case of all fines of more than two sheep and thirty oxen or, after the cattle-fines had been by the decree of the people in 324 commuted into money, of more than 3020 libral -asses- (30 pounds), the decision soon after the expulsion of the kings passed by way of appeal into the hands of the community;(2) and thus procedure by fine acquired an importance which it was far from originally possessing. Under the vague category of offences against order men might include any accusations they pleased, and by the higher grades in the scale of fines they might accomplish whatever they desired. The dangerous character of such arbitrary procedure was brought to light rather than obviated by the mitigating proviso, that these property-fines, where they were not fixed by law at a definite sum, should not amount to half the estate belonging to the person fined. To this class belonged the police-laws, which from the earliest times were especially abundant in the Roman community. Such were those enactments of the Twelve Tables, which prohibited the anointing of a dead body by persons hired for the purpose, the dressing it out with more than one cushion or more than three purple-edged coverings, the decorating it with gold or gaudy chaplets, the use of dressed wood for the funeral pile, and the perfuming or sprinkling of the pyre with frankincense or myrrh-wine; which limited the number of flute-players in the funeral procession to ten at most; and which forbade wailing women and funeral banquets—in a certain measure the earliest Roman legislation against luxury. Such also were the laws—originating in the conflicts of the orders—directed against usury as well as against an undue use of the common pasture and a disproportionate appropriation of the occupiable domain-land. But far more fraught with danger than these and similar fining-laws, which at any rate formulated once for all the trespass and often also the measure of punishment, was the general prerogative of every magistrate who exercised jurisdiction to inflict a fine for an offence against order, and, if the fine reached the amount necessary to found an appeal and the person fined did not submit to the penalty, to bring the case before the community. Already in the course of the fifth century quasi-criminal proceedings had been in this way instituted against immorality of life both in men and women, against the forestalling of grain, witchcraft, and similar matters. Closely akin to this was the quasi-jurisdiction of the censors, which likewise sprang up at this period. They were invested with authority to adjust the Roman budget and the burgess-roll, and they availed themselves of it, partly to impose of their own accord taxes on luxury which differed only in form from penalties on it, partly to abridge or withdraw the political privileges of the burgess who was reported to have been guilty of any infamous action.(3) The extent to which this surveillance was already carried is shown by the fact that penalties of this nature were inflicted for the negligent cultivation of a man's own land, and that such a man as Publius Cornelius Rufinus (consul in 464, 477) was struck off the list of senators by the censors of 479, because he possessed silver plate to the value of 3360 sesterces (34 pounds). No doubt, according to the rule generally applicable to the edicts of magistrates,(4) the sentences of the censors had legal force only during their censorship, that is on an average for the next five years, and might be renewed or not by the next censors at pleasure. Nevertheless this censorial prerogative was of so immense importance, that in virtue of it the censorship, originally a subordinate magistracy, became in rank and consideration the first of all.(5) The government of the senate rested essentially on this twofold police control supreme and subordinate, vested in the community and its officials, and furnished with powers as extensive as they were arbitrary. Like every such arbitrary government, it was productive of much good and much evil, and we do not mean to combat the view of those who hold that the evil preponderated. But we must not forget that—amidst the morality external certainly but stern and energetic, and the powerful enkindling of public spirit, that were the genuine characteristics of this period—these institutions remained exempt as yet from any really base misuse; and if they were the chief instruments in repressing individual freedom, they were also the means by which the public spirit and the good old manners and order of the Roman community were with might and main upheld.

Modifications in the Laws

Along with these changes a humanizing and modernizing tendency showed itself slowly, but yet clearly enough, in the development of Roman law. Most of the enactmerits of the Twelve Tables, which coincide with the laws of Solon and therefore may with reason be considered as in substance innovations, bear this character; such as the securing the right of free association and the autonomy of the societies that originated under it; the enactment that forbade the ploughing up of boundary-balks; and the mitigation of the punishment of theft, so that a thief not caught in the act might henceforth release himself from the plaintiff's suit by payment of double compensation. The law of debt was modified in a similar sense, but not till upwards of a century afterwards, by the Poetelian law.(6) The right freely to dispose of property, which according to the earliest Roman law was accorded to the owner in his lifetime but in the case of death had hitherto been conditional on the consent of the community, was liberated from this restriction, inasmuch as the law of the Twelve Tables or its interpretation assigned to the private testament the same force as pertained to that confirmed in the curies. This was an important step towards the breaking up of the clanships, and towards the full carrying out of individual liberty in the disposal of property. The fearfully absolute paternal power was restricted by the enactment, that a son thrice sold by his father should not relapse into his power, but should thenceforth be free; to which—by a legal inference that, strictly viewed, was no doubt absurd—was soon attached the possibility that a father might voluntarily divest himself of dominion over his son by emancipation. In the law of marriage civil marriage was permitted;(7) and although the full marital power was associated as necessarily with a true civil as with a true religious marriage, yet the permission of a connection instead of marriage,(8) formed without that power, constituted a first step towards relaxation of the full power of the husband. The first step towards a legal enforcement of married life was the tax on old bachelors (-aes uxorium-) with the introduction of which Camillus began his public career as censor in 351.

Administration of Justice—
Code of Common Law—
New Judicial Functionaries

Changes more comprehensive than those effected in the law itself were introduced into—what was more important in a political point of view, and more easily admitted of alteration—the system of judicial administration. First of all came the important limitation of the supreme judicial power by the embodiment of the common law in a written code, and the obligation of the magistrate thenceforth to decide no longer according to varying usage, but according to the written letter, in civil as well as in criminal procedure (303, 304). The appointment of a supreme magistrate in Rome exclusively for the administration of justice in 387,(9) and the establishment of separate police functionaries which took place contemporaneously in Rome, and was imitated under Roman influence in all the Latin communities,(10) secured greater speed and precision of justice. These police-magistrates or aediles had, of course, a certain jurisdiction at the same time assigned to them. On the one hand, they were the ordinary civil judges for sales concluded in open market, for the cattle and slave markets in particular; and on the other hand, they ordinarily acted in processes of fines and amercements as judges of first instance or—which was in Roman law the same thing—as public prosecutors. In consequence of this the administration of the laws imposing fines, and the equally indefinite and politically important right of fining in general, were vested mainly in them. Similar but subordinate functions, having especial reference to the poorer classes, pertained to the three night—or blood-masters (-tres viri nocturni- or -capitales-), first nominated in 465; they were entrusted with the duties of nocturnal police as regards fire and the public safety and with the superintendence of executions, with which a certain summary jurisdiction was very soon, perhaps even from the outset, associated.(11) Lastly from the increasing extent of the Roman community it became necessary, out of regard to the convenience of litigants, to station in the more remote townships special judges competent to deal at least with minor civil causes. This arrangement was the rule for the communities of burgesses -sine suffragio-,(12) and was perhaps even extended to the more remote communities of full burgesses,(13)—the first germs of a Romano-municipal jurisdiction developing itself by the side of that which was strictly Roman.

Changes in Procedure

In civil procedure (which, however, according to the ideas of that period included most of the crimes committed against fellow-citizens) the division of a process into the settlement of the question of law before the magistrate (-ius-), and the decision of the question of fact by a private person nominated by the magistrate (-iudicium-) —a division doubtless customary even in earlier times—was on the abolition of the monarchy prescribed by law;(14) and to that separation the private law of Rome was mainly indebted for its logical clearness and practical precision.(15) In actions regarding property, the decision as to what constituted possession, which hitherto had been left to the arbitrary caprice of the magistrate, was subjected gradually to legal rules; and, alongside of the law of property, a law of possession was developed—another step, by which the magisterial authority lost an important part of its powers. In criminal processes, the tribunal of the people, which hitherto had exercised the prerogative of mercy, became a court of legally secured appeal. If the accused after hearing (-quaestio-) was condemned by the magistrate and appealed to the burgesses, the magistrate proceeded in presence of these to the further hearing (-anquisitio-) and, when he after three times discussing the matter before the community had repeated his decision, in the fourth diet the sentence was confirmed or rejected by the burgesses. Modification was not allowed. A similar republican spirit breathed in the principles, that the house protected the burgess, and that an arrest could only take place out of doors; that imprisonment during investigation was to be avoided; and that it was allowable for every accused and not yet condemned burgess by renouncing his citizenship to withdraw from the consequences of condemnation, so far as they affected not his property but his person-principles, which certainly were not embodied in formal laws and accordingly did not legally bind the prosecuting magistrate, but yet were by their moral weight of the greatest influence, particularly in limiting capital punishment. But, if the Roman criminal law furnishes a remarkable testimony to the strong public spirit and to the increasing humanity of this epoch, it on the other hand suffered in its practical working from the struggles between the orders, which in this respect were specially baneful. The co-ordinate primary jurisdiction of all the public magistrates in criminal cases, that arose out of these conflicts,(16) led to the result, that there was no longer any fixed authority for giving instructions, or any serious preliminary investigation, in Roman criminal procedure. And, as the ultimate criminal jurisdiction was exercised in the forms and by the organs of legislation, and never disowned its origin from the prerogative of mercy; as, moreover, the treatment of police fines had an injurious reaction on the criminal procedure which was externally very similar; the decision in criminal causes was pronounced—and that not so much by way of abuse, as in some degree by virtue of the constitution—not according to fixed law, but according to the arbitrary pleasure of the judges. In this way the Roman criminal procedure was completely void of principle, and was degraded into the sport and instrument of political parties; which can the less be excused, seeing that this procedure, while especially applied to political crimes proper, was applicable also to others, such as murder and arson. The evil was aggravated by the clumsiness of that procedure, which, in concert with the haughty republican contempt for non-burgesses, gave rise to a growing custom of tolerating, side by side with the more formal process, a summary criminal, or rather police, procedure against slaves and common people. Here too the passionate strife regarding political processes overstepped natural limits, and introduced institutions which materially contributed to estrange the Romans step by step from the idea of a fixed moral order in the administration of justice.

Religion—
New Gods

We are less able to trace the progress of the religious conceptions of the Romans during this epoch. In general they adhered with simplicity to the simple piety of their ancestors, and kept equally aloof from superstition and from unbelief. How vividly the idea of spiritualizing all earthly objects, on which the Roman religion was based, still prevailed at the close of this epoch, is shown by the new "God of silver"

(-Argentinus-), who presumably came into existence only in consequence of the introduction of the silver currency in 485, and who naturally was the son of the older "God of copper" (-Aesculanus-).

The relations to foreign lands were the same as heretofore; but here, and here especially, Hellenic influences were on the increase. It was only now that temples began to rise in Rome itself in honour of the Hellenic gods. The oldest was the temple of Castor and Pollux, which had been vowed in the battle at lake Regillus(17) and was consecrated on 15th July 269. The legend associated with it, that two youths of superhuman size and beauty had been seen fighting on the battle-field in the ranks of the Romans and immediately after the battle watering their foaming steeds in the Roman Forum at the fountain of Iuturna, and announcing the great victory, bears a stamp thoroughly un-Roman, and was beyond doubt at a very early period modelled on the appearance of the Dioscuri—similar down to its very details—in the famous battle fought about a century before between the Crotoniates and Locrians at the river Sagras. The Delphic Apollo too was not only consulted—- as was usual with all peoples that felt the influence of Grecian culture—and presented moreover after special successes, such as the capture of Veii, with a tenth of the spoil (360), but also had a temple built for him in the city (323, renewed 401). The same honour was towards the close of this period accorded to Aphrodite (459), who was in some enigmatical way identified with the old Roman garden goddess, Venus;(18) and to Asklapios or Aesculapius, who was obtained by special request from Epidaurus in the Peloponnesus and solemnly conducted to Rome (463). Isolated complaints were heard in serious emergencies as to the intrusion of foreign superstition, presumably the art of the Etruscan -haruspices- (as in 326); but in such cases the police did not fail to take proper cognisance of the matter.

In Etruria on the other hand, while the nation stagnated and decayed in political nullity and indolent opulence, the theological monopoly of the nobility, stupid fatalism, wild and meaningless mysticism, the system of soothsaying and of mendicant prophecy gradually developed themselves, till they reached the height at which we afterwards find them.

Sacerdotal System

In the sacerdotal system no comprehensive changes, so far as we know, took place. The more stringent enactments, that were made about 465 regarding the collection of the process-fines destined to defray the cost of public worship, point to an increase in the ritual budget of the state—a necessary result of the increase in the number of its gods and its temples. It has already been mentioned as one of the evil effects of the dissensions between the orders that an illegitimate influence began to be conceded to the colleges of men of lore, and that they were employed for the annulling of political acts(19)—a course by which on the one hand the faith of the people was shaken, and on the other hand the priests were permitted to exercise a very injurious influence on public affairs.

Military System—
Manipular Legion—
Entrenchment of Camp—
Cavalry—
Officers—
Military Discipline—
Training and Classes of Soldiers—
Military Value of the Manipular Legion

A complete revolution occurred during this epoch in the military system. The primitive Graeco-Italian military organization, which was probably based, like the Homeric, on the selection of the most distinguished and effective warriors—who ordinarily fought on horseback—to form a special vanguard, had in the later regal period been superseded by the -legio—the old Dorian phalanx of hoplites, probably eight file deep.(20) This phalanx thenceforth undertook the chief burden of the battle, while the cavalry were stationed on the flanks, and, mounted or dismounted according to circumstances, were chiefly employed as a reserve. From this arrangement there were developed nearly at the same time the phalanx of -sarrissae- in Macedonia and the manipular arrangement in Italy, the former formed by closing and deepening, the latter by breaking up and multiplying, the ranks, in the first instance by the division of the old -legio- of 8400 into two -legiones- of 4200 men each. The old Doric phalanx had been wholly adapted to close combat with the sword and especially with the spear, and only an accessory and subordinate position in the order of battle was assigned to missile weapons. In the manipular legion the thrusting-lance was confined to the third division, and instead of it the first two were furnished with a new and peculiar Italian missile weapon, the -pilum- a square or round piece of wood, four and a half feet long, with a triangular or quadrangular iron point—which had been originally perhaps invented for the defence of the ramparts of the camp, but was soon transferred from the rear to the front ranks, and was hurled by the advancing line into the ranks of the enemy at a distance of from ten to twenty paces. At the same time the sword acquired far greater importance than the short knife of the phalangite could ever have had; for the volley of javelins was intended in the first instance merely to prepare the way for an attack sword in hand. While, moreover, the phalanx had, as if it were a single mighty lance, to be hurled at once upon the enemy, in the new Italian legion the smaller units, which existed also in the phalanx system but were in the order of battle firmly and indissolubly united, were tactically separated from each other. Not merely was the close square divided, as we have said, into two equally strong halves, but each of these was separated in the direction of its depth into the three divisions of the -hastati-, — principes-, and -triarii-, each of a moderate depth probably amounting in ordinary cases to only four files; and was broken up along the front into ten bands (-manipuli-), in such a way that between every two divisions and every two maniples there was left a perceptible interval. It was a mere continuation of the same process of individualizing, by which the collective mode of fighting was discouraged even in the diminished tactical unit and the single combat became prominent, as is evident from the (already mentioned) decisive part played by hand-to-hand encounters and combats with the sword. The system of entrenching the camp underwent also a peculiar development. The place where the army encamped, even were it only for a single night, was invariably provided with a regular circumvallation and as it were converted into a fortress. Little change took place on the other hand in the cavalry, which in the manipular legion retained the secondary part which it had occupied by the side of the phalanx. The system of officering the army also continued in the main unchanged; only now over each of the two legions of the regular army there were set just as many war-tribunes as had hitherto commanded the whole army, and the number of staff-officers was thus doubled. It was at this period probably that the clear line of demarcation became established between the subaltern officers, who as common soldiers had to gain their place at the head of the maniples by the sword and passed by regular promotion from the lower to the higher maniples, and the military tribunes placed at the head of whole legions—six to each—in whose case there was no regular promotion, and for whom men of the better class were usually taken. In this respect it must have become a matter of importance that, while previously the subaltern as well as the staff-officers had been uniformly nominated by the general, after 392 some of the latter posts were filled up through election by the burgesses.(21) Lastly, the old, fearfully strict, military discipline remained unaltered. Still, as formerly, the general was at liberty to behead any man serving in his camp, and to scourge with rods the staff-officer as well as the common soldier; nor were such punishments inflicted merely on account of common crimes, but also when an officer had allowed himself to deviate from the orders which he had received, or when a division had allowed itself to be surprised or had fled from the field of battle. On the other hand, the new military organization necessitated a far more serious and prolonged military training than the previous phalanx system, in which the solidity of the mass kept even the inexperienced in their ranks. If nevertheless no special soldier-class sprang up, but on the contrary the army still remained, as before, a burgess army, this object was chiefly attained by abandoning the former mode of ranking the soldiers according to property(22) and arranging them according to length of service. The Roman recruit now entered among the light-armed "skirmishers" (-rorarii-), who fought outside of the line and especially with stone slings, and he advanced from this step by step to the first and then to the second division, till at length the soldiers of long service and experience were associated together in the corps of the -triarii-, which was numerically the weakest but imparted its tone and spirit to the whole army.

The excellence of this military organization, which became the primary cause of the superior political position of the Roman community, chiefly depended on the three great military principles of maintaining a reserve, of combining the close and distant modes of fighting, and of combining the offensive and the defensive. The system of a reserve was already foreshadowed in the earlier employment of the cavalry, but it was now completely developed by the partition of the army into three divisions and the reservation of the flower of the veterans for the last and decisive shock. While the Hellenic phalanx had developed the close, and the Oriental squadrons of horse armed with bows and light missile spears the distant, modes of fighting respectively, the Roman combination of the heavy javelin with the sword produced results similar, as has justly been remarked, to those attained in modern warfare by the introduction of bayonet-muskets; the volley of javelins prepared the way for the sword encounter, exactly in the same way as a volley of musketry now precedes a charge with the bayonet. Lastly, the elaborate system of encampment allowed the Romans to combine the advantages of defensive and offensive war and to decline or give battle according to circumstances, and in the latter case to fight under the ramparts of their camp just as under the walls of a fortress—the Roman, says a Roman proverb, conquers by sitting still.

Origin of the Manipular Legion

That this new military organization was in the main a Roman, or at any rate Italian, remodelling and improvement of the old Hellenic tactics of the phalanx, is plain. If some germs of the system of reserve and of the individualizing of the smaller subdivisions of the army are found to occur among the later Greek strategists, especially Xenophon, this only shows that they felt the defectiveness of the old system, but were not well able to obviate it. The manipular legion appears fully developed in the war with Pyrrhus; when and under what circumstances it arose, whether at once or gradually, can no longer be ascertained. The first tactical system which the Romans encountered, fundamentally different from the earlier Italo-Hellenic system, was the Celtic sword-phalanx. It is not impossible that the subdivision of the army and the intervals between the maniples in front were arranged with a view to resist, as they did resist, its first and only dangerous charge; and it accords with this hypothesis that Marcus Furius Camillus, the most celebrated Roman general of the Gallic epoch, is presented in various detached notices as the reformer of the Roman military system. The further traditions associated with the Samnite and Pyrrhic wars are neither sufficiently accredited, nor can they with certainty be duly arranged;(23) although it is in itself probable that the prolonged Samnite mountain warfare exercised a lasting influence on the individual development of the Roman soldier, and that the struggle with one of the first masters of the art of war, belonging to the school of the great Alexander, effected an improvement in the technical features of the Roman military system.

National Economy—
The Farmers—
Farming of Estates

In the national economy agriculture was, and continued to be, the social and political basis both of the Roman community and of the new Italian state. The common assembly and the army consisted of Roman farmers; what as soldiers they had acquired by the sword, they secured as colonists by the plough. The insolvency of the middle class of landholders gave rise to the formidable internal crises of the third and fourth centuries, amidst which it seemed as if the young republic could not but be destroyed. The revival of the Latin farmer-class, which was produced during the fifth century partly by the large assignations of land and incorporations, partly by the fall in the rate of interest and the increase of the Roman population, was at once the effect and the cause of the mighty development of Roman power. The acute soldier's eye of Pyrrhus justly discerned the cause of the political and military ascendency of the Romans in the flourishing condition of the Roman farms. But the rise also of husbandry on a large scale among the Romans appears to fall within this period. In earlier times indeed there existed landed estates of—at least comparatively—large size; but their management was not farming on a large scale, it was simply a husbandry of numerous small parcels.(24) On the other hand the enactment in the law of 387, not incompatible indeed with the earlier mode of management but yet far more appropriate to the later, *viz.* that the landholder should be bound to employ along with his slaves a proportional number of free persons,(25) may well be regarded as the oldest trace of the later centralized farming of estates;(26) and it deserves notice that even here at its first emergence it essentially rests on slave-holding. How it arose, must remain an undecided point; possibly the Carthaginian plantations in Sicily served as models to the oldest Roman landholders, and perhaps even the appearance of wheat in husbandry by the side of spelt,(27) which Varro places about the period of the decemvirs, was connected with that altered style of management. Still less can we ascertain how far this method of husbandry had already during this period spread; but the history of the wars with Hannibal leaves no doubt that it cannot yet have become the rule, nor can it have yet absorbed the Italian farmer class. Where it did come into vogue, however, it annihilated the older clientship based on the -precarium-; just as the modern system of large farms has been formed in great part by the suppression of petty holdings and the conversion of hides into farm-fields. It admits of no doubt that the restriction of this agricultural clientship very materially contributed towards the distress of the class of small cultivators.

Inland Intercourse in Italy

Respecting the internal intercourse of the Italians with each other our written authorities are silent; coins alone furnish some information. We have already mentioned(28) that in Italy, with the exception of the Greek cities and of the Etruscan Populonia, there was no coinage during the first three centuries of Rome, and that cattle in the first instance, and subsequently copper by weight, served as the medium of exchange. Within the present epoch occurred the transition on the part of the Italians from the system of barter to that of money; and in their money they were naturally led at first to Greek models. The circumstances of central Italy led however to the adoption of copper instead of silver as the metal for their coinage, and the unit of coinage was primarily based on the previous unit of value, the copper pound; hence they cast their coins instead of stamping them, for no die would have sufficed for pieces so large and heavy. Yet there seems from the first to have been a fixed ratio for the relative value of copper and silver (250:1), and with reference to that ratio the copper coinage seems to have been issued; so that, for example, in Rome the large copper piece, the -as-, was equal in value to a scruple (1/288 of a pound) of silver. It is a circumstance historically more remarkable, that coining in Italy most probably originated in Rome, and in fact with the decemvirs, who found in the Solonian legislation a pattern for the regulation of their coinage; and that from Rome it spread over a number of Latin, Etruscan, Umbrian, and east-Italian communities, —a clear proof of the superior position which Rome from the beginning of the fourth century held in Italy. As all these communities subsisted side by side in formal independence, legally the monetary standard was entirely local, and the territory of every city had its own monetary system. Nevertheless the standards of copper coinage in central and northern Italy may be comprehended in three groups, within which the coins in common intercourse seem to have been treated as homogeneous. These groups are, first, the coins of the cities of Etruria lying north of the Ciminian Forest and those of Umbria; secondly, the coins of Rome and Latium; and lastly, those of the eastern seaboard. We have already observed that the Roman coins held a certain ratio to silver by weight; on the other hand we find those of the east coast of Italy placed in a definite proportional relation to the silver coins which were current from an early period in southern Italy, and the standard of which was adopted by the Italian immigrants, such as the Bruttians, Lucanians, and Nolans, by the Latin colonies in that quarter, such as Cales and Suessa, and even by the Romans themselves for their possessions in Lower Italy. Accordingly the inland traffic of Italy must have been divided into corresponding provinces, which dealt with one another like foreign nations.

In transmarine commerce the relations we have previously described(29) between Sicily and Latium, Etruria and Attica, the Adriatic and Tarentum, continued to subsist during the epoch before us or rather, strictly speaking, belonged to it; for although facts of this class, which as a rule are mentioned without a date, have been placed together for the purpose of presenting a general view under the first period, the statements made apply equally to the present. The clearest evidence in this respect is, of course, that of the coins. As the striking of Etruscan silver money after an Attic standard(30) and the penetrating of Italian and especially of Latin copper into Sicily(31) testify to the two former routes of traffic, so the equivalence, which we have just mentioned, between the silver money of Magna Graecia and the copper coinage of Picenum and Apulia, forms, with numerous other indications, an evidence of the active traffic which the Greeks of Lower Italy, the Tarentines in particular, held with the east Italian seaboard. The commerce again, which was at an earlier period perhaps still more active, between the Latins and the Campanian Greeks seems to have been disturbed by the Sabellian immigration, and to have been of no great moment during the first hundred and fifty years of the republic. The refusal of the Samnites in Capua and Cumae to supply the Romans with grain in the famine of 343 may be regarded as an indication of the altered relations which subsisted between Latium and Campania, till at the commencement of the fifth century the Roman arms restored and gave increased impetus to the old intercourse.

Touching on details, we may be allowed to mention, as one of the few dated facts in the history of Roman commerce, the notice drawn from the annals of Ardea, that in 454 the first barber came from Sicily to Ardea; and to dwell for a moment on the painted pottery which was sent chiefly from Attica, but also from Corcyra and Sicily, to Lucania, Campania, and Etruria, to serve there for the decoration of tombs—a traffic, as to the circumstances of which we are accidentally better informed than as to any other article of transmarine commerce. The commencement of this import trade probably falls about the period of the expulsion of the Tarquins; for the vases of the oldest style, which are of very rare occurrence in Italy, were probably painted in the second half of the third century of the city, while those of the chaste style, occurring in greater numbers, belong to the first half, those of the most finished beauty to the second half, of the fourth century; and the immense quantities of the other vases, often marked by showiness and size but seldom by excellence in workmanship, must be assigned as a whole to the following century. It was from the Hellenes undoubtedly that the Italians derived this custom of embellishing tombs;

but while the moderate means and fine discernment of the Greeks confined the practice in their case within narrow limits, it was stretched in Italy by barbaric opulence and barbaric extravagance far beyond its original and proper bounds. It is a significant circumstance, however, that in Italy this extravagance meets us only in the lands that had a Hellenic semi-culture. Any one who can read such records will perceive in the cemeteries of Etruria and Campania —the mines whence our museums have been replenished—a significant commentary on the accounts of the ancients as to the Etruscan and Campanian semi-culture choked amidst wealth and arrogance.(32) The homely Samnite character on the other hand remained at all times a stranger to this foolish luxury; the absence of Greek pottery from the tombs exhibits, quite as palpably as the absence of a Samnite coinage, the slight development of commercial intercourse and of urban life in this region. It is still more worthy of remark that Latium also, although not less near to the Greeks than Etruria and Campania, and in closest intercourse with them, almost wholly refrained from such sepulchral decorations. It is more than probable—especially on account of the altogether different character of the tombs in the unique Praeneste—that in this result we have to recognize the influence of the stern Roman morality or—if the expression be preferred—of the rigid Roman police. Closely connected with this subject are the already-mentioned interdicts, which the law of the Twelve Tables fulminated against purple bier-cloths and gold ornaments placed beside the dead; and the banishment of all silver plate, excepting the salt-cellar and sacrificial ladle, from the Roman household, so far at least as sumptuary laws and the terror of censorial censure could banish it: even in architecture we shall again encounter the same spirit of hostility to luxury whether noble or ignoble. Although, however, in consequence of these influences Rome probably preserved a certain outward simplicity longer than Capua and Volsinii, her commerce and trade—on which, in fact, along with agriculture her prosperity from the beginning rested—must not be regarded as having been inconsiderable, or as having less sensibly experienced the influence of her new commanding position.

Capital in Rome

No urban middle class in the proper sense of that term, no body of independent tradesmen and merchants, was ever developed in Rome. The cause of this was—in addition to the disproportionate centralization of capital which occurred at an early period—mainly the employment of slave labour. It was usual in antiquity, and was in fact a necessary consequence of slavery, that the minor trades in towns were very frequently carried on by slaves, whom their master established as artisans or merchants; or by freedmen, in whose case the master not only frequently furnished the capital, but also regularly stipulated for a share, often the half, of the profits. Retail trading and dealing in Rome were undoubtedly constantly on the increase; and there are proofs that the trades which minister to the luxury of great cities began to be concentrated in Rome—the Ficoroni casket for instance was designed in the fifth century of the city by a Praenestine artist and was sold to Praeneste, but was nevertheless manufactured in Rome.(33) But as the net proceeds even of retail business flowed for the most part into the coffers of the great houses, no industrial and commercial middle-class arose to an extent corresponding to that increase. As little were the great merchants and great manufacturers marked off as a distinct class from the great landlords. On the one hand, the latter were from ancient times(34) simultaneously traders and capitalists, and combined in their hands lending on security, trafficking on a great scale, the undertaking of contracts, and the executing of works for the state. On the other hand, from the emphatic moral importance which in the Roman commonwealth attached to the possession of land, and from its constituting the sole basis of political privileges—a basis which was infringed for the first time only towards the close of this epoch (35)—it was undoubtedly at this period already usual for the fortunate speculator to invest part of his capital in land. It is clear enough also from the political privileges given to freedmen possessing freeholds,(36) that the Roman statesmen sought in this way to diminish the dangerous class of the rich who had no land.

Development of Rome as A Great City

But while neither an opulent urban middle class nor a strictly close body of capitalists grew up in Rome, it was constantly acquiring more and more the character of a great city. This is plainly indicated by the increasing number of slaves crowded together in the capital (as attested by the very serious slave conspiracy of 335), and still more by the increasing multitude of freedmen, which was gradually becoming inconvenient and dangerous, as we may safely infer from the considerable tax imposed on manumissions in 397(37) and from the limitation of the political rights of freedmen in 450.(38) For not only was it implied in the circumstances that the great majority of the persons manumitted had to devote themselves to trade or commerce, but manumission itself among the Romans was, as we have already said, less an act of liberality than an industrial speculation, the master often finding it more for his interest to share the profits of the trade or commerce of the freedman than to assert his title to the whole proceeds of the labour of his slave. The increase of manumissions must therefore have necessarily kept pace with the increase of the commercial and industrial activity of the Romans.

Urban Police

A similar indication of the rising importance of urban life in Rome is presented by the great development of the urban police. To this period probably belong in great measure the enactments under which the four aediles divided the city into four police districts, and made provision for the discharge of their equally important and difficult functions—for the efficient repair of the network of drains small and large by which Rome was pervaded, as well as of the public buildings and places; for the proper cleansing and paving of the streets; for obviating the nuisances of ruinous buildings, dangerous animals, or foul smells; for the removing of waggons from the highway except during the hours of evening and night, and generally for the keeping open of the communication; for the uninterrupted supply of the market of the capital with good and cheap grain; for the destruction of unwholesome articles, and the suppression of false weights and measures; and for the special oversight of baths, taverns, and houses of bad fame.

Building—
Impulse Given to It

In respect to buildings the regal period, particularly the epoch of the great conquests, probably accomplished more than the first two centuries of the republic. Structures like the temples on the Capitol and on the Aventine and the great Circus were probably as obnoxious to the frugal fathers of the city as to the burgesses who gave their task-work; and it is remarkable that perhaps the most considerable building of the republican period before the Samnite wars, the temple of Ceres in the Circus, was a work of Spurius Cassius (261) who in more than one respect, sought to lead the commonwealth back to the traditions of the kings. The governing aristocracy moreover repressed private luxury with a rigour such as the rule of the kings, if prolonged, would certainly not have displayed. But at length even the senate was no longer able to resist the superior force of circumstances. It was Appius Claudius who in his epoch-making censorship (442) threw aside the antiquated rustic system of parsimonious hoarding, and taught his fellow-citizens to make a worthy use of the public resources. He began that noble system of public works of general utility, which justifies, if anything can justify, the military successes of Rome even from the point of view of the welfare of the nations, and which even now in its ruins furnishes some idea of the greatness of Rome to thousands on thousands who have never read a page of her history. To him the Roman state was indebted for its great military road, and the city of Rome for its first aqueduct. Following in the steps of Claudius, the Roman senate wove around Italy that network of roads and fortresses, the formation of which has already been described,(39) and without which, as the history of all military states from the Achaemenidae down to the creator of the road over the Simplon shows, no military hegemony can subsist. Following in the steps of Claudius, Manius Curius built from the proceeds of the Pyrrhic spoil a second aqueduct for the capital (482); and some years previously (464) with the gains of the Sabine war he opened up for the Velino, at the point above Terni where it falls into the Nera, that broader channel in which the stream still flows, with a view to drain the beautiful valley of Rieti and thereby to gain space for a large burgess settlement along with a modest farm for himself. Such works, in the eyes of persons of intelligence, threw into the shade the aimless magnificence of the Hellenic temples.

Embellishment of the City

The style of living also among the citizens now was altered. About the time of Pyrrhus silver plate began to make its appearance on Roman tables, and the chroniclers date the disappearance of shingle roofs in Rome from 470.(40) The new capital of Italy gradually laid aside its village-like aspect, and now began to embellish itself. It was not yet indeed customary to strip the temples in conquered towns of their ornaments for the decoration of Rome; but the beaks of the galleys of Antium were displayed at the orator's platform in the Forum(41) and on public festival days the gold-mounted shields brought home from the battle-fields of Samnium were exhibited along the stalls of the market.(42) The proceeds of fines were specially applied to the paving of the highways in and near the city, or to the erection and embellishment of public buildings. The wooden booths of the butchers, which stretched along the Forum on both sides, gave way, first on the Palatine side, then on that also which faced the Carinae, to the stone stalls of the money-changers; so that this place became the Exchange of Rome. Statues of the famous men of the past, of the kings, priests, and heroes of the legendary period, and of the Grecian - hospes- who was said to have interpreted to the decemvirs the laws of Solon; honorary columns and monuments dedicated to the great burgomasters who had conquered the Veientes, the Latins, the Samnites, to state envoys who had perished while executing their instructions, to rich women who had bequeathed their property to public objects, nay even to celebrated Greek philosophers and heroes such as Pythagoras and Alcibiades, were erected on the Capitol or in the Forum. Thus, now that the Roman community had become a great power, Rome itself became a great city.

Silver Standard of Value

Lastly Rome, as head of the Romano-Italian confederacy, not only entered into the Hellenistic state-system, but also conformed to the Hellenic system of moneys and coins. Up to this time the different communities of northern and central Italy, with few exceptions, had struck only a copper currency; the south Italian towns again universally had a currency of silver; and there were as many legal standards and systems of coinage as there were sovereign communities in Italy. In 485 all these local mints were restricted to the issuing of small coin; a general standard of currency applicable to all Italy was introduced, and the coining of the currency was centralized in Rome; Capua alone continued to retain its own silver coinage struck in the name of Rome, but after a different standard. The new monetary system was based on the legal ratio subsisting between the two metals, as it had long been fixed.(43) The common monetary unit was the piece of ten -asses- (which were no longer of a pound, but reduced to the third of a pound), the -denarius-, which weighed in copper 3 1/3 and in silver 1/72, of a Roman pound, a trifle more than the Attic —drachma—. At first copper money still predominated in the coinage; and it is probable that the earliest silver -denarius- was coined chiefly for Lower Italy and for intercourse with other lands. As the victory of the Romans over Pyrrhus and Tarentum and the Roman embassy to Alexandria could not but engage the thoughts of the contemporary Greek statesman, so the sagacious Greek merchant might well ponder as he looked on these new Roman drachmae. Their flat, unartistic, and monotonous stamping appeared poor and insignificant by the side of the marvellously beautiful contemporary coins of Pyrrhus and the Siceliots; nevertheless they were by no means, like the barbarian coins of antiquity, slavishly imitated and unequal in weight and alloy, but, on the contrary, worthy from the first by their independent and conscientious execution to be placed on a level with any Greek coin.

Extension of the Latin Nationality

Thus, when the eye turns from the development of constitutions and from the national struggles for dominion and for freedom which agitated Italy, and Rome in particular, from the banishment of the Tarquinian house to the subjugation of the

Samnites and the Italian Greeks, and rests on those calmer spheres of human existence which history nevertheless rules and pervades, it everywhere encounters the reflex influence of the great events, by which the Roman burgesses burst the bonds of patrician sway, and the rich variety of the national cultures of Italy gradually perished to enrich a single people. While the historian may not attempt to follow out the great course of events into the infinite multiplicity of individual detail, he does not overstep his province when, laying hold of detached fragments of scattered tradition, he indicates the most important changes which during this epoch took place in the national life of Italy. That in such an inquiry the life of Rome becomes still more prominent than in the earlier epoch, is not merely the result of the accidental blanks of our tradition; it was an essential consequence of the change in the political position of Rome, that the Latin nationality should more and more cast the other nationalities of Italy into the shade. We have already pointed to the fact, that at this epoch the neighbouring lands—southern Etruria, Sabina, the land of the Volscians, —began to become Romanized, as is attested by the almost total absence of monuments of the old native dialects, and by the occurrence of very ancient Roman inscriptions in those regions; the admission of the Sabines to full burgess-rights at the end of this period(44) betokens that the Latinizing of Central Italy was already at that time the conscious aim of Roman policy. The numerous individual assignations and colonial establishments scattered throughout Italy were, not only in a military but also in a linguistic and national point of view, the advanced posts of the Latin stock. The Latinizing of the Italians was scarcely at this time generally aimed at; on the contrary, the Roman senate seems to have intentionally upheld the distinction between the Latin and the other nationalities, and they did not yet, for example, allow the introduction of Latin into official use among the half-burgess communities of Campania. The force of circumstances, however, is stronger than even the strongest government: the language and customs of the Latin people immediately shared its predominance in Italy, and already began to undermine the other Italian nationalities.

Progress of Hellenism in Italy—
Adoption of Greek Habits at the Table

These nationalities were at the same time assailed from another quarter and by an ascendency resting on another basis—by Hellenism. This was the period when Hellenism began to become conscious of its intellectual superiority to the other nations, and to diffuse itself on every side. Italy did not remain unaffected by it. The most remarkable phenomenon of this sort is presented by Apulia, which after the fifth century of Rome gradually laid aside its barbarian dialect and silently became Hellenized. This change was brought about, as in Macedonia and Epirus, not by colonization, but by civilization, which seems to have gone hand in hand with the land commerce of Tarentum; at least that hypothesis is favoured by the facts, that the districts of the Poediculi and Daunii who were on friendly terms with the Tarentines carried out their Hellenization more completely than the Sallentines who lived nearer to Tarentum but were constantly at feud with it, and that the towns that were soonest Graecized, such as Arpi, were not situated on the coast. The stronger influence exerted by Hellenism over Apulia than over any other Italian region is explained partly by its position, partly by the slight development of any national culture of its own, and partly also perhaps by its nationality presenting a character less alien to the Greek stock than that of the rest of Italy.(45) We have already called attention(46) to the fact that the southern Sabellian stocks, although at the outset in concert with the tyrants of Syracuse they crushed and destroyed the Hellenism of Magna Graecia, were at the same time affected by contact and mingling with the Greeks, so that some of them, such as the Bruttians and Nolans, adopted the Greek language by the side of their native tongue, and others, such as the Lucanians and a part of the Campanians, adopted at least Greek writing and Greek manners. Etruria likewise showed tendencies towards a kindred development in the remarkable vases which have been discovered(47) belonging to this period, rivalling those of Campania and Lucania; and though Latium and Samnium remained more strangers to Hellenism, there were not wanting there also traces of an incipient and ever-growing influence of Greek culture. In all branches of the development of Rome during this epoch, in legislation and coinage, in religion, in the formation of national legend, we encounter traces of the Greeks; and from the commencement of the fifth century in particular, in other words, after the conquest of Campania, the Greek influence on Roman life appears rapidly and constantly on the increase. In the fourth century occurred the erection of the "-Graecostasis-"—remarkable in the very form of the word—a platform in the Roman Forum for eminent Greek strangers and primarily for the Massiliots.(48) In the following century the annals began to exhibit Romans of quality with Greek surnames, such as Philipus or in Roman form Pilipus, Philo, Sophus, Hypsaeus. Greek customs gained ground: such as the non-Italian practice of placing inscriptions in honour of the dead on the tomb—of which the epitaph of Lucius Scipio (consul in 456) is the oldest example known to us; the fashion, also foreign to the Italians, of erecting without any decree of the state honorary monuments to ancestors in public places —a system begun by the great innovator Appius Claudius, when he caused bronze shields with images and eulogies of his ancestors to be suspended in the new temple of Bellona (442); the distribution of branches of palms to the competitors, introduced at the Roman national festival in 461; above all, the Greek manners and habits at table. The custom not of sitting as formerly on benches, but of reclining on sofas, at table; the postponement of the chief meal from noon to between two and three o'clock in the afternoon according to our mode of reckoning; the institution of masters of the revels at banquets, who were appointed from among the guests present, generally by throwing the dice, and who then prescribed to the company what, how, and when they should drink; the table-chants sung in succession by the guests, which, however, in Rome were not -scolia-, but lays in praise of ancestors—all these were not primitive customs in Rome, but were borrowed from the Greeks at a very early period, for in Cato's time these usages were already common and had in fact partly fallen into disuse again. We must therefore place their introduction in this period at the latest. A characteristic feature also was the erection of statues to "the wisest and the bravest Greek" in the Roman Forum, which took place by command of the Pythian Apollo during the Samnite wars. The selection fell—evidently under Sicilian or Campanian influence—on Pythagoras and Alcibiades, the saviour and the Hannibal of the western Hellenes. The extent to which an acquaintance with Greek was already diffused in the fifth century among Romans of quality is shown by the embassies of the Romans to Tarentum—when their mouthpiece spoke, if not in the purest Greek, at any rate without an interpreter—and of Cineas to Rome. It scarcely admits of a doubt that from the fifth century the young Romans who devoted themselves to state affairs universally acquired a knowledge of what was then the general language of the world and of diplomacy.

Thus in the intellectual sphere Hellenism made advances quite as incessant as the efforts of the Romans to subject the earth to their sway; and the secondary nationalities, such as the Samnite, Celt, and Etruscan, hard pressed on both sides, were ever losing their inward vigour as well as narrowing their outward bounds.

Rome and the Romans of This Epoch

When the two great nations, both arrived at the height of their development, began to mingle in hostile or in friendly contact, their antagonism of character was at the same time prominently and fully brought out—the total want of individuality in the Italian and especially in the Roman character, as contrasted with the boundless variety, lineal, local, and personal, of Hellenism. There was no epoch of mightier vigour in the history of Rome than the epoch from the institution of the republic to the subjugation of Italy. That epoch laid the foundations of the commonwealth both within and without; it created a united Italy; it gave birth to the traditional groundwork of the national law and of the national history; it originated the -pilum- and the maniple, the construction of roads and of aqueducts, the farming of estates and the monetary system; it moulded the she-wolf of the Capitol and designed the Ficoroni casket. But the individuals, who contributed the several stones to this gigantic structure and cemented them together, have disappeared without leaving a trace, and the nations of Italy did not merge into that of Rome more completely than the single Roman burgess merged in the Roman community. As the grave closes alike over all whether important or insignificant, so in the roll of the Roman burgomasters the empty scion of nobility stands undistinguishable by the side of the great statesman. Of the few records that have reached us from this period none is more venerable, and none at the same time more characteristic, than the epitaph of Lucius Cornelius Scipio, who was consul in 456, and three years afterwards took part in the decisive battle of Sentinum.(49) On the beautiful sarcophagus, in noble Doric style, which eighty years ago still enclosed the dust of the conqueror of the Samnites, the following sentence is inscribed:—

-Cornelius Lucius—Scipio Barbatus,
Gnaivod patre prognatus, —fortis vir sapiensque,
Quoius forma virtu—tei parisuma fuit,
Consol censor aidilis—quei fuit apud vos,
Taurasia Cisauna—Samnio cepit,
Subigit omne Loucanum—opsidesque abdoucit.-

_-'_-'_-'_‖-'_-'_-'_

Innumerable others who had been at the head of the Roman commonwealth, as well as this Roman statesman and warrior, might be commemorated as having been of noble birth and of manly beauty, valiant and wise; but there was no more to record regarding them. It is doubtless not the mere fault of tradition that no one of these Cornelii, Fabii, Papirii, or whatever they were called, confronts us in a distinct individual figure. The senator was supposed to be no worse and no better than other senators, nor at all to differ from them. It was not necessary and not desirable that any burgess should surpass the rest, whether by showy silver plate and Hellenic culture, or by uncommon wisdom and excellence. Excesses of the former kind were punished by the censor, and for the latter the constitution gave no scope. The Rome of this period belonged to no individual; it was necessary for all the burgesses to be alike, that each of them might be like a king.

Appius Claudius

No doubt, even now Hellenic individual development asserted its claims by the side of that levelling system; and the genius and force which it exhibited bear, no less than the tendency to which it opposed itself, the full stamp of that great age. We can name but a single man in connection with it; but he was, as it were, the incarnation of the idea of progress. Appius Claudius (censor 442; consul 447, 458), the great-great-grandson of the decemvir, was a man of the old nobility and proud of the long line of his ancestors; but yet it was he who set aside the restriction which confined the full franchise of the state to the freeholders,(50) and who broke up the old system of finance.(51) From Appius Claudius date not only the Roman aqueducts and highways, but also Roman jurisprudence, eloquence, poetry, and grammar. The publication of a table of the -legis actiones-, speeches committed to writing and Pythagorean sentences, and even innovations in orthography, are attributed to him. We may not on this account call him absolutely a democrat or include him in that opposition party which found its champion in Manius Curius;(52) in him on the contrary the spirit of the ancient and modern patrician kings predominated —the spirit of the Tarquins and the Caesars, between whom he forms a connecting link in that five hundred years' interregnum of extraordinary deeds and ordinary men. So long as Appius Claudius took an active part in public life, in his official conduct as well as his general carriage he disregarded laws and customs on all hands with the hardihood and sauciness of an Athenian; till, after having long retired from the political stage, the blind old man, returning as it were from the tomb at the decisive Moment, overcame king Pyrrhus in the senate, and first formally and solemnly proclaimed the complete sovereignty of Rome over Italy.(53) But the gifted man came too early or too late; the gods made him blind on account of his untimely wisdom. It was not individual genius that ruled in Rome and through Rome in Italy; it was the one immoveable idea of a policy—propagated from generation to generation in the senate—with the leading maxims of which the sons of the senators became already imbued, when in the company of their fathers they went to the council and there at the door of the hall listened to the wisdom of the men whose seats they were destined at some future time to fill. Immense successes were thus obtained at an immense price; for Nike too is followed by her Nemesis. In the Roman commonwealth there was no special dependence on any one man, either on soldier or on general, and under the rigid discipline of its moral police all the idiosyncrasies of human character were extinguished. Rome reached a greatness such as no other state of antiquity attained; but she dearly purchased her greatness at the sacrifice of the graceful variety, of the easy abandon and of the inward freedom of Hellenic life.

Notes for Book II Chapter VIII

1. I. XI. Punishment of Offenses against Order

2. II. I. Right of Appeal

3. II. III. The Senate, Its Composition

4. II. I. Law and Edict

5. II. III. Censorship, the Magistrates, Partition and Weakening of the Consular Powers

6. II. III. Laws Imposing Taxes

7. I. VI. Class of —Metoeci— Subsisting by the Side of the Community

8. I. V. The Housefather and His Household, note

9. II. III. Praetorship

10. II. III. Praetorship, *ii.* V. Revision of the Municipal Constitutions, Police Judges

11. The view formerly adopted, that these -tres viri- belonged to the earliest period, is erroneous, for colleges of magistrates with odd numbers are foreign to the oldest state-arrangements (Chronol. p. 15, note 12). Probably the well-accredited account, that they were first nominated in 465 (Liv. Ep. 11), should simply be retained, and the otherwise suspicious inference of the falsifier Licinius Macer (in Liv. vii. 46), which makes mention of them before 450, should be simply rejected. At first undoubtedly the -tres viri- were nominated by the superior magistrates, as was the case with most of the later -magistratus minores-; the Papirian -plebiscitum-, which transferred the nomination of them to the community (Festus, -v. sacramentum-, p. 344, Niall.), was at any rate not issued till after the institution of the office of -praetor peregrinus-, or at the earliest towards the middle of the sixth century, for it names the praetor -qui inter jus cives ius dicit-.

12. II. VII. Subject Communities

13. This inference is suggested by what Livy says (ix. 20) as to the reorganization of the colony of Antium twenty years after it was founded; and it is self-evident that, while the Romans might very well impose on the inhabitant of Ostia the duty of settling all his lawsuits in Rome, the same course could not be followed with townships like Antium and Sena.

14. II. I. Restrictions on the Delegation of Powers

15. People are in the habit of praising the Romans as a nation specially privileged in respect to jurisprudence, and of gazing with wonder on their admirable law as a mystical gift of heaven; presumably by way of specially excusing themselves for the worthlessness of their own legal system. A glance at the singularly fluctuating and undeveloped criminal law of the Romans might show the untenableness of ideas so confused even to those who may think the proposition too simple, that a sound people has a sound law, and a morbid people an unsound. Apart from the more general political conditions on which jurisprudence also, and indeed jurisprudence especially, depends, the causes of the excellence of the Roman civil law lie mainly in two features: first, that the plaintiff and defendant were specially obliged to explain and embody in due and binding form the grounds of the demand and of the objection to comply with it; and secondly, that the Romans appointed a permanent machinery for the edictal development of their law, and associated it immediately with practice. By the former the Romans precluded the pettifogging practices of advocates, by the latter they obviated incapable law-making, so far as such things can be prevented at all; and by means of both in conjunction they satisfied, as far as is possible, the two conflicting requirements, that law shall constantly be fixed, and that it shall constantly be in accordance with the spirit of the age.

16. II. II. Relation of the Tribune to the Consul

17. V. V. The Hegemony of Rome over Latium Shaken and Re-established

18. Venus probably first appears in the later sense as Aphrodite on occasion of the dedication of the temple consecrated in this year (Liv. x. 31; Becker, Topographie, p. 472).

19. II. III. Intrigues of the Nobility

20. I. VI. Organization of the Army

21. II. III. Increasing Powers of the Burgesses

22. I. VI. the Five Classes

23. According to Roman tradition the Romans originally carried quadrangular shields, after which they borrowed from the Etruscans the round hoplite shield (-clupeus-, —aspis—), and from the Samnites the later square shield (-scutum-, —-thureos—), and the javelin (-veru-) (Diodor. Vat. Fr. p. 54; Sallust, Cat. 51, 38; Virgil, Aen. vii. 665; Festus, Ep. v. Samnites, p. 327, Mull.; and the authorities cited in Marquardt, Handb. iii. 2, 241). But it may be regarded as certain that the hoplite shield or, in other words, the tactics of the Doric phalanx were imitated not from the Etruscans, but directly from the Hellenes, As to the -scutum-, that large, cylindrical, convex leather shield must certainly have taken the place of the flat copper -clupeus-,

when the phalanx was broken up into maniples; but the undoubted derivation of the word from the Greek casts suspicion on the derivation of the thing itself from the Samnites. From the Greeks the Romans derived also the sling (-funda- from —-sphendone—). (like -fides- from —sphion—),(I. XV. Earliest Hellenic Influences). The pilum was considered by the ancients as quite a Roman invention.

24. I. XIII. Landed Proprietors

25. II. III. Combination of the Plebian Aristocracy and the Farmers against the Nobility

26. Varro (De R. R. i. 2, 9) evidently conceives the author of the Licinian agrarian law as fanning in person his extensive lands; although, we may add, the story may easily have been invented to explain the cognomen (-Stolo-).

27. I. XIII. System of Joint Cultivation

28. I. XIII. Inland Commerce of the Italians

29. I. XIII. Commerce in Latium Passive, in Etruria Active

30. I. XIII. Etrusco-Attic, and Latino-Sicilian Commerce

31. I. XIII. Etrusco-Attic, and Latino-Sicilian Commerce

32. II. IV. Etruria at Peace and on the Decline, *ii*. V. Campanian Hellenism

33. The conjecture that Novius Flautius, the artist who worked at this casket for Dindia Macolnia, in Rome, may have been a Campanian, is refuted by the old Praenestine tomb-stones recently discovered, on which, among other Macolnii and Plautii, there occurs also a Lucius Magulnius, son of Haulms (L. Magolnio Pla. f.).

34. I. XIII. Etrusco-Attic, and Latino-Sicilian Commerce, *ii*. II. Rising Power of the Capitalists

35. II. III. The Burgess Body

36. II. III. The Burgess Body

37. II. III. Laws Imposing Taxes

38. II. III. The Burgess Body

39. II. VII. Construction of New Fortresses and Roads

184

40. We have already mentioned the censorial stigma attached to Publius Cornelius Rufinus (consul 464, 477) for his silver plate.(II. VIII. Police) The strange statement of Fabius (in Strabo, v. p. 228) that the Romans first became given to luxury (—aisthesthae tou plouton—) after the conquest of the Sabines, is evidently only a historical version of the same matter; for the conquest of the Sabines falls in the first consulate of Rufinus.

41. II. V. Colonizations in the Land of the Volsci

42. II. VI. Last Campaigns in Samnium

43. II. VIII. Inland Intercourse in Italy

44. I. III. Localities of the Oldest Cantons

45. I. II. Iapygians

46. II. V. Campanian Hellenism

47. II. VIII. Transmarine Commerce

48. II. VII. The Full Roman Franchise

49. II. VI. Battle of Sentinum

50. II. III. The Burgess-Body

51. II. VIII. Impulse Given to It

52. II. III. New Opposition

53. II. VII. Attempts at Peace

CHAPTER IX

Art and Science

The Roman National Festival— The Roman Stage

The growth of art, and of poetic art especially, in antiquity was intimately associated with the development of national festivals. The thanksgiving-festival of the Roman community, which had been already organized in the previous period essentially under Greek influence and in the first instance as an extraordinary festival, —the -ludi maximi- or -Romani-,(1) —acquired during the present epoch a longer duration and greater variety in the amusements. Originally limited to one day, the festival was prolonged by an additional day after the happy termination of each of the three great revolutions of 245, 260, and 387, and thus at the close of this period it had already a duration of four days.(2)

A still more important circumstance was, that, probably on the institution of the curule aedileship (387) which was from the first entrusted with the preparation and oversight of the festival,(3) it lost its extraordinary character and its reference to a special vow made by the general, and took its place in the series of the ordinary annually recurring festivals as the first of all. Nevertheless the government adhered to the practice of allowing the spectacle proper —namely the chariot-race, which was the principal performance—to take place not more than once at the close of the festival. On the other days the multitude were probably left mainly to furnish amusement for themselves, although musicians, dancers, rope-walkers, jugglers, jesters and such like would not fail to make their appearance on the occasion, whether hired or not But about the year 390 an important change occurred, which must have stood in connection with the fixing and prolongation of the festival, that took place perhaps about the same time. A scaffolding of boards was erected at the expense of the state in the Circus for the first three days, and suitable representations were provided on it for the entertainment of the multitude. That matters might not be carried too far however in this way, a fixed sum of 200,000 -asses- (2055 pounds) once for all appropriated from the exchequer for the expenses of the festival; and the sum was not increased up to the period of the Punic wars. The aediles, who had to expend this sum, were obliged to defray any additional amount out of their own pockets; and it is not probable that they at this time contributed often or considerably from their own resources. That the new stage was generally under Greek influence, is proved by its very name (-scaena-, —skene—). It was no doubt at first designed merely for musicians and buffoons of all sorts, amongst whom the dancers to the flute, particularly those then so celebrated from Etruria, were probably the most distinguished; but a public stage had at any rate now arisen in Rome and it soon became open also to the Roman poets.

Ballad Singers, -Satura- —
Censure of Art

There was no want of such poets in Latium. Latin "strolling minstrels" or "ballad-singers" (-grassatores-, -spatiatores-) went from town to town and from house to house, and recited their chants (-saturae-(4)), gesticulating and dancing to the accompaniment of the flute. The measure was of course the only one that then existed, the so-called Saturnian.(5) No distinct plot lay at the basis of the chants, and as little do they appear to have been in the form of dialogue. We must conceive of them as resembling those monotonous —sometimes improvised, sometimes recited—ballads and -tarantelle-, such as one may still hear in the Roman hostelries. Songs of this sort accordingly early came upon the public stage, and certainly formed the first nucleus of the Roman theatre. But not only were these beginnings of the drama in Rome, as everywhere, modest and humble; they were, in a remarkable manner, accounted from the very outset disreputable. The Twelve Tables denounced evil and worthless song-singing, imposing severe penalties not only upon incantations but even on lampoons composed against a fellow-citizen or recited before his door, and forbidding the employment of wailing-women at funerals. But far more severely, than by such legal restrictions, the incipient exercise of art was affected by the moral anathema, which was denounced against these frivolous and paid trades by the narrowminded earnestness of the Roman character. "The trade of a poet," says Cato, "in former times was not respected; if any one occupied himself with it or was a hanger-on at banquets, he was called an idler." But now any one who practised dancing, music, or ballad-singing for money was visited with a double stigma, in consequence of the more and more confirmed disapproval of gaining a livelihood by services rendered for remuneration. While accordingly the taking part in the masked farces with stereotyped characters, that formed the usual native amusement,(6) was looked upon as an innocent youthful frolic, the appearing on a public stage for money and without a mask was considered as directly infamous, and the singer and poet were in this respect placed quite on a level with the rope-dancer and the harlequin. Persons of this stamp were regularly pronounced by the censors(7) incapable of serving in the burgess-army and of voting in the burgess-assembly. Moreover, not only was the direction of the stage regarded as pertaining to the province of the city police—a fact significant enough even in itself—but the police was probably, even at this period, invested with arbitrary powers of an extraordinary character against professional stage-artists. Not only did the police magistrates sit in judgment on the performance after its conclusion—on which occasion wine flowed as copiously for those who had acquitted themselves well, as stripes fell to the lot of the bungler—but all the urban magistrates were legally entitled to inflict bodily chastisement and imprisonment on any actor at any time and at any place. The necessary effect of this was that dancing, music, and poetry, at least so far as they appeared on the public stage, fell into the hands of the lowest classes of the Roman burgesses, and especially into those of foreigners; and while at this period poetry still played altogether too insignificant a part to engage the attention of foreign artists, the statement on the other hand, that in Rome all the music, sacred and profane, was essentially Etruscan, and consequently the ancient Latin art of the flute, which was evidently at one time held in high esteem,(8) had been supplanted by foreign music, may be regarded as already applicable to this period.

There is no mention of any poetical literature. Neither the masked plays nor the recitations of the stage can have had in the proper sense fixed texts; on the contrary, they were ordinarily improvised by the performers themselves as circumstances required. Of works composed at this period posterity could point to nothing but a sort of Roman "Works and Days"—counsels of a farmer to his son,(9) and the already-mentioned Pythagorean poems of Appius Claudius(10) the first commencement of Roman poetry after the Hellenic type. Nothing of the poems of this epoch has survived but one or two epitaphs in Saturnian measure.(11)

Roman Historical Composition

Along with the rudiments of the Roman drama, the rudiments of Roman historical composition belong to this period; both as regards the contemporary recording of remarkable events, and as regards the conventional settlement of the early history of the Roman community.

Registers of Magistrates

The writing of contemporary history was associated with the register of the magistrates. The register reaching farthest back, which was accessible to the later Roman inquirers and is still indirectly accessible to us, seems to have been derived from the archives of the temple of the Capitoline Jupiter; for it records the names of the annual presidents of the community onward from the consul Marcus Horatius, who consecrated that temple on the 13th Sept. in his year of office, and it also notices the vow which was made on occasion of a severe pestilence under the consuls Publius Servilius and Lucius Aebutius (according to the reckoning now current, 291), that thenceforward a nail should be driven every hundredth year into the wall of the Capitoline temple. Subsequently it was the state officials who were learned in measuring and in writing, or in other words, the pontifices, that kept an official record of the names of the annual chief magistrates, and thus combined an annual, with the earlier monthly, calendar. Both these calendars were afterwards comprehended under the name of Fasti—which strictly belonged only to the list of court-days. This arrangement was probably adopted not long after the abolition of the monarchy; for in fact an official record of the annual magistrates was of urgent practical necessity for the purpose of authenticating the order of succession of official documents. But, if there was an official register of the consuls so old, it probably perished in the Gallic conflagration (364); and the list of the pontifical college was subsequently completed from the Capitoline register which was not affected by that catastrophe, so far as this latter reached back. That the list of presidents which we now have —although in collateral matters, and especially in genealogical statements, it has been supplemented at pleasure from the family pedigrees of the nobility—is in substance based from the beginning on contemporary and credible records, admits of no doubt. But it reproduces the calendar years only imperfectly and approximately: for the consuls did not enter on office with the new year, or even on a definite day fixed once for all; on the contrary from various causes the day of entering on office was fluctuating, and the -interregna-that frequently occurred between two consulates were entirely omitted in the reckoning by official years. Accordingly, if the calendar years were to be reckoned by this list of consuls, it was necessary to note the days of entering on and of demitting office in the case of each pair, along with such -interregna- as occurred; and this too may have been early done. But besides this, the list of the annual magistrates was adjusted to the list of calendar years in such a way that a pair of magistrates were by accommodation assigned to each calendar year, and, where the list did not suffice, intercalary years were inserted, which are denoted in the later (Varronian) table by the figures 379, 383, 421, 430, 445, 453. From 291 u. c. (463 B. C.) the Roman list demonstrably coincides, not indeed in detail but yet on the whole, with the Roman calendar, and is thus chronologically certain, so far as the defectiveness of the calendar itself allows. The 47 years preceding that date cannot be checked, but must likewise be at least in the main correct.(12) Whatever lies beyond 245 remains, chronologically, in oblivion.

Capitoline Era

No era was formed for ordinary use; but in ritual matters they reckoned from the year of the consecration of the temple of the Capitoline Jupiter, from which the list of magistrates also started.

Annals

The idea naturally suggested itself that, along with the names of the magistrates, the most important events occurring under their magistracy might be noted; and from such notices appended to the catalogue of magistrates the Roman annals arose, just as the chronicles of the middle ages arose out of the memoranda marginally appended to the table of Easter. But it was not until a late period that the pontifices formed the scheme of a formal chronicle (-liber annalis-), which should steadily year by year record the names of all the magistrates and the remarkable events. Before the eclipse of the sun noticed under the 5th of June 351, by which is probably meant that of the 20th June 354, no solar eclipse was found recorded from observation in the later chronicle of the city: its statements as to the numbers of the census only begin to sound credible after the beginning of the fifth century,(13) the cases of fines brought before the people, and the prodigies expiated on behalf of the community, appear to have been regularly introduced into the annals only after the second half of the fifth century began. To all appearance the institution of an organized book of annals, and—what was certainly associated with it—the revision (which we have just explained) of the earlier list of magistrates so as to make it a year-calendar by the insertion, where chronologically necessary, of intercalary years, took place in the first half of the fifth century. But even after it became a practically recognized duty of the -pontifex maximus- to record year after year campaigns and colonizations, pestilences and famines, eclipses and portents, the deaths of priests and other men of note, the new decrees of the people, and the results of the census, and to deposit these records in his official residence for permanent preservation and for any one's inspection, these records were still far removed from the character of real historical writings. How scanty the contemporary record still was at the close of this period and how ample room is left for the caprice of subsequent annalists, is shown with incisive clearness by a comparison of the accounts as to the campaign of 456 in the annals and in the epitaph of the consul Scipio.(14) The later historians were evidently unable to construct a readable and in some measure connected narrative out of these notices from the book of annals; and we should have difficulty, even if the book of annals still lay before us with its original contents, in writing from it in duly connected sequence the history of the times. Such chronicles, however, did not exist merely in Rome; every Latin city possessed its annals as well as its pontifices, as is clear from isolated notices relative to Ardea for instance, Ameria, and Interamna on the Nar; and from the collective mass of these city-chronicles some result might perhaps have been attained similar to what has been accomplished for the earlier middle ages by the comparison of different monastic chronicles. Unfortunately the Romans in later times preferred to supply the defect by Hellenic or Hellenizing falsehoods.

Family Pedigrees

Besides these official arrangements, meagrely planned and uncertainly handled, for commemorating past times and past events, there can scarcely have existed at this epoch any other records immediately serviceable for Roman history. Of private chronicles we find no trace. The leading houses, however, were careful to draw up genealogical tables, so important in a legal point of view, and to have the family pedigree painted for a perpetual memorial on the walls of the entrance-hall. These lists, which at least named the magistracies held by the family, not only furnished a basis for family tradition, but doubtless at an early period had biographical notices attached to them. The memorial orations, which in Rome could not be omitted at the funeral of any person of quality, and were ordinarily pronounced by the nearest relative of the deceased, consisted essentially not merely in an enumeration of the virtues and excellencies of the dead, but also in a recital of the deeds and virtues of his ancestors; and so they were doubtless, even in the earliest times, transmitted traditionally from one generation to another. Many a valuable notice may by this means have been preserved; but many a daring perversion and falsification also may have been in this way introduced into tradition.

Roman Early History of Rome

But as the first steps towards writing real history belonged to this period, to it belonged also the first attempts to record, and conventionally distort, the primitive history of Rome. The sources whence it was formed were of course the same as they are everywhere. Isolated names like those of the kings Numa, Ancus, Tullus, to whom the clan-names were probably only assigned subsequently, and isolated facts, such as the conquest of the Latins by king Tarquinius and the expulsion of the Tarquinian royal house, may have continued to live in true general tradition orally transmitted. Further materials were furnished by the traditions of the patrician clans, such as the various tales that relate to the Fabii. Other tales gave a symbolic and historic shape to primitive national institutions, especially setting forth with great vividness the origin of rules of law. The sacredness of the walls was thus illustrated in the tale of the death of Remus, the abolition of blood-revenge in the tale of the end of king Tatius(15), the necessity of the arrangement as to the -pons sublicius- in the legend of Horatius Cocles,(15) the origin of the -provocatio- in the beautiful tale of the Horatii and Curiatii, the origin of manumission and of the burgess-rights of freedmen in the tale of the Tarquinian conspiracy and the slave Vindicius. To the same class belongs the history of the foundation of the city itself, which was designed to connect the origin of Rome with Latium and with Alba, the general metropolis of the Latins. Historical glosses were annexed to the surnames of distinguished Romans; that of Publius Valerius the "servant of the people" (-Poplicola-), for instance, gathered around it a whole group of such anecdotes. Above all, the sacred fig-tree and other spots and notable objects in the city were associated with a great multitude of sextons' tales of the same nature as those out of which, upwards of a thousand years afterwards, there grew up on the same ground the Mirabilia Urbis. Some attempts to link together these different tales—the adjustment of the series of the seven kings, the setting down of the duration of the monarchy at 240 years in all, which was undoubtedly based on a calculation of the length of generations,(16) and even the commencement of an official record of these assumed facts—probably took place already in this epoch. The outlines of the narrative, and in particular its quasi-chronology, make their appearance in the later tradition so unalterably fixed, that for that very reason the fixing of them must be placed not in, but previous to, the literary epoch of Rome. If a bronze casting of the twins Romulus and Remus sucking the teats of the she-wolf was already placed beside the sacred fig-tree in 458, the Romans who subdued Latium and Samnium must have heard the history of the origin of their ancestral city in a form not greatly differing from what we read in Livy. Even the Aborigines—i. e. "those from the very beginning"—that simple rudimental form of historical speculation as to the Latin race—are met with about 465 in the Sicilian author Callias. It is of the very nature of a chronicle that it should attach prehistoric speculation to history and endeavour to go back, if not to the origin of heaven and earth, at least to the origin of the community; and there is express testimony that the table of the pontifices specified the year of the foundation of Rome. Accordingly it may be assumed that, when the pontifical college in the first half of the fifth century proceeded to substitute for the former scanty records—ordinarily, doubtless, confined to the names of the magistrates—the scheme of a formal yearly chronicle, it also added what was wanting at the beginning, the history of the kings of Rome and of their fall, and, by placing the institution of the republic on the day of the consecration of the Capitoline temple, the 13th of Sept. 245, furnished a semblance of connection between the dateless and the annalistic narrative. That in this earliest record of the origin of Rome the hand of Hellenism was at work, can scarcely be doubted. The speculations as to the primitive and subsequent population, as to the priority of pastoral life over agriculture, and the transformation of the man Romulus into the god Quirinus,(17) have quite a Greek aspect, and even the obscuring of the genuinely national forms of the pious Numa and the wise Egeria by the admixture of alien elements of Pythagorean primitive wisdom appears by no means to be one of the most recent ingredients in the Roman prehistoric annals.

The pedigrees of the noble clans were completed in a manner analogous to these -origines- of the community, and were, in the favourite style of heraldry, universally traced back to illustrious ancestors. The Aemilii, for instance, Calpurnii, Pinarii, and Pomponii professed to be descended from the four sons of Numa, Mamercus, Calpus, Pinus, and Pompo; and the Aemilii, yet further, from Mamercus, the son of Pythagoras, who was named the "winning speaker" (—aimulos—)

But, notwithstanding the Hellenic reminiscences that are everywhere apparent, these prehistoric annals of the community and of the leading houses may be designated at

192

least relatively as national, partly because they originated in Rome, partly because they tended primarily to form links of connection not between Rome and Greece, but between Rome and Latium.

Hellenic Early History of Rome

It was Hellenic story and fiction that undertook the task of connecting Rome and Greece. Hellenic legend exhibits throughout an endeavour to keep pace with the gradual extension of geographical knowledge, and to form a dramatized geography by the aid of its numerous stories of voyagers and emigrants. In this, however, it seldom follows a simple course. An account like that of the earliest Greek historical work which mentions Rome, the "Sicilian History" of Antiochus of Syracuse (which ended in 330)—that a man named Sikelos had migrated from Rome to Italia, that is, to the Bruttian peninsula —such an account, simply giving a historical form to the family affinity between the Romans, Siculi, and Bruttians, and free from all Hellenizing colouring, is a rare phenomenon. Greek legend as a whole is pervaded—and the more so, the later its rise—by a tendency to represent the whole barbarian world as having either issued from the Greeks or having been subdued by them; and it early in this sense spun its threads also around the west. For Italy the legends of Herakles and of the Argonauts were of less importance—although Hecataeus (after 257) is already acquainted with the Pillars of Herakles, and carries the Argo from the Black Sea into the Atlantic Ocean, from the latter into the Nile, and thus back to the Mediterranean—than were the homeward voyages connected with the fall of Ilion. With the first dawn of information as to Italy Diomedes begins to wander in the Adriatic, and Odysseus in the Tyrrhene Sea;(18) as indeed the latter localization at least was naturally suggested by the Homeric conception of the legend. Down to the times of Alexander the countries on the Tyrrhene Sea belonged in Hellenic fable to the domain of the legend of Odysseus; Ephorus, who ended his history with the year 414, and the so-called Scylax (about 418) still substantially follow it. Of Trojan voyages the whole earlier poetry has no knowledge; in Homer Aeneas after the fall of Ilion rules over the Trojans that remained at home.

Stesichorus

It was the great remodeller of myths, Stesichorus (122-201) who first in his "Destruction of Ilion" brought Aeneas to the land of the west, that he might poetically enrich the world of fable in the country of his birth and of his adoption, Sicily and Lower Italy, by the contrast of the Trojan heroes with the Hellenic. With him originated the poetical outlines of this fable as thenceforward fixed, especially the group of the hero and his wife, his little son and his aged father bearing the household gods, departing from burning Troy, and the important identification of the Trojans with the Sicilian and Italian autochthones, which is especially apparent in the case of the Trojan trumpeter Misenus who gave his name to the promontory of Misenum.(19) The old poet was guided in this view by the feeling that the barbarians of Italy were less widely removed from the Hellenes than other barbarians were, and that the relation between the Hellenes and Italians might, when measured poetically, be conceived as similar to that between the Homeric Achaeans and the Trojans. This new Trojan fable soon came to be mixed up with the earlier legend of Odysseus, while it spread at the same time more widely over Italy. According to Hellanicus (who wrote about 350) Odysseus and Aeneas came through the country of the Thracians and Molottians (Epirus) to Italy, where the Trojan women whom they had brought with them burnt the ships, and Aeneas founded the city of Rome and named it after one of these Trojan women. To a similar effect, only with less absurdity, Aristotle (370-432) related that an Achaean squadron cast upon the Latin coast had been set on fire by Trojan female slaves, and that the Latins had originated from the descendants of the Achaeans who were thus compelled to remain there and of their Trojan wives. With these tales were next mingled elements from the indigenous legend, the knowledge of which had been diffused as far as Sicily by the active intercourse between Sicily and Italy, at least towards the end of this epoch. In the version of the origin of Rome, which the Sicilian Callias put on record about 465, the fables of Odysseus, Aeneas, and Romulus were intermingled.(20)

Timaeus

But the person who really completed the conception subsequently current of this Trojan migration was Timaeus of Tauromenium in Sicily, who concluded his historical work with 492. It is he who represents Aeneas as first founding Lavinium with its shrine of the Trojan Penates, and as thereafter founding Rome; he must also have interwoven the Tyrian princess Elisa or Dido with the legend of Aeneas, for with him Dido is the foundress of Carthage, and Rome and Carthage are said by him to have been built in the same year. These alterations were manifestly suggested by certain accounts that had reached Sicily respecting Latin manners and customs, in conjunction with the critical struggle which at the very time and place where Timaeus wrote was preparing between the Romans and the Carthaginians. In the main, however, the story cannot have been derived from Latium, but can only have been the good-for-nothing invention of the old "gossip-monger" himself. Timaeus had heard of the primitive temple of the household gods in Lavinium; but the statement, that these were regarded by the Lavinates as the Penates brought by the followers of Aeneas from Ilion, is as certainly an addition of his own, as the ingenious parallel between the Roman October horse and the Trojan horse, and the exact inventory taken of the sacred objects of Lavinium—there were, our worthy author affirms, heralds' staves of iron and copper, and an earthen vase of Trojan manufacture! It is true that these same Penates might not at all be seen by any one for centuries afterwards; but Timaeus was one of the historians who upon no matter are so fully informed as upon things unknowable. It is not without reason that Polybius, who knew the man, advises that he should in no case be trusted, and least of all where, as in this instance, he appeals to documentary proofs. In fact the Sicilian rhetorician, who professed to point out the grave of Thucydides in Italy, and who found no higher praise for Alexander than that he had finished the conquest of Asia sooner than Isocrates finished his "Panegyric," was exactly the man to knead the naïve fictions of the earlier time into that confused medley on which the play of accident has conferred so singular a celebrity.

194

How far the Hellenic play of fable regarding Italian matters, as it in the first instance arose in Sicily, gained admission during this period even in Italy itself, cannot be ascertained with precision. Those links of connection with the Odyssean cycle, which we subsequently meet with in the legends of the foundation of Tusculum, Praeneste, Antium, Ardea, and Cortona, must probably have been already concocted at this period; and even the belief in the descent of the Romans from Trojan men or Trojan women must have been established at the close of this epoch in Rome, for the first demonstrable contact between Rome and the Greek east is the intercession of the senate on behalf of the "kindre" Ilians in 472. That the fable of Aeneas was nevertheless of comparatively recent origin in Italy, is shown by the extremely scanty measure of its localization as compared with the legend of Odysseus; and at any rate the final redaction of these tales, as well as their reconciliation with the legend of the origin of Rome, belongs only to the following age.

While in this way historical composition, or what was so called among the Hellenes, busied itself in its own fashion with the prehistoric times of Italy, it left the contemporary history of Italy almost untouched—a circumstance as significant of the sunken condition of Hellenic history, as it is to be for our sakes regretted. Theopompus of Chios (who ended his work with 418) barely noticed in passing the capture of Rome by the Celts; and Aristotle,(21) Clitarchus,(22) Theophrastus,(23) Heraclides of Pontus (about 450), incidentally mention particular events relating to Rome. It is only with Hieronymus of Cardia, who as the historian of Pyrrhus narrated also his Italian wars, that Greek historiography becomes at the same time an authority for the history of Rome.

Jurisprudence

Among the sciences, that of jurisprudence acquired an invaluable basis through the committing to writing of the laws of the city in the years 303, 304. This code, known under the name of the Twelve Tables, is perhaps the oldest Roman document that deserves the name of a book. The nucleus of the so-called -leges regiae- was probably not much more recent. These were certain precepts chiefly of a ritual nature, which rested upon traditional usage, and were probably promulgated to the general public under the form of royal enactments by the college of pontifices, which was entitled not to legislate but to point out the law. Moreover it may be presumed that from the commencement of this period the more important decrees of the senate at any rate—if not those of the people—were regularly recorded in writing; for already in the earliest conflicts between the orders disputes took place as to their preservation.(24)

Opinions—
Table of Formulae for Actions

While the mass of written legal documents thus increased, the foundations of jurisprudence in the proper sense were also firmly laid. It was necessary that both the magistrates who were annually changed and the jurymen taken from the people should be enabled to resort to men of skill, who were acquainted with the course of law and knew how to suggest a decision accordant with precedents or, in the absence of these, resting on reasonable grounds. The pontifices who were wont to be consulted by the people regarding court-days and on all questions of difficulty and of legal observance relating to the worship of the gods, delivered also, when asked, counsels and opinions on other points of law, and thus developed in the bosom of their college that tradition which formed the basis of Roman private law, more especially the formulae of action proper for each particular case. A table of formulae which embraced all these actions, along with a calendar which specified the court-days, was published to the people about 450 by Appius Claudius or by his clerk, Gnaeus Flavius. This attempt, however, to give formal shape to a science, that as yet hardly recognized itself, stood for a long time completely isolated.

That the knowledge of law and the setting it forth were even now a means of recommendation to the people and of attaining offices of state, may be readily conceived, although the story, that the first plebeian pontifex Publius Sempronius Sophus (consul 450), and the first plebeian pontifex maximus Tiberius Coruncanius (consul 474), were indebted for these priestly honours to their knowledge of law, is probably rather a conjecture of posterity than a statement of tradition.

Language

That the real genesis of the Latin and doubtless also of the other Italian languages was anterior to this period, and that even at its commencement the Latin language was substantially an accomplished fact, is evident from the fragments of the Twelve Tables, which, however, have been largely modernized by their semi-oral tradition. They contain doubtless a number of antiquated words and harsh combinations, particularly in consequence of omitting the indefinite subject; but their meaning by no means presents, like that of the Arval chant, any real difficulty, and they exhibit far more agreement with the language of Cato than with that of the ancient litanies. If the Romans at the beginning of the seventh century had difficulty in understanding documents of the fifth, the difficulty doubtless proceeded merely from the fact that there existed at that time in Rome no real, least of all any documentary, research.

Technical Style

On the other hand it must have been at this period, when the indication and redaction of law began, that the Roman technical style first established itself—a style which at least in its developed shape is nowise inferior to the modern legal phraseology of England in stereotyped formulae and turns of expression, endless enumeration of particulars, and long-winded periods; and which commends itself to the initiated by its clearness and precision, while the layman who does not understand it listens, according to his character and humour, with reverence, impatience, or chagrin.

Philology

Moreover at this epoch began the treatment of the native languages after a rational method. About its commencement the Sabellian as well as the Latin idiom

196

threatened, as we saw,(25) to become barbarous, and the abrasion of endings and the corruption of the vowels and more delicate consonants spread on all hands, just as was the case with the Romanic languages in the fifth and sixth centuries of the Christian era. But a reaction set in: the sounds which had coalesced in Oscan, -d and -r, and the sounds which had coalesced in Latin, -g and -k, were again separated, and each was provided with its proper sign; -o and -u, for which from the first the Oscan alphabet had lacked separate signs, and which had been in Latin originally separate but threatened to coalesce, again became distinct, and in Oscan even the -i was resolved into two signs different in sound and in writing; lastly, the writing again came to follow more closely the pronunciation—the -s for instance among the Romans being in many cases replaced by -r. Chronological indications point to the fifth century as the period of this reaction; the Latin -g for instance was not yet in existence about 300 but was so probably about 500; the first of the Papirian clan, who called himself Papirius instead of Papisius, was the consul of 418; the introduction of that -r instead of -s is attributed to Appius Claudius, censor in 442. Beyond doubt the re-introduction of a more delicate and precise pronunciation was connected with the increasing influence of Greek civilization, which is observable at this very period in all departments of Italian life; and, as the silver coins of Capua and Nola are far more perfect than the contemporary asses of Ardea and Rome, writing and language appear also to have been more speedily and fully reduced to rule in the Campanian land than in Latium. How little, notwithstanding the labour bestowed on it, the Roman language and mode of writing had become settled at the close of this epoch, is shown by the inscriptions preserved from the end of the fifth century, in which the greatest arbitrariness prevails, particularly as to the insertion or omission of -m, -d and -s in final sounds and of -n in the body of a word, and as to the distinguishing of the vowels -o -u and -e -i.(26) It is probable that the contemporary Sabellians were in these points further advanced, while the Umbrians were but slightly affected by the regenerating influence of the Hellenes.

Instruction

In consequence of this progress of jurisprudence and grammar, elementary school-instruction also, which in itself had doubtless already emerged earlier, must have undergone a certain improvement. As Homer was the oldest Greek, and the Twelve Tables was the oldest Roman, book, each became in its own land the essential basis of instruction; and the learning by heart the juristico-political catechism was a chief part of Roman juvenile training. Alongside of the Latin "writing-masters" (-litteratores-) there were of course, from the time when an acquaintance with Greek was indispensable for every statesman and merchant, also Greek "language-masters" (-grammatici-)(27)—partly tutor-slaves, partly private teachers, who at their own dwelling or that of their pupil gave instructions in the reading and speaking of Greek. As a matter of course, the rod played its part in instruction as well as in military discipline and in police.(28) The instruction of this epoch cannot however have passed beyond the elementary stage: there was no material shade of difference, in a social respect, between the educated and the non-educated Roman.

That the Romans at no time distinguished themselves in the mathematical and mechanical sciences is well known, and is attested, in reference to the present epoch, by almost the only fact which can be adduced under this head with certainty—the regulation of the calendar attempted by the decemvirs. They wished to substitute for the previous calendar based on the old and very imperfect -trieteris-(29) the contemporary Attic calendar of the -octaeteris-, which retained the lunar month of 29 1/2 days but assumed the solar year at 365 1/4 days instead of 368 3/4, and therefore, without making any alteration in the length of the common year of 354 days, intercalated, not as formerly 59 days every 4 years, but 90 days every 8 years. With the same view the improvers of the Roman calendar intended—while otherwise retaining the current calendar—in the two inter-calary years of the four years' cycle to shorten not the intercalary months, but the two Februaries by 7 days each, and consequently to fix that month in the intercalary years at 22 and 21 days respectively instead of 29 and 28. But want of mathematical precision and theological scruples, especially in reference to the annual festival of Terminus which fell within those very days in February, disarranged the intended reform, so that the Februaries of the intercalary years came to be of 24 and 23 days, and thus the new Roman solar year in reality ran to 366 1/4 days. Some remedy for the practical evils resulting from this was found in the practice by which, setting aside the reckoning by the months or ten months of the calendar (30) as now no longer applicable from the inequality in the length of the months, wherever more accurate specifications were required, they accustomed themselves to reckon by terms of ten months of a solar year of 365 days or by the so-called ten-month year of 304 days. Over and above this, there came early into use in Italy, especially for agricultural purposes, the farmers' calendar based on the Egyptian solar year of 365 1/4 days by Eudoxus (who flourished 386).

Structural and Plastic Art

A higher idea of what the Italians were able to do in these departments is furnished by their works of structural and plastic art, which are closely associated with the mechanical sciences. Here too we do not find phenomena of real originality; but if the impress of borrowing, which the plastic art of Italy bears throughout, diminishes its artistic interest, there gathers around it a historical interest all the more lively, because on the one hand it preserves the most remarkable evidences of an international intercourse of which other traces have disappeared, and on the other hand, amidst the well-nigh total loss of the history of the non-Roman Italians, art is almost the sole surviving index of the living activity which the different peoples of the peninsula displayed. No novelty is to be reported in this period; but what we have already shown(31) may be illustrated in this period with greater precision and on a broader basis, namely, that the stimulus derived from Greece powerfully affected the Etruscans and Italians on different sides, and called forth among the former a richer and more luxurious, among the latter—where it had any influence at all—a more intelligent and more genuine, art.

Architecture—
Etruscan

We have already shown how wholly the architecture of all the Italian lands was, even in its earliest period, pervaded by Hellenic elements. Its city walls, its aqueducts, its tombs with pyramidal roofs, and its Tuscanic temple, are not at all, or not materially, different from the oldest Hellenic structures. No trace has been preserved of any advance in architecture among the Etruscans during this period; we find among them neither any really new reception, nor any original creation, unless we ought to reckon as such the magnificent tombs, e. g. the so-called tomb of Porsena at Chiusi described by Varro, which vividly recalls the strange and meaningless grandeur of the Egyptian pyramids.

Latin—
The Arch

In Latium too, during the first century and a half of the republic, it is probable that they moved solely in the previous track, and it has already been stated that the exercise of art rather sank than rose with the introduction of the republic.(32) There can scarcely be named any Latin building of architectural importance belonging to this period, except the temple of Ceres built in the Circus at Rome in 261, which was regarded in the period of the empire as a model of the Tuscanic style. But towards the close of this epoch a new spirit appeared in Italian and particularly in Roman architecture;(33) the building of the magnificent arches began. It is true that we are not entitled to pronounce the arch and the vault Italian inventions. It is well ascertained that at the epoch of the genesis of Hellenic architecture the Hellenes were not yet acquainted with the arch, and therefore had to content themselves with a flat ceiling and a sloping roof for their temples; but the arch may very well have been a later invention of the Hellenes originating in more scientific mechanics; as indeed the Greek tradition refers it to the natural philosopher Democritus (294-397). With this priority of Hellenic over Roman arch-building the hypothesis, which has been often and perhaps justly propounded, is quite compatible, that the vaulted roof of the Roman great -cloaca-, and that which was afterwards thrown over the old Capitoline well-house which originally had a pyramidal roof,(34) are the oldest extant structures in which the principle of the arch is applied; for it is more than probable that these arched buildings belong not to the regal but to the republican period,(35) and that in the regal period the Italians were acquainted only with flat or overlapped roofs.(34) But whatever may be thought as to the invention of the arch itself, the application of a principle on a great scale is everywhere, and particularly in architecture, at least as important as its first exposition; and this application belongs indisputably to the Romans. With the fifth century began the building of gates, bridges, and aqueducts based mainly on the arch, which is thenceforth inseparably associated with the Roman name. Akin to this was the development of the form of the round temple with the dome-shaped roof, which was foreign to the Greeks, but was held in much favour with the Romans and was especially applied by them in the case of the cults peculiar to them, particularly the non-Greek worship of Vesta.(37)

Something the same may be affirmed as true of various subordinate, but not on that account unimportant, achievements in this field. They do not lay claim to originality or artistic accomplishment; but the firmly-jointed stone slabs of the Roman streets, their indestructible highways, the broad hard ringing tiles, the everlasting mortar of their buildings, proclaim the indestructible solidity and the energetic vigour of the Roman character.

Plastic and Delineative Art

Like architectural art, and, if possible, still more completely, the plastic and delineative arts were not so much matured by Grecian stimulus as developed from Greek seeds on Italian soil. We have already observed(38) that these, although only younger sisters of architecture, began to develop themselves at least in Etruria, even during the Roman regal period; but their principal development in Etruria, and still more in Latium, belongs to the present epoch, as is very evident from the fact that in those districts which the Celts and Samnites wrested from the Etruscans in the course of the fourth century there is scarcely a trace of the practice of Etruscan art. The plastic art of the Tuscans applied itself first and chiefly to works in terra-cotta, in copper, and in gold-materials which were furnished to the artists by the rich strata of clay, the copper mines, and the commercial intercourse of Etruria. The vigour with which moulding in clay was prosecuted is attested by the immense number of bas-reliefs and statuary works in terra-cotta, with which the walls, gables, and roofs of the Etruscan temples were once decorated, as their still extant ruins show, and by the trade which can be shown to have existed in such articles from Etruria to Latium. Casting in copper occupied no inferior place. Etruscan artists ventured to make colossal statues of bronze fifty feet in height, and Volsinii, the Etruscan Delphi, was said to have possessed about the year 489 two thousand bronze statues. Sculpture in stone, again, began in Etruria, as probably everywhere, at a far later date, and was prevented from development not only by internal causes, but also by the want of suitable material; the marble quarries of Luna (Carrara) were not yet opened. Any one who has seen the rich and elegant gold decorations of the south-Etruscan tombs, will have no difficulty in believing the statement that Tyrrhene gold cups were valued even in Attica. Gem-engraving also, although more recent, was in various forms practised in Etruria. Equally dependent on the Greeks, but otherwise quite on a level with the workers in the plastic arts, were the Etruscan designers and painters, who manifested extraordinary activity both in outline-drawing on metal and in monochromatic fresco-painting.

Campanian and Sabellian

On comparing with this the domain of the Italians proper, it appears at first, contrasted with the Etruscan riches, almost poor in art. But on a closer view we cannot fail to perceive that both the Sabellian and the Latin nations must have had far more capacity and aptitude for art than the Etruscans. It is true that in the proper Sabellian territory, in Sabina, in the Abruzzi, in Samnium, there are hardly found any works of art at all, and even coins are wanting. But those Sabellian stocks, which reached the coasts of the Tyrrhene or Ionic seas, not only appropriated Hellenic art externally, like the Etruscans, but more or less completely acclimatized it. Even in Velitrae, where probably alone in the former land of the Volsci their language and peculiar character were afterwards maintained, painted terra-cottas have been found, displaying vigorous and characteristic treatment. In Lower Italy Lucania was to a less degree influenced by Hellenic art; but in Campania and in the land of the Bruttii, Sabellians and Hellenes became completely intermingled not only in language and nationality, but also and especially in art, and the Campanian and Bruttian coins in particular stand so entirely in point of artistic treatment on a level with the contemporary coins of Greece, that the inscription alone serves to distinguish the one from the other.

Latin

It is a fact less known, but not less certain, that Latium also, while inferior to Etruria in the copiousness and massiveness of its art, was not inferior in artistic taste and practical skill. Evidently the establishment of the Romans in Campania which took place about the beginning of the fifth century, the conversion of the town of Cales into a Latin community, and that of the Falernian territory near Capua into a Roman tribe,(39) opened up in the first instance Campanian art to the Romans. It is true that among these the art of gem-engraving so diligently prosecuted in luxurious Etruria is entirely wanting, and we find no indication that the Latin workshops were, like those of the Etruscan goldsmiths and clay-workers, occupied in supplying a foreign demand. It is true that the Latin temples were not like the Etruscan overloaded with bronze and clay decorations, that the Latin tombs were not like the Etruscan filled with gold ornaments, and their walls shone not, like those of the Tuscan tombs, with paintings of various colours. Nevertheless, on the whole the balance does not incline in favour of the Etruscan nation. The device of the effigy of Janus, which, like the deity itself, may be attributed to the Latins,(40) is not unskilful, and is of a more original character than that of any Etruscan work of art. The beautiful group of the she-wolf with the twins attaches itself doubtless to similar Greek designs, but was—-as thus worked out—certainly produced, if not in Rome, at any rate by Romans; and it deserves to be noted that it first appears on the silver moneys coined by the Romans in and for Campania. In the above-mentioned Cales there appears to have been devised soon after its foundation a peculiar kind of figured earthenware, which was marked with the name of the masters and the place of manufacture, and was sold over a wide district as far even as Etruria. The little altars of terra-cotta with figures that have recently been brought to light on the Esquiline correspond in style of representation as in that of ornament exactly to the similar votive gifts of the Campanian temples. This however does not exclude Greek masters from having also worked for Rome. The sculptor Damophilus, who with Gorgasus prepared the painted terra-cotta figures for the very ancient temple of Ceres, appears to have been no other than Demophilus of Himera, the teacher of Zeuxis (about 300). The most instructive illustrations are furnished by those branches of art in which we are able to form a comparative judgment, partly from ancient testimonies, partly from our own observation. Of Latin works in stone scarcely anything else survives than the stone sarcophagus of the Roman consul Lucius Scipio, wrought at the close of this period in the Doric style; but its noble simplicity puts to shame all similar Etruscan works. Many beautiful bronzes of an antique chaste style of art, particularly helmets, candelabra, and the like articles, have been taken from Etruscan tombs; but which of these works is equal to the bronze she-wolf erected from the proceeds of fines in 458 at the Ruminal fig-tree in the Roman Forum, and still forming the finest ornament of the Capitol? And that the Latin metal-founders as little shrank from great enterprises as the Etruscans, is shown by the colossal bronze figure of Jupiter on the Capitol erected by Spurius Carvilius (consul in 461) from the melted equipments of the Samnites, the chisellings of which sufficed to cast the statue of the victor that stood at the feet of the Colossus; this statue of Jupiter was visible even from the Alban Mount. Amongst the cast copper coins by far the finest belong to southern Latium; the Roman and Umbrian are tolerable, the Etruscan almost destitute of any image and often really barbarous. The fresco-paintings, which Gaius Fabius executed in the temple of Health on the Capitol, dedicated in 452, obtained in design and colouring the praise even of connoisseurs trained in Greek art in the Augustan age; and the art-enthusiasts of the empire commended the frescoes of Caere, but with still greater emphasis those of Rome, Lanuvium, and Ardea, as masterpieces of painting. Engraving on metal, which in Latium decorated not the hand-mirror, as in Etruria, but the toilet-casket with its elegant outlines, was practised to a far less extent in Latium and almost exclusively in Praeneste. There are excellent works of art among the copper mirrors of Etruria as among the caskets of Praeneste; but it was a work of the latter kind, and in fact a work which most probably originated in the workshop of a Praenestine master at this epoch,(41) regarding which it could with truth be affirmed that scarcely another product of the graving of antiquity bears the stamp of an art so finished in its beauty and characteristic expression, and yet so perfectly pure and chaste, as the Ficoroni -cista-.

Character of Etruscan Art

The general character of Etruscan works of art is, on the one hand, a sort of barbaric extravagance in material as well as in style; on the other hand, an utter absence of original development. Where the Greek master lightly sketches, the Etruscan disciple lavishes a scholar's diligence; instead of the light material and moderate proportions of the Greek works, there appears in the Etruscan an ostentatious stress laid upon the size and costliness, or even the mere singularity, of the work. Etruscan art cannot imitate without exaggerating; the chaste in its hands becomes harsh, the graceful effeminate, the terrible hideous, and the voluptuous obscene; and these features become more prominent, the more the original stimulus falls into the background and Etruscan art finds itself left to its own resources. Still more surprising is the adherence to traditional forms and a traditional style. Whether it was that a more friendly contact with Etruria at the outset allowed the Hellenes to scatter there the seeds of art, and that a later epoch of hostility impeded the admission into Etruria of the more recent developments of Greek art, or whether, as is more probable, the intellectual torpor that rapidly came over the nation was the main cause of the phenomenon, art in Etruria remained substantially stationary at the primitive stage which it had occupied on its first entrance. This, as is well known, forms the reason why Etruscan art, the stunted daughter, was so long regarded as the mother, of Hellenic art. Still more even than the rigid adherence to the style traditionally transmitted in the older branches of art, the sadly inferior handling of those branches that came into vogue afterwards, particularly of sculpture in stone and of copper-casting as applied to coins, shows how quickly the spirit of Etruscan art evaporated. Equally instructive are the painted vases, which are found in so enormous numbers in the later Etruscan tombs. Had these come into current use among the Etruscans as early as the metal plates decorated with contouring or the painted terra-cottas, beyond doubt they would have learned to manufacture them at home in considerable quantity, and of a quality at least relatively good; but at the period at which this luxury arose, the power of independent reproduction wholly failed—as the isolated vases provided with Etruscan inscriptions show—and they contented themselves with buying instead of making them.

North Etruscan and South Etruscan Art

But even within Etruria there appears a further remarkable distinction in artistic development between the southern and northern districts. It is South Etruria, particularly in the districts of Caere, Tarquinii, and Volci, that has preserved the great treasures of art which the nation boasted, especially in frescoes, temple decorations, gold ornaments, and painted vases. Northern Etruria is far inferior; no painted tomb, for example, has been found to the north of Chiusi. The most southern Etruscan cities, Veii, Caere, and Tarquinii, were accounted in Roman tradition the primitive and chief seats of Etruscan art; the most northerly town, Volaterrae, with the largest territory of all the Etruscan communities, stood most of all aloof from art While a Greek semi-culture prevailed in South Etruria, Northern Etruria was much more marked by an absence of all culture. The causes of this remarkable contrast may be sought partly in differences of nationality—South Etruria being largely peopled in all probability by non-Etruscan elements(42)—partly in the varying intensity of Hellenic influence, which must have made itself very decidedly felt at Caere in particular. The fact itself admits of no doubt. The more injurious on that account must have been the early subjugation of the southern half of Etruria by the Romans, and the Romanizing—which there began very early—of Etruscan art. What Northern Etruria, confined to its own efforts, was able to produce in the way of art, is shown by the copper coins which essentially belong to it.

Character of Latin Art

Let us now turn from Etruria to glance at Latium. The latter, it is true, created no new art; it was reserved for a far later epoch of culture to develop on the basis of the arch a new architecture different from the Hellenic, and then to unfold in harmony with that architecture a new style of sculpture and painting. Latin art is nowhere original and often insignificant; but the fresh sensibility and the discriminating tact, which appropriate what is good in others, constitute a high artistic merit. Latin art seldom became barbarous, and in its best products it comes quite up to the level of Greek technical execution. We do not mean to deny that the art of Latium, at least in its earlier stages, had a certain dependence on the undoubtedly earlier Etruscan;(43) Varro may be quite right in supposing that, previous to the execution by Greek artists of the clay figures in the temple of Ceres,(44) only "Tuscanic" figures adorned the Roman temples; but that, at all events, it was mainly the direct influence of the Greeks that led Latin art into its proper channel, is self-evident, and is very obviously shown by these very statues as well as by the Latin and Roman coins. Even the application of graving on metal in Etruria solely to the toilet mirror, and in Latium solely to the toilet casket, indicates the diversity of the art-impulses that affected the two lands. It does not appear, however, to have been exactly at Rome that Latin art put forth its freshest vigour; the Roman -asses- and Roman -denarii- are far surpassed in fineness and taste of workmanship by the Latin copper, and the rare Latin silver, coins, and the masterpieces of painting and design belong chiefly to Praeneste, Lanuvium, and Ardea. This accords completely with the realistic and sober spirit of the Roman republic which we have already described—a spirit which can hardly have asserted itself with equal intensity in other parts of Latium. But in the course of the fifth century, and especially in the second half of it, there was a mighty activity in Roman art. This was the epoch, in which the construction of the Roman arches and Roman roads began; in which works of art like the she-wolf of the Capitol originated; and in which a distinguished man of an old Roman patrician clan took up his pencil to embellish a newly constructed temple and thence received the honorary surname of the "Painter." This was not accident. Every great age lays grasp on all the powers of man; and, rigid as were Roman manners, strict as was Roman police, the impulse received by the Roman burgesses as masters of the peninsula or, to speak more correctly, by Italy united for the first time as one state, became as evident in the stimulus given to Latin and especially to Roman art, as the moral and political decay of the Etruscan nation was evident in the decline of art in Etruria. As the mighty national vigour of Latium subdued the weaker nations, it impressed its imperishable stamp also on bronze and on marble.

Notes for Book II Chapter IX

1. I. XV. Earliest Hellenic Influences

2. The account given by Dionysius (vi. 95; comp. Niebuhr, ii. 40) and by Plutarch (Camill. 42), deriving his statement from another passage in Dionysius regarding the Latin festival, must be understood to apply rather to the Roman games, as, apart from other grounds, is strikingly evident from comparing the latter passage with Liv. vi. 42 (Ritschl, Parerg. i. p. 313). Dionysius has—and, according to his wont when in error, persistently—misunderstood the expression -ludi maximi-.

There was, moreover, a tradition which referred the origin of the national festival not, as in the common version, to the conquest of the Latins by the first Tarquinius, but to the victory over the Latins at the lake Regillus (Cicero, de Div. i. 26, 55; Dionys. vii. 71). That the important statements preserved in the latter passage from Fabius really relate to the ordinary thanksgiving-festival, and not to any special votive solemnity, is evident from the express allusion to the annual recurrence of the celebration, and from the exact agreement of the sum of the expenses with the statement in the Pseudo-Asconius (p. 142 Or.).

3. II. III. Curule Aedileship

4. I. II. Art

5. I. XV. Metre

6. I. XV. Masks

7. II. VIII. Police f.

8. I. XV. Melody

9. A fragment has been preserved:

-Hiberno pulvere, verno luto, grandia farra Camille metes-

We do not know by what right this was afterwards regarded as the oldest Roman poem (Macrob. Sat. v. 20; Festus, Ep. v. Flaminius, p. 93, M.; Serv. on Virg. Georg, i. 101; Plin. xvii. 2. 14).

10. II. VIII. Appius Claudius

11. II. VIII. Rome and the Romans of This Epoch

12. The first places in the list alone excite suspicion, and may have been subsequently added, with a view to round off the number of years between the flight of the king and the burning of the city to 120.

13. I. VI. Time and the Occasion of the Reform, *ii*. VII. System of Government

14. II. VIII Rome and the Romans of This Epoch. According to the annals Scipio commands in Etruria and his colleague in Samnium, and Lucania is during this year in league with Rome; according to the epitaph Scipio conquers two towns in Samnium and all Lucania.

15. I. XI. Jurisdiction, second note.

16. They appear to have reckoned three generations to a hundred years and to have rounded off the figures 233 1/3 to 240, just as the epoch between the king's flight and the burning of the city was rounded off to 120 years (*ii*. IX. Registers of Magistrates, note). The reason why these precise numbers suggested themselves, is apparent from the similar adjustment (above explained, I. XIV. The Duodecimal System) of the measures of surface.

17. I. XII. Spirits

18. I. X. Relations of the Western Italians to the Greeks

19. The "Trojan colonies" in Sicily, mentioned by Thucydides, the pseudo-Scylax, and others, as well as the designation of Capua as a Trojan foundation in Hecataeus, must also be traced to Stesichorus and his identification of the natives of Italy and Sicily with the Trojans.

20. According to his account Rome, a woman who had fled from Ilion to Rome, or rather her daughter of the same name, married Latinos, king of the Aborigines, and bore to him three sons, Romos, Romylos, and Telegonos. The last, who undoubtedly emerges here as founder of Tusculum and Praeneste, belongs, as is well known, to the legend of Odysseus.

21. II. IV. Fruitlessness of the Celtic Victory

22. II. VII. Relations between the East and West

23. II. VII. The Roman Fleet

24. II. II. Political Value of the Tribunates, *ii*. II. The Valerio-Horatian Laws

25. I. XIV. Corruption of Language and Writing

26. In the two epitaphs, of Lucius Scipio consul in 456, and of the consul of the same name in 495, -m and -d are ordinarily wanting in the termination of cases, yet -Luciom- and -Gnaivod- respectively occur once; there occur alongside of one another in the nominative -Cornelio- and -filios-; -cosol-, -cesor-, alongside of -consol-, -censor-; -aidiles-, -dedet-, -ploirume- (= -plurimi-) -hec- (nom. sing.) alongside of -aidilis-, -cepit-, -quei-, -hic-. Rhotacism is already carried out completely; we find -duonoro-(= -bonorum-), -ploirume-, not as in the chant of the Salii -foedesum-, -plusima-. Our surviving inscriptions do not in general precede the age of rhotacism; of the older -s only isolated traces occur, such as afterwards -honos-, -labos- alongside of -honor-, -labor-; and the similar feminine -praenomina-, -Maio- (= -maios- -maior-) and -Mino-in recently found epitaphs at Praeneste.

27. -Litterator- and -grammaticus- are related nearly as elementary teacher and teacher of languages with us; the latter designation belonged by earlier usage only to the teacher of Greek, not to a teacher of the mother-tongue. -Litteratus- is more recent, and denotes not a schoolmaster but a man of culture.

28. It is at any rate a true Roman picture, which Plautus (Bacch. 431) produces as a specimen of the good old mode of training children:—

... -ubi revenisses domum, Cincticulo praecinctus in sella apud magistrum adsideres; Si, librum cum legeres, unam peccavisses syllabam, Fieret corium tam maculosum, quam est nutricis pallium-.

29. I. XIV. The Oldest Italo-Greek Calendar

30. I. XIV. The Oldest Italo-Greek Calendar

31. I. XV. Plastic Art in Italy

32. II. VIII. Building

33. II. VIII. Building

34. I. XV. Earliest Hellenic Influences

35. I. VII. Servian Wall

36. I. XV. Earliest Hellenic Influences

37. The round temple certainly was not, as has been supposed, an imitation of the oldest form of the house; on the contrary, house architecture uniformly starts from the square form. The later Roman theology associated this round form with the idea of the terrestrial sphere or of the universe surrounding like a sphere the central sun (Fest. v. -rutundam-, p. 282; Plutarch, Num. 11; Ovid, Fast. vi. 267, seq.). In reality

it may be traceable simply to the fact, that the circular shape has constantly been recognized as the most convenient and the safest form of a space destined for enclosure and custody. That was the rationale of the round —thesauroi— of the Greeks as well as of the round structure of the Roman store-chamber or temple of the Penates. It was natural, also, that the fireplace—that is, the altar of Vesta—and the fire-chamber—that is, the temple of Vesta —should be constructed of a round form, just as was done with the cistern and the well-enclosure (-puteal-). The round style of building in itself was Graeco-Italian as was the square form, and the former was appropriated to the store-place, the latter to the dwelling-house; but the architectural and religious development of the simple -tholos-into the round temple with pillars and columns was Latin.

38. I. XV. Plastic Art in Italy

39. II. V. Complete Submission of the Campanian and Volscian Provinces

40. I. XII. Nature of the Roman Gods

41. Novius Plautius (*ii*. VIII. Capital in Rome) cast perhaps only the feet and the group on the lid; the casket itself may have proceeded from an earlier artist, but hardly from any other than a Praenestine, for the use of these caskets was substantially confined to Praeneste.

42. I. IX. Settlements of the Etruscans in Italy

43. I. XV. Earliest Hellenic Influences

44. I. VI. Time and Occasion of the Reform

TABLE OF CALENDAR EQUIVALENTS

```
A.U.C.*              B.C.     B.C.                A.U.C.
-------------------------------------------------------
000          753              753          000
025      728                  750      003
050  703                      725  028
075 678      700               053
100          653              675          078
125      628                  650  103
150  603                      625 128
175 578      600               153
200          553              575          178
225      528                  550  203
250  503                      525 228
275 478      500               253
300          453              475          278
325      428                  450  303
350  303                      425 328
375 378      400               353
400          353              375          378
425      328                  350  403
450  303                      325 428
475 278      300               453
500          253              275          478
525      228                  250  503
550  203                      225 528
575 178      200               553
600          153              175          578
625      128                  150  603
650  103                      125 628
675 078      100               653
700          053              075          678
725      028                  050  703
750  003                      025 728
753 000      000               753
```

A. U. C. — Ab Urbe Condita (from the founding of the City of Rome)

Made in the USA
Lexington, KY
11 February 2010